THE SHI'I IMAMATE

The Institute of Ismaili Studies
Ismaili Texts and Translations Series, 20

Previously published titles:

1. Ibn al-Haytham. *The Advent of the Fatimids: A Contemporary Shi'i Witness.* An edition and English translation of Ibn al-Haytham's *Kitāb al-Munāẓarāt*, by Wilferd Madelung and Paul E. Walker (2000).
2. Muḥammad b. ʿAbd al-Karīm al-Shahrastānī. *Struggling with the Philosopher: A Refutation of Avicenna's Metaphysics.* A new Arabic edition and English translation of al-Shahrastānī's *Kitāb al-Muṣāraʿa*, by Wilferd Madelung and Toby Mayer (2001).
3. Jaʿfar b. Manṣūr al-Yaman. *The Master and the Disciple: An Early Islamic Spiritual Dialogue.* Arabic edition and English translation of Jaʿfar b. Manṣūr al-Yaman's *Kitāb al-ʿālim wa'l-ghulām*, by James W. Morris (2001).
4. Idrīs ʿImād al-Dīn. *The Fatimids and their Successors in Yaman: The History of an Islamic Community.* Arabic edition and English summary of Idrīs ʿImād al-Dīn's *ʿUyūn al-akhbār*, vol. 7, by Ayman F. Sayyid, in collaboration with Paul E. Walker and Maurice A. Pomerantz (2002).
5. Naṣīr al-Dīn Ṭūsī. *Paradise of Submission: A Medieval Treatise on Ismaili Thought.* A new Persian edition and English translation of Naṣīr al-Dīn Ṭūsī's *Rawḍa-yi taslīm*, by S. J. Badakhchani with an introduction by Hermann Landolt and a philosophical commentary by Christian Jambet (2005).
6. al-Qāḍī al-Nuʿmān. *Founding the Fatimid State: The Rise of an Early Islamic Empire.* An annotated English translation of al-Qāḍī al-Nuʿmān's *Iftitāḥ al-daʿwa*, by Hamid Haji (2006).
7. Idrīs ʿImād al-Dīn. *ʿUyūn al-akhbār wa-funūn al-āthār.* Arabic critical edition in 7 volumes by Ahmad Chleilat, Mahmoud Fakhoury, Yousef S. Fattoum, Muhammad Kamal, Ma'moun al-Sagherji and Ayman F. Sayyid (2007–2009).

8. Aḥmad b. Ibrāhīm al-Naysābūrī. *Degrees of Excellence: A Fatimid Treatise on Leadership in Islam*. A new Arabic edition and English translation of Aḥmad b. Ibrāhīm al-Naysābūrī's *Kitāb ithbāt al-imāma*, by Arzina Lalani (2010).

9. Ḥamīd al-Dīn Aḥmad b. ʿAbd Allāh al-Kirmānī. *Master of the Age: An Islamic Treatise on the Necessity of the Imamate*. A critical edition of the Arabic text and English translation of Ḥamīd al-Dīn al-Kirmānī's *al-Maṣābīḥ fī ithbāt al-imāma*, by Paul E. Walker (2007).

10. *Orations of the Fatimid Caliphs: Festival Sermons of the Ismaili Imams*. An edition of the Arabic texts and English translation of Fatimid *khuṭbas*, by Paul E. Walker (2009).

11. Taqī al-Dīn Aḥmad b. ʿAlī al-Maqrīzī. *Towards a Shiʿi Mediterranean Empire: Fatimid Egypt and the Founding of Cairo*. The reign of the Imam-caliph al-Muʿizz, from al-Maqrīzī's *Ittiʿāẓ al-ḥunafāʾ bi-akhbār al-aʾimma al-Fāṭimiyyīn al-khulafāʾ*, translated by Shainool Jiwa (2009).

12. Taqī al-Dīn Aḥmad b. ʿAlī al-Maqrīzī. *Ittiʿāẓ al-ḥunafāʾ bi-akhbār al-aʾimma al-Fāṭimiyyīn al-khulafāʾ*. Arabic critical edition in 4 volumes, with an English introduction by Paul E. Walker and notes by Ayman F. Sayyid (2010).

13. Naṣīr al-Dīn Ṭūsī. *Shiʿi Interpretations of Islam: Three Treatises on Theology and Eschatology*. A Persian edition and English translation of Naṣīr al-Dīn Ṭūsī's *Tawallā wa tabarrā, Maṭlūb al-muʾminīn and Āghāz wa anjām*, by S. J. Badkhchani (2010).

14. al-Muʾayyad al-Shīrāzī. *Mount of Knowledge, Sword of Eloquence: Collected Poems of an Ismaili Muslim Scholar in Fatimid Egypt*. A translation from the original Arabic of al-Muʾayyad al-Shīrāzī's *Dīwān*, translated by Mohamad Adra (2011).

15. Aḥmad b. Ibrāhīm al-Naysābūrī. *A Code of Conduct: A Treatise on the Etiquette of the Fatimid Ismaili Mission*. A critical edition of the Arabic text and English translation of Aḥmad b. Ibrāhīm al-Naysābūrī's *al-Risāla al-mūjaza al-kāfiya fī ādāb al-duʿāt*, by Verena Klemm and Paul E. Walker with Susanne Karam (2011).

16. Manṣūr al-ʿAzīzī al-Jawdharī. *Inside the Immaculate Portal: A History from Early Fatimid Archives.* A new edition and English translation of Manṣūr al-ʿAzīzī al-Jawdharī's biography of al-Ustādh Jawdhar, the *Sīrat al-Ustādh Jawdhar,* by Hamid Haji (2012).

17. Nāṣir-i Khusraw. *Between Reason and Revelation: Twin Wisdoms Reconciled.* An annotated English translation of Nāṣir-i Khusraw's *Kitāb-i jāmiʿ al-ḥikmatayn,* by Eric Ormsby (2012).

18. al-Qāḍī al-Nuʿmān. *The Early History of Ismaili Jurisprudence: Law under the Fatimids.* A critical edition of the Arabic text and English translation of al-Qāḍī al-Nuʿmān's *Minhāj al-farāʾiḍ,* by Agostino Cilardo (2012).

19. Ḥātim b. Ibrāhīm al-Ḥāmidī. *The Precious Gift of the Hearts and Good Cheer for Those in Distress. On the Organisation and History of the Yamanī Fatimid Daʿwa.* A critical edition of the Arabic text and summary English translation of Ḥātim b. Ibrāhīm al-Ḥāmidī's *Tuḥfat al-qulūb wa furjat al-makrūb* by Abbas Hamdani (2012).

The Shiʻi Imamate

A Fatimid Interpretation

An Arabic edition and English translation
of the *Tathbīt al-imāma*, attributed to the
Fatimid Caliph-Imam al-Manṣūr

by
Sami Makarem

I.B.Tauris Publishers
LONDON • NEW YORK
in association with
The Institute of Ismaili Studies
LONDON

Published in 2013 by I.B.Tauris & Co Ltd
6 Salem Rd, London W2 4BU
175 Fifth Avenue, New York NY 10010
www.ibtauris.com

in association with The Institute of Ismaili Studies
210 Euston Road, London NW1 2DA
www.iis.ac.uk

Distributed in the United States of America and in Canada
Exclusively by Palgrave Macmillan, 175 Fifth Avenue, NY 10010

ISBN 978 1 78076 679 9

A full CIP record for this book is available from the British Library
A full CIP record for this book is available from the Library of
Congress

Library of Congress catalog card: available

Typeset in Minion Tra for The Institute of Ismaili Studies
Printed and bound in Great Britain by T.J. International, Padstow,
Cornwall

The Institute of Ismaili Studies

The Institute of Ismaili Studies was established in 1977 with the object of promoting scholarship and learning on Islam, in the historical as well as contemporary contexts, and a better understanding of its relationship with other societies and faiths.

The Institute's programmes encourage a perspective which is not confined to the theological and religious heritage of Islam, but seeks to explore the relationship of religious ideas to broader dimensions of society and culture. The programmes thus encourage an interdisciplinary approach to the materials of Islamic history and thought. Particular attention is also given to issues of modernity that arise as Muslims seek to relate their heritage to the contemporary situation.

Within the Islamic tradition, the Institute's programmes promote research on those areas which have, to date, received relatively little attention from scholars. These include the intellectual and literary expressions of Shi'ism in general, and Ismailism in particular.

In the context of Islamic societies, the Institute's programmes are informed by the full range and diversity of cultures in which Islam is practised today, from the Middle East, South and Central Asia, and Africa to the industrialised societies of the West, thus taking into consideration the variety of contexts which shape the ideals, beliefs and practices of the faith.

These objectives are realised through concrete programmes and activities organised and implemented by various departments of the Institute. The Institute also collaborates periodically, on a programme-specific basis, with other institutions of learning in the United Kingdom and abroad.

The Institute's academic publications fall into a number of inter-related categories:

1. Occasional papers or essays addressing broad themes of the relationship between religion and society, with special reference to Islam.
2. Monographs exploring specific aspects of Islamic faith and culture, or the contributions of individual Muslim thinkers or writers.
3. Editions or translations of significant primary or secondary texts.
4. Translations of poetic or literary texts which illustrate the rich heritage of spiritual, devotional and symbolic expressions in Muslim history.
5. Works on Ismaili history and thought, and the relationship of the Ismailis to other traditions, communities and schools of thought in Islam.
6. Proceedings of conferences and seminars sponsored by the Institute.
7. Bibliographical works and catalogues which document manuscripts, printed texts and other source materials.

This book falls into category three listed above.

In facilitating these and other publications, the Institute's sole aim is to encourage original research and analysis of relevant issues. While every effort is made to ensure that the publications are of a high academic standard, there is naturally bound to be a diversity of views, ideas and interpretations. As such, the opinions expressed in these publications must be understood as belonging to their authors alone.

Table of Contents

An Editorial Note

Professor Makarem sadly passed away on 21 August 2012, before he had the opportunity to see the final draft of this text. The editorial team at the IIS and in Beirut took special care to see this work through to press.

The son of Sheikh Nassib Makarem, the most celebrated Arab calligrapher of his generation, Professor Sami Makarem (1931–2012) was himself an expert on calligraphy and a renowned Islamic scholar.

He obtained a BA in Literature and Philosophy in 1954 and an MA in Arabic Literature in 1957, both from the American University of Beirut (AUB), followed by a PhD in Middle Eastern Studies from the University of Michigan at Ann Arbor in 1963.

Upon returning to Lebanon, Professor Makarem taught at the Lebanese University before taking up an appointment as an assistant professor at AUB, where he taught Arabic Literature and Islamic Thought. He was promoted to the rank of Associate Professor in 1970 and full professor in 1985. A part-time professor at the Lebanese University from 1977–1981, he twice held the position of chair of the Department of Arabic Literature and Near Eastern Languages (1975–1978 and 1993–1996) at AUB, and also served as director of its Center for Arab and Middle Eastern Studies (1975–1978).

Aside from creating various works of art, Professor Makarem wrote over 20 books and numerous academic papers, as well as three volumes of poetry, including *Mir'at 'ala Jabal Qaf* (A Mirror on Mount Qaf, 1996). His academic publications include *The Doctrine of the Ismailis* (1972) and *The Druze Faith* (1974). Professor Makarem also had a good knowledge of Ismaili literature; he edited and translated Abu'l-Fawāris Aḥmad's *al-Risāla fi'l-imāma* under the title of *The Political Doctrine of the Ismā'īlīs (The Imamate)*, published in 1977.

Profesor Makarem was a member of the Board of Regents of the Lebanese Foundation for Permanent Peace; secretary general of the Druze Council for Research and Development; and head of the Department of Scientific Studies and Research at the Druze Heritage Foundation. During his career, he received many awards and honours, from the Union of Arab Historians, the Lebanese Ministry of Culture, and the Antelias Cultural Movement, among others.

Acknowledgements

I am grateful to The Institute of Ismaili Studies in London for providing me with the two manuscripts of *Tathbīt al-imāma* that I relied upon in preparing this work and for sponsoring this project. I am especially grateful to Dr Nader El-Bizri and Dr Arzina Lalani, both of The Institute of Ismaili Studies, for their encouragement and assistance.

My gratitude goes also to Adrian Basheer who offered me great help in improving the English translation and in typing both the Arabic manuscript and its English version. He was assisted by two dear friends, Nabil Emad and Mira El Masri. I greatly appreciate their help.

Finally, my deepest thanks go to my wife, Leila Makarem, for her understanding and patience throughout the preparation of this work.

S. N. Makarem
American University of Beirut

Introduction

The importance of the *Tathbīt al-imāma*

The *Tathbīt al-imāma* attributed to the Fatimid Caliph-Imam al-Manṣūr bi'llāh[1] Ismāʿīl (334–341/946–953) is an important early Ismaili treatise on the legitimacy of the imamate of ʿAlī b. Abī Ṭālib and that of the Ismaili imams from among his progeny. As one of the earliest Ismaili works on this crucial and fundamental subject, it can thus be considered a major treatise on the doctrine of the imamate.

In his classical work *Daʿāʾim al-Islām* (Chapter 1, 'Allegiance to the Imam (*al-walāya*)', in a section entitled 'The declaration of divine appointment of the Imam from among the house of Muḥammad (may God bless them)') al-Qāḍī al-Nuʿmān, the Supreme Judge during the reign of the fourth Fatimid Caliph-Imam al-Muʿizz li-Dīn Allāh, writes about this treatise:

> Al-Manṣūr bi'llāh (may God grant him His blessings and mercy, His benedictions and sanctions, and may He vindicate him for all that he did) devoted a comprehensive book on the subject of the imamate in which he inquired into its significance thoroughly and probed the depths of all its grounds.[2]

Al-Manṣūr's *Tathbīt al-imāma* does not deal with the metaphysical significance of the imamate. Rather, it concentrates on its legal and historical aspects and uses proofs derived from the Qurʾān, the

---

1. In one of the two manuscripts (MS ⟨أ⟩) that the editor has relied upon (see below), al-Manṣūr's caliphal title is al-Manṣūr bi-Naṣr Allāh, rather than al-Manṣūr bi'llāh.

2. al-Qāḍī al-Nuʿmān, *Daʿāʾim al-Islām*, vol. 1, ed. Āṣaf b. ʿAlī Aṣghar Fayḍī (Cairo: Dār al-Maʿārif, 1370/1951), p. 48.

Traditions and logical arguments. It is, therefore, directed at the Islamic public in all its different religious affiliations without calling them by name. The most important of these religious factions, however, are mentioned later by al-Qāḍī al-Nuʿmān. He continues his passage quoted above by enumerating and describing them as follows:

1. *Al-ʿĀmma*. By *al-ʿāmma* al-Qāḍī al-Nuʿmān does not mean the lower class of the Sunni Muslims as compared to *al-khāṣṣa* or the upper class as it may appear at first glance. Rather, he means the multitude of those who profess Sunni Islam. The *ʿāmma* believe that the imams should be chosen by the people. Although the multitudes of the Sunni Muslims differ among themselves on the imam's qualifications, they all deny the fact that the Prophet had nominated anyone in particular to be so. A faction of them, however, believes that the Prophet, on his death bed, when designating Abū Bakr to lead the prayer, was alluding to him without naming him in person. Hence, as the Companions of the Prophet chose Abū Bakr to be imam, he became by right the legal successor of the Prophet.[3]

   However, the majority of those *ʿāmma* of the Sunni Muslims had become, by the time of al-Manṣūr biʾllāh, followers of Abuʾl-Ḥasan al-Ashʿarī (d. 324/935–936). In fact, the author of *Tathbīt al-imāma*, in his arguments against the Sunni theory of imamate, was most probably aiming at refuting al-Ashʿarī in particular, especially in the latter's two books, *al-Ibāna* and *al-Lumaʿ fīʾl-radd ʿalā ahl al-ziyagh waʾl-bidāʾ*.[4] It is interesting that the Fatimid Caliph-Imam al-Manṣūr surprisingly refers in his treatise (fol. 104r) to Abū Bakr and ʿUmar by their honorific titles ʿal-Ṣiddīqʾ (the truthful) and ʿal-Fārūqʾ (the one who distinguishes truth from falsehood). Such titles cannot possibly be used as such by a Fatimid imam in a treatise dispraising Abū Bakr and ʿUmar and considering them to be usurpers. By referring to them with these honorific titles, al-Manṣūr must, therefore, have been using in an ironic way the same terminology that

---

3. Ibid., p. 49.

4. See Yusuf Ibish, *Nuṣūṣ al-fikr al-siyāsī al-Islāmī, al-imāma ʿind al-sunna* (Beirut: Dār aṭ-Ṭalīʿa, 1966), pp. 20–26.

was found in the two aforementioned works of al-Ashʿarī, especially in the chapter 'Bāb al-kalām fī imāmat Abī Bakr al-Ṣiddīq' of his book *al-Ibāna*[5] and the chapter entitled 'Bāb al-kalām fi'l-imāma' of his other book, *al-Lumaʿ*.[6]

2. The Murjiʿa. They also believe that the imam should be chosen by the people. He should, however, be deserving of being vicegerent of the Prophet as well as being knowledgeable. He should rule in accordance with the Qur'ān and the Traditions of the Prophet; in case he does not find for his statements anything in the Scriptures to rely on, he can formulate independent judgments, provided they do not contradict the Qur'ān and the Traditions. The Murjiʿa, however, maintain that obedience to the imam is incumbent on everybody unless he disobeys God. In such a case the *umma* should depose him and install another imam.

3. The Muʿtazila. They believe that the Prophet had not nominated any successor, nor had he alluded to anyone. He had merely called on the people to choose someone to be in authority over them, so they chose Abū Bakr.

4. The Khawārij. They maintain that no one knows whether the Prophet had called on the people to choose anyone or not, nor if he alluded to anyone or not. However, there should be necessarily an imam installed by the people, so that he may apply the religious laws and implement legal punishments.[7] Such an imam should be obeyed as long as he capably performs his duties or else he should be deposed.

The *Tathbīt al-imāma* is addressed to these different factions. Although al-Manṣūr, as Wilferd Madelung states, 'was faced in the few years of his reign right after his military triumph [over the Khārijī rebel Abū Yazīd], with the need to gain the loyal allegiance of his Sunni, mostly Mālikī, subjects, many of whom had for a time sided with the Khariji rebel',[8] he found it necessary to refute the Sunni and

---

5. Ibid., pp. 20–23.

6. Ibid., pp. 24–26.

7. Al-Nuʿmān, *Daʿāʾim*, p. 49.

8. Wilferd Madelung, 'A treatise on the Imamate of the Fatimid Caliph al-Manṣūr bi-Allāh', in *Texts, Documents and Artifacts: Ismaili Studies in*

Khāriji theories of the imamate and to convince such factions and others that whatever tolerance he showed, it would never be on the account of the ideological principles of the Fatimid state.

The different theories concerning the vicegerency of the Prophet were, therefore, discussed by al-Manṣūr in the *Tathbīt*. Hence, this treatise could have also meant to serve as a guide book for the Ismailis in proving the *raison d'être* of the Fatimid state.

The right of the Ismaili imams to the vicegerency of the Prophet is, therefore, discussed at length. Also discussed are the necessity of the imamate from the Ismaili point of view, the validity of installing the imam by appointment from above rather than through election by the *umma* and, consequently, the illegitimacy of the imamate of the first three caliphs and the Umayyad and Abbasid dynasties.

The author begins by asserting that the imamate is a religious commandment. It is not imposed by any human authority or by any conjectural opinion. Therefore, Abū Bakr and ‘Umar were illegitimate imams.

He then argues that the imam's appointment is a divine commandment. It is neither a mere convenience, nor is the imam simply commissioned by the *umma*.

The author then proceeds to refute the following arguments:

1. Abū Bakr deserves to be appointed as imam because of his previous designation by the Prophet to lead the prayer.
2. The imamate should go to the victor.
3. Even if it is assigned to a certain person at a certain time, the imamate should not necessarily be always implemented by assignment.
4. The imamate can go to a less deserving person.
5. The imamate is not necessarily a permanent institution.
6. The Messenger of God did not assign an imam to succeed him.

The author then goes on to demonstrate that the Prophet did designate ‘Alī b. Abī Ṭālib to be vicegerent and to prove that those who do not acknowledge ‘Alī as imam are going astray.

Confirming that ‘Alī was the one appointed by the Prophet, he goes on to refute the Sunni belief in the legitimacy of electing an

---

Honour of D.S. Richards, ed. Chase F. Robinson (Leiden: Brill, 2003), p. 69.

imam who is less deserving in knowledge and piety.

Al-Manṣūr goes on to argue that by letting the institution of the imamate be a tool in the hands of different and contradicting factions, the *umma* would be subjected to the various contradicting interests of those factions. The institution of the imamate would thus be ruined and chaos would prevail. The imam should therefore, by necessity, be appointed from above.

The author comes to the conclusion that the imam's appointment from above is divinely decreed and is, therefore, a divine commandment just like any other cardinal pillar of Islam. It is, therefore, ordained in the Scriptures.

However, the fact that the Qur'ān was not explicit about this matter, and consequently it was not agreed upon unanimously, does not mean that no mention of a divine appointment exists. Here, the author endeavours to prove that the Qur'ān and the Traditions did in fact mention the divine appointment of 'Alī as imam. If such an appointment was indirectly mentioned in the Qur'ān, it was explicitly mentioned in the Traditions. The author thus confirms the fact that the Traditions of the Prophet are considered a main source in Islam, second only to the Qur'ān.

He then proceeds to point out that the fact that some of the common people of the *umma* are unaware of such a commandment and other revealed divine favours (*nawāzil*) does not invalidate them. In fact the Prophet was keen, says the author, not to divulge such favours to the masses owing to their ignorance. Therefore, it is necessary to have an imam who would be chosen by God through the Prophet so that he may guide the *umma* according to these divine favours. Had the masses been allowed to receive these divine favours they would have been required to do more than they were supposed to. Their role in life would thus be impeded. However, since they are supposed to implement God's utterances and relish these divine favours, there should be an imam who is cognizant of what others are not cognizant of, and who is able to endure what others cannot. Such an imam, by necessity, cannot likely be subject to sinfulness or liable to make mistakes.

In implementing God's commandments and receiving divine favours, which are also revealed to the Prophet, such an imam should be in authority over mankind. As the Prophet is divinely appointed, so should be those in authority after him.

However, this does not make the imam, says the author, equal to the Prophet. He mentions three points of difference between the Prophet and the imam. First, unlike the Prophet, the imam is denied revelation from God. Second, the Prophet is superior to the imam. Third, abrogation of Qurʾānic verses occurred only during the Prophet's lifetime, not during the lifetime of the imam. It is worth noting that the author does not elaborate on the second point and takes it for granted in a treatise addressed to the common people, be they believers in Ismaili Shiʿism or not. As mentioned earlier, this work aims to address the religio-political confirmation of the imamate of ʿAlī b. Abī Ṭālib and that of the imams from his progeny, and refute logically the different non-Ismaili theories of the imamate. The author thus devotes a considerable portion of the work to prove the necessity and validity of ʿAlī b. Abī Ṭālib's appointment as imam and to show that every other person contemporary with him was not eligible to become imam.

The author then moves on to establish that it is impossible for the Prophet not to have appointed an imam to succeed him. He also points out that it is impossible for the Prophet to have left this important matter to the discretion of the *umma*. This is because it is impossible for the *umma*, even for the learned, to come to a consensus on the matter owing to their lack of familiarity with those who would look to occupy the post. Hence, they would never come to a unanimous agreement, and even if they did, they would be basing their decision on an inauthentic Tradition. Furthermore, even if all the *umma* unanimously agreed on one imam because he was found to be the best, it would still be likely that some other person unknown to the *umma* would be superior to the one chosen. Additionally, when *ijmāʿ* is based on a Tradition short of being authentic, it would be categorically invalid. In fact, the *umma* will never unanimously consent on one imam, and even the learned in the *umma* cannot come to such a decision, for the following reasons: the great number of factions in the *umma*, the wide range of provinces, the various beliefs among the members of the *umma*, the enmity among them, and their constant accusation of unbelief by each other.

As such, it is imperative that the imam be appointed from above, just as the Prophet was. The people, says the author, have no right to choose either one of them; it is the Messenger of God who is entitled to appoint the imam who in turn will appoint his successor, and so on. The Messenger of God, the author says, is the imam of imams. He was divinely appointed. He, in turn, appointed ʿAlī b. Abī Ṭālib as imam, who in turn appointed his successor. Consequently, appointment to the imamate runs from father to son. It follows that God has imposed on the *umma* obedience to the imam.

However, the author explains, because of the discontinuity of the previous cycle, that is, of Jesus, as well as of the predominance of tyrants in the present cycle of Muḥammad and, consequently, the imams going underground with their lieutenants acting as façade imams, it became necessary to have the rank of imamate restricted to the Prophet's progeny.

Although the bloodline from the Prophet became necessary for the validity of the imamate of the cycle of Muḥammad, such ancestry, the author insinuates, is not imperative in the absolute sense, except in this very cycle. Be that as it may, the author finds it necessary to emphasise such a bloodline in this cycle. He logically defends the necessity of this bloodline from the Prophet by using the following arguments:

1. In matters related to God's religion, neither individuals nor the *umma* at large have the right to sanction independent judgements. Such matters are out of their reach. Those who claim such a right should be dispraised. The fact that they were previously praised for the good deeds they undertook in the past does not make them immune from sinfulness, for which they should be dispraised.
2. Piety, goodness and blood relation to the Prophet are not enough to make a person such as al-ʿAbbās, the Prophet's uncle, deserve to be imam. Many people possess such qualities.
3. Not every Tradition praising a certain Companion of the Prophet can be an indication of the right to the imamate. Such Traditions cannot be put on the same level as that of the Pond of Ghadīr Khumm whose authenticity is recognised by everyone, unlike other Traditions related by a single person.
4. Since Abū Bakr could not fit howsoever for the Prophet's vicegerency, he had no right to nominate ʿUmar b. al-Khaṭṭāb for the

imamate. 'Umar's imamate is therefore, by necessity, groundless and invalid.

5.   Those who believed in the validity of Abū Bakr's vicegerency and in the nomination of 'Umar to be vicegerent after him were, therefore, sure that the Prophet empowered the *umma* to choose the fittest among them as imam. Had this been true it would necessarily mean either that the Prophet was ignorant of who was the fittest after him or that he had refrained from installing the fittest. Both alternatives were degrading to the Prophet.

6.   As a logical consequence, by appointing a consultative committee to choose the imam after him, 'Umar committed a similar sin. He founded his decision on neither the Qur'ān nor the Traditions. It was a decision based solely on his own personal conjecture. This was absolutely forbidden in Islam.

7.   'Alī was accused of having consented to such a decision. Even if this accusation were true, it would be simply out of dissimulation, a practice made permissible by both the Qur'ān and the Traditions.

8.   In reply to those who say that no one can equal the Prophet in knowledge, certitude and wise judgement, the author clearly condemns all exaggerations in 'Alī, as well as in putting him on equal footing with the Prophet. Anything of this kind is pure delusion, deceit and unbelief.

9.   'Alī is no more than the Prophet's cousin, legatee, successor and heir of his knowledge. He was a sure vestige of the Prophet's knowledge, a sound way out from doubt, a true understanding of good judgement and a clear way to explain concrete and abstract religious matters. Evidence for 'Alī possessing all these qualities was the fact that his appointment was by the Prophet. Following the same logic, no one can be a true imam unless one is appointed to the imamate by the previous imam.

10.   As for the qualities and miracles ascribed to some of the Companions, including 'Alī, the author makes it a point to prove that these are not enough to claim the position of imam. Such a position is won only by appointment by the previous imam. The chain ends with the Prophet, who is considered the first imam and who is invested by God Himself.

Descriptions of the manuscripts used
in editing the *Tathbīt al-imāma*

Two manuscripts were used in editing al-Manṣūr bi'llāh's *Tathbīt*, both of which are now in the collections of the library of The Institute of Ismaili Studies. The first ('ب') is from the Hamdani collection. In the colophon, the scribe has mentioned neither his name nor the place where the manuscript was copied. From the wordings of the colophon, however, one can judge that the scribe was Ismaili, but without any definite hint as to which denomination he belonged. He referred only to 'the lord and imam of time' without mentioning his name, which suggests that he did not belong to the Nizārī Ismailis who alone among the Ismailis believe that the imam is not concealed. The copying of the manuscript was completed in 1310/1892; the month is referred to as the revered (*muʿazzam*) month, and the day is not mentioned. The manuscript contains 145 folios, and is paginated with Persian numerals by a later hand. It is 18.5 x 13.2 cm in size, and every page contains 10 lines except for the first page which contains six lines plus the title of the treatise, without mentioning its author's name. However, the manuscript is headed by an independent title page where the name of the author reads 'al-Manṣūr bi'llāh the prince of Believers our lord Ismāʿīl, son [instead of father] of our lord Maʿadd al-Muʿizz li-Dīn Allāh'. The length of each line is approximately 6.5 cm. The manuscript is written in neat unvocalised *naskhī* with no rubrication. It contains a number of grammatical mistakes, and occasionally words and whole sentences and phrases are omitted out of negligence by the scribe.

The second manuscript ('أ') is from the Zāhid ʿAlī collection. Unlike the previous manuscript, the colophon contains the scribe's name, Aḥmad ʿAlī b. Mullā Yūsuf ʿAlī, but it does not mention the place where he copied his manuscript. This scribe completed the copying of the manuscript on 28 Dhu'l-Ḥijja, 1329/18 December 1911. As in manuscript 'ب' one can judge from the wording of the colophon that the scribe is an Ismaili, although his denomination is also unknown. Since the imam in the scribe's lifetime is not mentioned by name he, too, may not belong to the Nizārī Ismaili denomination. This, however, may not necessarily be true, for not every Nizārī scribe mentions the imam's name. The manuscript contains 123 folios. It is 18.5 x 11 cm in size and every page contains 13 lines except for the first page which contains 11. On this page the caliphal title of the author is al-Manṣūr bi-Naṣr Allāh instead of the usual title al-Manṣūr bi'llāh. The length of each line is approximately 6 cm. The manuscript is written in readable unvocalised *naskhī* with little rubrication. Though it contains grammatical mistakes, and words and sentences are sometimes omitted, it can be considered more reliable than manuscript 'ب'.

The mistakes made by the scribes of both manuscripts are corrected in the Arabic text but designated in the footnotes.

Methods used in editing and translating

I have attempted to reproduce the words and sentences of the author as closely as possible to the original work although I was sometimes obliged to paraphrase the translation so as to keep its sense as closely as possible to the context of the original treatise. In this regard, the last part of the *Tathbīt*, as it appears in both manuscripts, seems to lack smoothness in style. This is probably due to negligence on the part of the various scribes who copied the original manuscript.

I have also inserted punctuation, paragraphed the text and introduced subheadings to render it easier to understand by the contemporary reader. I have also supplied enough *hamza*s, *shadda*s and vowel marks to make the text easier to read. Trivial mistakes due to slips of the pen and orthographic improficiency on the part of the scribes have been corrected without pointing them out in the footnotes.

Historical events referred to in the text that are not directly related to the subject of the treatise are not commented on in the footnotes so that the reader is not distracted by matters unconnected directly to the core subject.

The numbers in the margins of the Arabic text and the English translation refer to the folios of 'أ', while the notes to the Arabic text mark up all significant mistakes, readings, and versions of both 'أ' and 'ب'.

Care was taken to translate the Arabic text into idiomatic English as much as possible, without abusing the spirit of the Arabic text. Also, some polemical passages written in the exigencies of the time, especially of the revolt of the Ibaḍī Abū Yazid, supported by the Sunni jurists, have been omitted from the translation.

Qur'ānic passages quoted in the translation are based on the *The Koran Interpreted* by A.J. Arberry. In rare cases, however, I have modified these. Reference to the Qur'ān cite *sūra* and verse of the official Egyptian version.

Translation of the *Tathbīt al-imāma*

[1v] Preface

This book, *The Confirmation of the Imamate*, is authored by the magnanimous imam, the shadow of the Lord of mankind, our lord Ismā'īl al-Manṣūr bi-Naṣr Allāh, God's blessings be on him and his virtuous forefathers and most noble descendants.

Introduction

In the name of God, the Merciful, the Compassionate. May God bless and give peace to His Messenger and his family. May He increase your desire for knowledge and want for understanding, and may He dispose you to be thankful for his blessings. You have asked me, may God guide all your affairs, about the confirmation of the imamate of the Prince of Believers, 'Alī b. Abī Ṭālib (God's blessing be on him) and his right to it before anyone else. I shall clarify this matter to you in a way that cannot be refuted by any of the foes, and attest it with proof that cannot be denied by any of the opponents **[2r]** and enemies. So, [I ask you], may God have mercy on you, to use it in good thinking and right judgement in a way enjoined by demonstrative reason and not by mere hearsay or according to the allegations of those who have confused the institution of the imamate and assumed the necessity of having an imam presiding over mankind.

Is the imamate confirmed by conjecture or by one's authority or by divine commandment?

The first thing to do is to ask them about their belief in the necessity of having an imam. To such people one should say: Is this a belief that you hold by conjecture, or is it a judgement that you prescribe on mankind, or is it a commandment that is divinely imposed?

If you say it is a commandment, then who is, in your opinion, the appointee among you to that position that God (Glory be to Him) has designated over mankind and associated his obedience with that of the Messenger of God (God's blessings be on him and his family)? If they say he is Abū Bakr, we reply: you have been refuted by Abū Bakr himself.

[2v] He said: 'I nominate one of these two men to the imamate: Abū 'Ubayda b. al-Jarrāḥ and 'Umar b. al-Khaṭṭāb, so pledge allegiance to the one of your choice.' He also said: 'Release me, release me [from my post]!' Then he said: 'I wish I had asked the Messenger of God (God's blessings be on him) who should be in authority after him'. He also said: 'Now the Muslims have requested that I may be vicegerent over them.' He took a salary of two *dirhams* a day from the State treasury. You have also been refuted by 'Umar saying: 'The promise of allegiance to Abū Bakr was a lapse. May God protect the Muslims from its evil consequences ... ' and by his saying: 'If I leave you [without a will], so did he who was better than I, and if I nominate a successor, so did he who was better than I.'[9] By this statement he meant that the Messenger of God (God's blessings be on him) did not nominate any successor, whereas

[3r] 'Abū Bakr did nominate me before his death'. You were also refuted by the *Anṣār* who said: 'One emir from amongst us and one from amongst you.' Likewise, you have related that the Messenger of God (God's blessings be on him) said: 'If I were to nominate anyone as my successor, without counsel, I would nominate Ibn Mas'ūd.' How then was it permissible for Abū Bakr to change the Scripture, abrogate the divine precepts and move the matter from where God has placed it? And, how can he release himself from something which God (Exalted be He) and His Messenger have allegedly ordained him to do? How can this ordinance be from God and His Messenger to Abū Bakr, when Abū Bakr thought he should alter it by replacing himself with Abū 'Ubayda or 'Umar b. al-Khaṭṭāb? How can something ordained and sanctioned by God be a lapse, as was mentioned by 'Umar b. al-Khaṭṭāb, knowing that a lapse in 'Umar b. al-Khaṭṭāb's statement can only be the opposite of the truth.

If this were an opinion you conjectured or an assumption [3v] you imagined, how then would it be permissible for you to think that God did not heed the welfare of His creation, nor did He spare them what is necessary? As if you consider yourselves, in what you have done, to be more truthful and sincere to the *umma* than God (Exalted be He) and His Messenger (God's blessings be on him). To such people one must say: Don't you see, if God had ordered

---

9. For the relevant context, see Abu'l Fawāris, *al-Risāla fi'l imāma*, ed. and tr. Sami Makarem as *The Political Doctrine of the Ismā'īlīs (The Imamate)* (Delmar, NY, 1977), p. 37 of the English trans. and p. 23 of the Arabic text, with notes 87 and 88 on p. 80. See also *Sahih Bukhari*, vol. 9, Book 89, no. 325.

His Prophet (God's blessings be on him) to install one over you and he did not respond, would he not be violating and disobeying His order? If He had forbidden him from doing that, then who gave you permission to do what was forbidden for the Messenger of God (God's blessings be on him)? If that was a sway over mankind, who then authorised you to sway over them, so that you shed blood that God (Exalted be He) has spared, allowed yourselves to their women when God had prohibited it, and warranted their property when God had forbidden it? You declared jurisdiction over God's religion and over His people in a way that was not allowed by God; is there [4r] any reward for what you have done, or is there punishment? Also, is this permissible to you in matters other than that of the imamate as it is in matters of the imamate? Otherwise, who permitted you in matters of the imamate and prohibited you in other matters?

Then one must say to those people: Which was more proper, what the Messenger of God (God's blessings be on him) did in refraining from doing so, or what you did in installing those you had nominated? If they answer: What we did is more proper, then they should be told: Do you claim to be more worthy and more righteous than the Messenger of God (God's blessings be on him)?

Then they are told: Tell us about the appointment of the imam; is it a religious duty or not? If they say it is not a religious duty, we say: Then what do we need it for? If they say it is a religious duty, we reply: Should God, therefore, reveal it and should the Messenger of God convey it? If they say yes, the answer would be: Did they fail to fulfill their duty? If they say no, then one should say: This is an intrusion [4v] into God's religion and an imprudence which you committed against the Messenger of God. Have you considered what it would mean if this was supposed to be a religious duty but was forsaken by God who failed to reveal it or His Messenger who failed to convey it? If so, it may be that many other religious duties that are important to Muslims may not have been sent down by God or conveyed by His Messenger. In fact, you have conducted yourselves to such a conclusion in matters of *fatwas* concerning divine duties, jurisdictions, the lawful, the unlawful, and cases of homicide and religious observances. Moreover, you claimed that God had decreed religious duties, ordered and prohibited things that He had not sent down in His Book or by way of His Messenger, so you were impelled to rely on analogy, personal opinion and discretion. This is indeed utter blasphemy and disgrace of God and His Messenger.

Is the imam's appointment a divine commandment or a *sunna*, or was it mere commission?

To such people one must say: Tell us about the appointment of the imam; is it a divine obligation

[5r] or a *sunna* of the Prophet? If it is a divine obligation, then who among you are we ordered to obey? If they say it is Abū Bakr, we reply: Was Abū Bakr aware or was he not aware of his being designated to be obeyed? If he was aware of it, then why did he say: 'I wish I asked the Messenger of God (God's blessings be on him), "Who will be in authority after you?" and why did he say: 'I nominate one of these two men to the imamate: Abū ʿUbayda b. al-Jarrāḥ and ʿUmar b. al-Khaṭṭāb, so pledge allegiance to the one of your choice', and why did he say: 'Release me, release me [from my post]!', and why did he say: 'Now the Muslims have requested that I may be vicegerent over them.' Moreover, why did he take his salary from the state treasury? And why did ʿUmar b. al-Khaṭṭāb say: 'The promise of allegiance to Abū Bakr was a lapse. May God protect the Muslims from its evil consequences … ' and why did the *Anṣār* say: 'One emir from amongst us and one

[5v] from amongst you', and why [did Abū Bakr] say: 'I was put in charge of you, yet I am not the best of you.' Why did he not say instead: Verily God has put me in charge of you, desired me to guard you, and ordered me to administer you and has given me such and such or has done such and such with me? On the contrary, he related things about himself which proved that God could not possibly accept anyone like him to guard the *umma*, especially what he said about himself … How can it, thus, be possible that God appoints as imam anyone of such characteristics, or to choose for His religion any one with such defects and fluctuating qualities? How can He accept for the Muslims a person who has accepted for them someone who is not accepted by God, such as Abū ʿUbayda b. al-Jarrāḥ or ʿUmar b. al-Khaṭṭāb, and who admits that he does not resemble any of the believers, either in knowledge or in person, and who fails to

assume the affairs of the Muslims better than they do? Such a person
[6r] is not capable of giving them legal opinion on lawful and unlawful matters, or on their religious duties, traditions, legal judgements,
and what God has prescribed of religious and civil affairs. How can
it be possible that God (Exalted be He) appoints a guardian whose
obedience is incumbent on all His creation without informing both
him and the subjects about such assignment and [without] teaching
the guardian how to rule properly, especially when He enjoined the
guardian to administer the affairs of the subjects and enjoined the
subjects to obey him and yield to his knowledge? On the other hand,
if such a person does not know about his appointment as imam,
whose obedience was enjoined on the *umma*, then what has made
him do and say what he did and said? Furthermore, why did he not
justify his appointment as imam in the manner we have mentioned
above? Why did he not inform the people of his appointment if it
was really announced by God and His Messenger, especially if God
and His Messenger had commanded him to be in charge
[6v] of the affairs of all people and called upon them to obey him,
submit to his judgement and accept his knowledge, or was the
matter a mere commission rather than that of religious duty? If it
was merely a commission, then how was it possible for the people
to address such a person as vicegerent of the Messenger of God?
Did they say the truth or did they lie? If they said the truth, then
what did Abū Bakr and the others really mean by saying what they
said? If they lied, then why did Abū Bakr willingly approve of such
a saying and not deny and reject it, especially after they were proven
with certainty by all people to be utterly false testimony? How did he
manage to let the people testify falsely against the Messenger of God
(God's blessings be on him)? How did he manage to go along with
them all the way in their testimony until he passed into perdition?
[One should ask those people]: What to you is the difference between
a witness who gives a false testimony
[7r] and a person who is falsely testified against? And it is said to
them: Do you know? In addition to the question of the imamate,
they most probably departed from many religious tenets by deviat-
ing from their correct sense, obstructing them from their goal and
assigning them to the wrong people. Observances of such tenets were
ruled out, either intentionally or because of wrongfulness, error and

forgetfulness. If this is acceptable in matters of the imamate, which is considered to be the foremost religious tenet whose observance is most incumbent on man, then what of the other tenets that you were unable to discern either by analogy, opinion or personal judgement, even to the point of passing one hundred different and contradicting judgements for a single case? In fact, had you passed one thousand different judgements instead, you would have only gone further from the truth. This is because neither opinion nor analogy nor personal judgement

[7v] can lead them, in God's eyes, to the truth, nor does it deviate them from the path of the imam, as it did not deviate them from that of the Messenger (God's blessings be on him). Perhaps, most of the religious statutes have been ramified by being likened to what is contrary to their very nature. Had those people been given the chance, they would have forsaken these tenets as they did with the previous ones. For if this can happen in regard to some tenets, it could happen to all the tenets. What can happen to some can happen to all and *vice versa*. To such people one should therefore say: Do you realise that most of what people were ordered to follow and were enjoined to consider as religious duties – such as paying allegiance to the imam they appointed and making his obedience incumbent on all creation – could have not been spiritually stipulated by God and His Messenger, as you would like to think? In fact, all the affairs of the *umma* used

[8r] to run and be administered in such a way. Furthermore, one should say to such people: Tell us, is there any alternative concerning this matter other than it being either a constraint or a divine ordinance? If it is a constraint, then why do we need to burden ourselves with something we are spared of doing, when neither God nor His Messenger had allowed it? Furthermore, following such matters causes disgraceful derogation and blame and leads to cardinal offence and major sinning. This is because constraint is reprehensible to God in all cases, especially in those cases in which forcefulness is prohibited. Such cases have already been sanctioned by God and carried through. They can never be amended or changed. Any one of us who does that would be considered disobedient to God and his Messenger. [As for the other alternative], that is, being a binding religious ordinance, then God has decisively solved it and spared us

its burden. On the other hand, if it is not binding, then we are spared [8v] any judicial error, even if it contained obedience to God and His Messenger. This is because by rejecting it we spare ourselves of all analogies and ungrounded opinions on legal judgements and *fatwas* concerning what is religiously allowed or disallowed. We return thus to relying solely on divine judgement. This is exactly what true devotion to God is. Then we should say to them: Tell us, had you chosen Abū ʿUbayda b. al-Jarrāḥ or ʿUmar b. al-Khaṭṭāb, would you have addressed him as the vicegerent of the Messenger of God? Would you have any doubt that such an address is an utter lie, even if you did not actually give him priority over others? In fact, many people were at fault concerning this issue, as they relied on those considerations mentioned above. Such issues have occurred before God and His Messenger. Many verdicts were presumably passed according to God's religion, and were inflicted on the people, and were concerned with matters not in line with the teachings of God and His Messenger.

[9r] [In this respect one may ask:] Do you see any difference between a person who willingly takes money in spite of knowing he does not own it, and who willingly has intercourse with a woman in spite of knowing she belongs to someone else, and who willingly sheds blood that is legally spared, and a person who is forced to take forbidden money, and forced to have unlawful intercourse, and forced to shed illegal blood, though he knows that such acts are neither of his will nor ordained by God and His Messenger? Both people are equally responsible before the law whether the act is done willingly or not. This is because it is well known indeed that such acts, whatever the cause of their commitment, are far from God's righteous Volition. No one who commits such acts may claim any right, neither for himself nor for those in authority [9v] over him. Wrong begets wrong and right begets right. Such are the characteristics of he who says: I shall implement that which was sent down by God. As for those who do not act and engage themselves in accordance with the teachings of God and His Messenger, they are at evident fault. The more they increase in their knowledge the more they increase in their error, disparity and disobedience to God and His Messenger.

To those people one should say: Tell us about the call to prayer in your country; is it more important than the instalment of the imam? The rituals of ablution, prayer, almsgiving and other duties and principles of religion – are they more important than the instalment of the imam? The duty of the *khums*, together with that concerning the offering to those whose hearts are brought together – are they more important than the duty of installing the imam? Do you consider such things to be abrogated and deviated from their aims or neglected and no longer observed? Also, what is the difference between the abrogation of the imam and the abrogation of

[10r] prayers, the *khums* and the duty of offering to those whose hearts are brought together, and the abrogation of pilgrimage and the benefit of *'umra* until the pilgrimage, and other practices the injunction of which was revealed by God and decreed in the Scripture? No one has disagreed that they were sent down by God, or that they were enjoined and made incumbent on everyone in spite of them declaring that which was unlawful to be lawful and that which was lawful to be unlawful. This was the produce of their predecessors and leaders who even refused to be questioned about their deeds. It was obvious that such behaviour of theirs was not out of dissimulation, since they were certain that whatever they said was accepted and whatever they decreed was considered lawful. As a matter of fact, when they allowed themselves to do away with the imamate, it became easy for them to do away with all the aforementioned religious ordinances. By doing so they were defying God and the Messenger.

To be an imam in prayer is different from being an imam of the *umma*

Then one should say to them: Tell us about your saying, 'When we saw the Messenger of God (God's blessings be on him) inviting and sanctioning Abū Bakr to lead the prayer, we made him our leader and sanctioned him as our superior', but is your statement more accountable

[10v] than that of others who said, 'When we saw the Messenger of God (God's blessings be on him) depose him publicly from leading the prayers, we deposed him. When we saw that God and His Messenger drove him back from conveying a part of a *sūra* of the Qur'ān, we denied him the right of conveying anything at all. When we saw that the Messenger of God (God's blessings be on him) took

heed and disapproved of him and ordered him to join Usāma's army with his comrades, we disapproved of him.' What kind of free will would such a thing be? Do you have, in regard to such matters, something different from those who discredited him and found that he is not fit to be an imam deserving any priority?

Should the imamate be divinely appointed or should it go to the victor?

Then one should say to those people: Tell us about the imamate. Is it a religious obligation to allot it to a certain person, or does it belong to the victor? If it is a religious obligation to be given to a certain person once and for all without being reassigned afterwards, then such an argument of yours would be refuted as well, because that which is right concerning the first imam is right concerning

[11r] the second, the third, the fourth, the fifth ... and the tenth until the end of time. On the other hand, if the imamate was supposed to be the prerogative of the vanquisher, then the provision, according to you, would be that the imamate goes to the vanquisher either by virtue of a written decree issued by God and His Messenger or on account of a personal opinion or an arbitrary action of yours over the whole *umma*. No other argument can be given except these two: either on the basis of being a religious tenet or of being a mere allegiance to a certain man that you know in person or a man who has seized it by force.

Hence, you have no alternative but to have a definite standpoint concerning the appointment and instalment of the imam. However, any standpoint you decide upon must be supported by evidence showing that God and His Messenger had definitely ordered you to adopt it in both word and deed. So give us a clear proof that your standpoint, which you claimed to be true, is really so. (There is no power except in God) (18:39) the All-High, the All-Glorious.

Then one should say to them: What do you say about what is concealed from you

[11v] and from us? Is it applicable to that which is apparent to you and to us, or not? If the same laws apply to the one who is absent as to the one who is present, then we would be seeing, just as you do, that the imamate would be a *fait accompli* whether it is effected by appointment or election, regardless of it being deserved. Was it ever

other than that? What we witness happening in the present time is clear evidence of what happened in the past. Is this not sufficient evidence for (a people who reflect)? (2:164; 13:4; 16:12 and 16:67; 29:35; 30:24 and 30:28; 45:5)

Can the imamate go to the lesser person?

Then one should say to them: Tell us about the fact that people pay allegiance to the imam for all epochs and times. Is this because the imam is better and more knowledgeable than any one of them and more deserving? Or is it because they cannot be righteous and cannot follow the right path unless they obey and are guided by him? Or is it because they are afraid of his power and authority? Or is it because he is supported by the evil doers and their associates? If this were the case, then Muʿāwiya b. Abī Sufyān, Yazīd

[12r] b. Muʿāwiya, Marwān b. al-Hakam, ʿAbd al-Malik b. Marwān, al-Walīd, Sulaymān, Hishām, and others, and all the tyrants of the clan of Umayya would be the best and most righteous of all mankind and the most deserving of the station of the Messenger of God (God's blessings be on him). If the case were otherwise and the people were obeying those who have power over them and their affairs, would their pretence concerning the imam of the epoch and time be different? Would things not take but the same course? Would their arguments concerning Abū Bakr and his appointment and instalment as imam not be the same? Would their plea for his right not be like yours, and like that of your fellow men, rulers, men of knowledge, jurists, leaders and traditionalists whose arguments you rely upon concerning the supremacy of those we have mentioned from the clan of Umayya, and others? What would the difference be? You will never find

[12v] any difference.

The permanence of the imamate

Then to such people we should say: Tell us about the imamate, no matter in which epoch or time. Did its provisions, whether coming from God or from you, ever differ? If they say no, neither in themselves nor in the eyes of God, because God (Exalted be He) never contradicts His stipulations, then we would say to them: If God's stipulations concerning the imamate are always the same, and if such

an institution was, to you, valid only by appointment, then where is such a testament of appointment now? If the imamate was in your opinion valid by election, then what election have you carried out and where did it end up? Who has been ordered to implement it? If they claim that God has given contradictory stipulations and has done away with an appointed imam – for He does not force His creation to obey one who does not obey Him, nor does He impose obedience of one who disobeys Him, violates His orders and transgresses His prescriptions – we say to them: Therefore, your institution of imamate has absolutely fallen into disuse
[13r] and God would necessarily have abolished the imam and ordered you to relinquish him. Such conclusions are definitely based on personal judgement. Now, would you tell us which of the following alternatives was better: To believe in the first, which is the appointment of the imam in such a way, or to believe in the second, which results in the relinquishing of the imam? How can it be possible for mankind either to appoint or to release an imam as it wishes? Give us a decisive proof of the validity of such a claim of yours. Or do you claim that God (Blessed and Exalted be He) was in the past more heedful of His creation than He is now? God is too highly Exalted for that.

Did the Messenger appoint a vicegerent or not?
Then, one should say to them: Tell us what you thought of the Messenger of God (God's blessings be on him)? That he left behind a will naming his vicegerent or that he did not? If they say: our belief is that
[13v] he left a testament stating that he appointed a vicegerent, we would ask: What made you refrain from such a belief and claim that he relinquished his testament of appointing a vicegerent? This means that either you believe that God has ordered him not to leave a testament or a statement of appointment, and has warned him of doing so, and that he obeyed (and this is a contradiction to what he has related from God), or that the Messenger of God was overcome by error, oblivion and ignorance, far be it from him! This would be contrary to the interest of all mankind. In fact, the purpose of such a claim would be non-compliance with the Messenger's orders and disobedience to his will. God has deemed His Prophet (God's

blessings be on him) too high to commit an error or to fall under such a pretext. Since we do not find the matter as we have described, what then would be your excuse for installing

[14r] a man you claim to be the vicegerent of the Messenger of God (God's blessings be on him), who has inherited both the post of vicegerent and that of leadership from the Prophet, declared the Prophet's belongings and properties lawful for him, and ruled over his immediate family and his inheritance? How can you do that when you have witnessed before God that the Prophet has appointed neither a legatee nor a vicegerent? Such an act of yours highly discredits and defames the Prophet of God (God's blessings be on him). Do you have any other argument against those who do not agree with you? In fact, you addressed him as vicegerent of the Messenger of God when he originally did not make such a claim about himself, and did not say: 'The Messenger of God appointed me as his vicegerent.' Instead he said: 'The Muslims appointed me and accepted me as such.' He also said: 'I was put in charge of you, yet I am not the best among you.' He did not say: 'God (Exalted be He) and his Messenger put me in charge of you.' He took a salary of two *dirham*s per day from the state treasury.

[14v] ... Furthermore, you know that he did not read the Qur'ān, and he who does not read the Qur'ān does not know its interpretation, nor does he know the verses which abrogate others and those which are abrogated, nor does he know the clear verses from the ambiguous ones. How can a person with such shortcomings differentiate between what is lawful and what is unlawful? Moreover, we have seen you classify mankind into categories; yet, he was not in any category that entitles him to be known by any virtue, be it religious or worldly. In fact, you have related that when the Prophet (God's blessings be on him) mentioned the truthful, he identified Abū Dharr; when he mentioned the people of the Qur'ān, he identified Abdallah b. Mas'ūd and Ubayy b. Ka'b; when he mentioned the people of religious obligation, he identified Zayd b. Thābit; when he mentioned the people of justice,

[15r] he identified 'Alī b. Abī Ṭālib; and when he mentioned the knowledgeable in the lawful and the unlawful, he identified Mu'ādh b. Jabal. How then did you assent to the instalment of someone in place of the Messenger of God (God's blessings be on him) who

would be in need of everyone without being needed by anyone in anything? In fact, you have reached the epitome of choosing the worst and in defaming the Messenger (God's blessings be on him).

Other reasons discrediting Abū Bakr's and 'Umar's imamate

To such people one should say: Tell us, what should people do after acknowledging the imamate of Abū Bakr and 'Umar? If they say they should pay allegiance to them, we say: Paying allegiance to them means complying with them, obeying them, yielding to their orders and believing that everything they say, and everything they decree [15v] and sentence is correct, and is a duty and a necessity, in the same way that a religious imposition is. Or, one can be in doubt of what they say. In this case one should notice whether or not they committed a mistake or passed an unrighteous verdict contrary to the revealed Scriptures and the Muslim beliefs. If they say: It is not for us to judge them, we must rather accept what they say, believe in their deeds and never infringe on their commands, then we say: He of you who does that would be committing either a sin or an injustice, or would be an unbeliever or would be going astray; he would be restrained by no laws and abide by no responsibility, be it religious or worldly. If such people are considered sinful and unjust, or unbelievers and going astray, for having taken such a stand, then that will also apply to every one of the Prophet's Companions, starting with 'Umar b. al-Khaṭṭāb by succeeding Abū Bakr, and the rest of the *umma* (as everyone was involved in such a dispute), and if all of the *umma* [16r] would be counted among the sinful and the infidels or among those who fall in between, then none of them would be reliable enough or even worthy of being trusted. If, on the other hand, they say: We have the right to find out whether they are wrong or right, to consider their decrees and appraise their analogies, then we say to them: If we disagree among each other, who would then look into our issues? Where do we find our conventions? To whom do we take refuge from our problems? Whose words should we follow so that we may not fall into confusion, sin, going astray, and disbelief? Who could respond to our act of obedience and disobedience? Have we not promised God to follow His word with no discord or contrariety? Has the Messenger of God not referred every divergent issue to

God, His Messenger and the one in authority among you? So, if you go back to the one

[16v] in authority, you certainly go back to what is not in discord, just as if you went back to God and His Messenger. When many people have differences it may be that they are all wrong, but it may not be that they are all right; and it may be that some of them are right and some are wrong. You have seen people with differences but none of them claim that God has ordered him to rule with justice, nor given him power over others nor entrusted him with authority over the *umma*, except, in the case of the Messenger of God (God's blessings be on him) whom God entrusted with absolute power. He alone was given absolute authority. This is because he alone never related but truth and never ruled but with justice and never spoke out of caprice. Then the Messenger of God (God's blessings be on him)

[17r] passed away. Did he appoint anyone to take his place and be an example for you to follow? And ordered you to obey and follow him? Did he put him in the Prophet's stead and refer to such a person what had been referred to him? If they say yes, then we say to them: Who is that man? If they say [that] he is 'Alī, then, by not following him, they would profess unbelief in God, since they disobeyed him after he was appointed as imam and did not heed what he decided, nor go back to what he judged, nor accepted what he said. If, on the other hand, they say: He did not appoint anyone, our reply would be: Then the saying of God (Glory be to Him): 'Obey God, and obey the Messenger and those in authority among you' (4:59) and His saying: 'If you should quarrel on anything, refer it to God and

[17v] the Messenger (and to those in authority among you)' [10] (4:59), would be meaningless. Hence you relied on personal opinion and analogy, on independent judgement and discretion, or on approximation and assumption. To rely on such things was forbidden to the Messenger of God (God's blessings be on him). How then can you claim that God has relieved you of such things and permitted you to do what He prohibited the Messenger of God to do? Give us clear proof that what you have unduly claimed is true and never forge falsehood against God; 'Surely those who forge against God falsehood shall not prosper' (16:116).

---

10. The latter phrase is not repeated in the Qur'ānic verse.

To such people one should say: Tell us, did the Messenger of God (God's blessings and peace be on him) order the dispatching of Usāma's army and those who were in it? If they say yes, then we say to them: How come you did not carry out his order of dispatching the army

[18r] and those in it, and you accepted, as you have claimed, his order of appointing the imam? Tell us, had you dispatched the army as you were ordered by the Messenger of God, would you have been obeying or disobeying his orders? Also tell us, had you been obeying God (Exalted be He) and His Messenger in dispatching the army and those who were in it by order of the Messenger of God (God's blessings be on him), would Abū Bakr have won the imamate? Or do you claim that the Messenger of God (God's blessings be on him) did not know that God would take him unto Him and that the *umma* was in need of Abū Bakr? Or that he knew, and was certain that the *umma* was, after his death, in need of Abū Bakr? And that the people could not be good and fair except through him? So he dispatched Usāma's army and kept Abū Bakr behind? If God and His Messenger did order the dispatching of Abū Bakr

[18v] and 'Umar with the army, then who gave you the authority to summon them or any other person back? Did you know about this matter what the Messenger of God (God's blessings be on him) did not? Do you not know that the Messenger of God (God's blessings be on him) does not commit anything except by order of his Lord? In summoning Usāma and his companions back, were you obeying the orders of God and His Messenger? Did you not hear God's saying 'And whoso rebels against God and His Messenger, for him there awaits the Fire of Gehenna; therein they shall dwell forever' (72:23) or His saying: 'Say: Obey God, and obey the Messenger' (24:54).

To them one should say: Tell us, what would be more appropriate for the Messenger of God (God's blessings be on him), knowing that he would be dying – to carry out God's greatest and most honourable and significant command, which mankind cannot be good and fair

[19r] except by obeying it, or to neglect such a command and delay it and do what is inferior to it in a way so impeccable and sure? If they say: It was more appropriate for him to first carry out the most important and then the less important, we reply: In fact he did do

what was more appropriate. Then we say to them: How then could you claim that he neglected the question of the imam in spite of his knowledge that it was necessary for the *umma* to have an imam who would take care of their affairs, unite them, judge between them, flog the adulterers and cut off [the hands] of the thieves, lead them in conquering the enemy, divide the booty among them and teach them what they did not know about religion, and about the lawful and the unlawful, and in spite of all that, he would not designate, install nor declare anyone as imam, so that no one, whether minor or senior, would have any doubt about the appointed person? How could he neglect such an issue to give priority to the dispatching of Usāma's army and to forsake

[19v] the most important and noteworthy issue, even though he was certain that the imam, whose obedience is incumbent on the people, is that one who would dispatch the armies, lead the people to *jihād* and replace the Prophet (God's blessings be upon him), in his capacity as an appointee by God and His Messenger, in handling the affairs with thoroughness and concern? How could you claim that the Prophet dropped the issue of appointing an imam? Did he not know how righteous and accordant it was, and how ignominious and distracting his failure to appoint an imam would be? Or did you think that he forsook that issue out of forgetfulness, ignorance or negligence? If this were the case, then forgetting all the commandments, in spite of their being ordered by God, would be possible. The Prophet's erring and forgetting one religious duty would be a clear proof that he might err and forget all necessary things commanded by God. This is because

[20r] having an imam is imperative to all mankind. It follows that your very claim that the Prophet failed to name an imam was by itself a testimony on your part that this was in utmost contrariety and disobedience to God's ordering him to guide you to righteousness. Had it not been so, the Prophet would not have pointed to the imam's indispensability. Likewise, he would not be aware of the ignobleness and distrustfulness that might result from his failing to assign an imam. Also, he would not have known that God had ordered him to appoint an imam after him and had enjoined everyone to obey him and pay allegiance to him. Indeed, God did not describe him as such. On the contrary, He described him as being

merciful, faithful and compassionate.

It was thus certain that the Prophet (God's blessings be upon him) did order the dispatch of Usāma's army and that he was acquainted with everyone enlisted whether low or high in rank. Every one of them was certain that God had ordered him to man the army and dispatch the men to war. This was to give clear proof before God (Exalted be He) against those who denied that. This is so that the *umma* might be witness to the Prophet (God's blessings be on him) against those who renounced that and rejected his command by opposing and disobeying him.

[20v] This is evident in the Book of God, indeed, where He said (Exalted be He): 'How then shall it be, when We bring forward from every nation a witness, and bring there to witness against those? Upon that day the unbelievers, those who have disobeyed the Messenger, will wish that the earth might be levelled with them; and they will not conceal from God one tiding' (4:41–42).

Then to those people one should say: Tell us about the religious duties that God (Exalted be He) mentioned in His Book, and ordered mankind to follow as stated. Everyone consented that they had been sent down and enjoined as religious duties that should be carried out, such as pilgrimage and striving in God's way, together with divine ordinances and punishment, and the laws concerning murder, adultery, property, and stipulations urging people to be fair with the oppressed, to give to the kinsmen, the travellers and the needy their rights. Can such religious duties be put into practice or can anyone bear to do them without a just imam

[21r] who is virtuous and knowledgeable? Then, why did you say that Abū Bakr could do this task? Did you not witness that he said: 'I wish I had asked the Messenger of God (God's blessings be on him) whom he would appoint to be in authority after him', and 'I nominate one of these two men to the imamate: Abū 'Ubayda b. al-Jarrāḥ and 'Umar b. al-Khaṭṭāb, so pledge allegiance to the one of your choice', and 'Now, the Muslims have asked me requesting that I be vicegerent over them,' and, 'Release me, release me.' Did you not witness that he took a salary from the state treasury? Did you not witness that 'Umar said: 'The promise of allegiance to Abū Bakr was a lapse. May God protect the Muslims from its evil consequences ...' and 'If I nominate a successor, so did he who was better

than I', meaning Abū Bakr, 'and if I leave you without a will
[21v] so did he who was better than I.' He meant the Prophet (God's
blessings and peace be on him and his family). This was after Abū
Bakr's saying: 'I have been put in charge of you, yet I am not the best
among you.' Why did he not say: 'Verily God has put me in charge
of you and ordered me to manage your affairs?' The very saying of
Abū Bakr: 'I wish I had asked the Messenger of God (God's blessings
be on him) whom would you appoint to be in authority after you?',
is a clear proof that both he and you did know for sure that God and
His Messenger had not left to him any of the nation's affairs, and
that such a post was left for someone else who would rule in accordance with the commands of God and His Messenger (God's blessings be on him). This is with you consenting that it is incumbent on
mankind to have an imam. If an imam is incumbent, it would be
necessary to appoint one. If it is necessary, then those who should
appoint and designate him should be none other than God and His
Messenger. In fact Abū Bakr did admit that God and His Messenger
[22r] did not prefer him nor install him, nor did they invest him
with authority.

Moreover, we see that the Messenger of God (God's blessings be
on him) assigned Usāma b. Zayd as commander-in-chief over Abū
Bakr and his fellows, and did not assign them over Usāma b. Zayd.
Who then would be more appropriate, both from the theoretical
and practical points of view, to be imam: he who was assigned as
commander by the Messenger of God (God's blessings be on him)
or he who was put under another's command, but whom you put
in charge of you? How was it possible for Abū Bakr to command
Usāma b. Zayd when God made Usāma the commander over him?
Knowing that the Messenger of God (God's blessings be on him) did
so only by God's order, how then was it lawful for you to untie a knot
fastened by God and His Messenger, or to reject an order issued by
God? How can you claim that bringing Abū Bakr back from Usāma's
army so that he would be installed as imam
[22v] was better than what God and His Messenger chose for him,
to draft him and his fellows in the army. Do you not conceive the
idea that if the Messenger of God (God's blessings be on him) were
wrong in forsaking and refraining from installing the imam, then he
could be wrong in all things? The mere fact that he may be wrong in

one matter is proof that he may be wrong in all other matters. I take refuge in God from such a statement! How did you not condemn him for that? Why did you refrain from confronting the Prophet by calling his attention to such a matter? Why did you not choose for the imamate someone else whom the Messenger of God (God's blessings be on him) did not order to join Usāma's expedition? You could have easily found among the Muslims someone who could have been worthy of such a position. Or did the Prophet (God's blessings be on him) not know what you know now so as to choose him for the position that you chose him for, and to install him as his successor and refrain from ordering him to join the army, in view
[23r] of his endeavour to serve mankind?

The mere fact that he was ordered by the Messenger to join the army means either that the Messenger was right and you were wrong, or that he was wrong and you were right. In such a case one should say to them: Tell us, did you carry on God's Will in installing whom you had appointed and in doing what you did or were you wrong? If you were right, then the Messenger of God (God's blessings be on him) was wrong – far be it from him, and if you were wrong, which should be the case, then the Messenger of God (God's blessings be on him) was right? How then did you forsake what you called the Tradition of the Messenger of God (God's blessings be on him) to follow your own judgement? How could you tell that what was done by God's Messenger (God's blessing be on him) was wrong and sinful, while what you did was right and pious? Do you testify that what the Messenger of God (God's blessings be on him) did was wrong
[23v] and what you did was right? There is no reason for you not to answer.

The necessity that the imam be appointed by the Messenger

Then one should say to them: Tell us, if the Messenger of God (God's blessings be on him) was relieved from appointing an imam, then who gave you that responsibility? We also ask the same question to you and your fellow men concerning the *fatwa*s, the judicial decisions, the judgements concerning the lawful and the unlawful, and what was forbidden by God and His Messenger to do or engage in or to advocate. In fact, God put a curse on those who pass a sentence without relying on the revelation of God (Exalted be He). He charged such people with blasphemy, injustice and deviation from the truth. All that is taken from your religion and is in line with what you profess, with what you call for, and with the laws according to which you pass your sentences. You have heard God (Exalted be He) say: 'And do not say, as to what your tongues describes, "this is lawful and this is forbidden"' (16:116). He also said: 'Surely those who forge [24r] against God falsehood shall not prosper' (16:116). He also said (Exalted be He): 'And pursue not that thou hast no knowledge of' (17:36). He also said (Exalted be He): 'And say not as to God but the truth' (4:171). He also said: 'Whoso forges has ever failed' (20:61) ['Whose boundaries of] evil doing' (20:111), and many other similar sayings.

One should say to them: Why did you abstain from following the Messenger of God if, as you falsely claim, he waived the issue of the imam and revoked its religious injunction and statute? If they say: Because the *umma* cannot hold true, and religion cannot hold nor can it be completed except by an imam. For without an imam, religion would be corrupted and the *umma* and all mankind would be ruined and laws would cease to exist. We respond: If the Messenger of God (God's blessings be on him) knew what you had known and still relinquished it intentionally, would he not be unjust and wrongful to his *umma*? On the other hand, if he did not know what you had known, then he would definitely [24v] be ignorant of the commandments of God (Exalted be He) and short of implementing His religious tenets. Which one of you, therefore, is more deserving of being characterised by such qualities – you or the Messenger of God (God's blessings be on him)?

Then to those who have justified the imamate of Abū Bakr by claiming that Bilāl came to them on behalf of 'Ā'isha saying, 'Tell Abū Bakr to lead the prayer': Do you think that if God and His Messenger were to order the people to obey 'Ā'isha's demand, would you have accepted Bilāl's saying on behalf of 'Ā'isha, even if you consider Bilāl to be the fairest of mankind and the foremost in excellence? How could this happen when you definitely admit that if one hundred women of the faithful Emigrants came with 'Ā'isha to give witness on a two-*dirham* case, their witness would not be considered unless they would be accompanied by one trustworthy man. Hence, had

'Ā'isha approached

[25r] the people and told them, whether she was representing herself or the Messenger of God (God's blessings be on him), that Abū Bakr was to lead them to prayer they should refuse, unless there is a valid proof justifying such an act.

Then one should tell those people: Suppose the Prophet (God's blessings be on him) called you so that all of you, whether young or old, heard him, to tell you that Abū Bakr was to lead you to prayer, and you obeyed, would you imagine him walking between 'Alī b. Abī Ṭālib (God's blessings be on him) and al-Faḍl b. al-'Abbās b. 'Abd al-Muṭṭalib with his feet firmly on the ground, then the Messenger dismissed him and ordered him to leave the scene? Was this not enough evidence that he disapproved of your promoting him? Which is more preferable and appropriate in your opinion: The Messenger's deed (God's blessings be on him), when he dismissed, released

[25v] and demoted him, or your deed when you promoted him? Moreover, your appointing and promoting him are by no means equal to his being dismissed and demoted by God (Exalted be He) and His Messenger. Also, you know very well that the Messenger of God (God's blessings be on him) was against any state of disorder and weakness that might inflict anyone of his people, so how can you claim that [Abū Bakr's] imamate and authority were from God and not from the *umma* at large? In fact, he exerted a power that can be exerted both by the righteous and the unrighteous alike. This was against the Will of God and His Messenger, who never left you in doubt. So how did you accept such a state while the Messenger of God (God's blessings be on him) did not? Did you not relate his dismissal, even though the Messenger of God did stop him from delivering the record from the *sūra* of the Acquital, like

[26r] you related his dismissal from leading the prayer? Did you not relate likewise that the Prophet (God's blessings be on him) prayed behind 'Abd al-Raḥmān b. 'Awf who was, in your opinion, lower in rank than Abū Bakr? Did the Prophet not give orders to 'Attāb b. Usayd to lead the prayer in Mecca while the Messenger of God (God's blessings be on him) was away in al-Abṭaḥ? Likewise, was it not reported that Ibn Umm Maktūm and Abū Majdūda, in addition to innumerable people, used to do the same. After all, the fact that Abū Bakr has led the prayer, which is not historically certain, is not valid proof for him to lead the *umma*. Even if it were true that he led the prayer, it would in no respect mean that he had the merit or knowledge. How could this be, when you all know that prayer could be just as valid and true whether it was led by the Prophet himself or anyone else? Moreover, it is very well known to you that the position of the imamate and vicegerency of the Messenger of God (God's blessings be on him) is not appropriate for you. How then did you allow yourselves to install into such a position

[26v] the weakest among you in religion, faith and knowledge, and in opinion and administration, when this position requires the best in learning and cognizance, and in knowledge of religious and temporal matters? Think of what I explained and you will verily find it the same as I described. 'There is no power except in God' (18:39) 'the All-High, the All-Glorious' (2:255)

Then one should say to them: Tell us, what would be more useful, more proper, more unifying, more distant from disunity and discord, and more suited for both our beginning and our end than that God and His Messenger appoint an imam for us, who would be known to us like we know our own fathers and children. He would be obeyed by those from among us who obey God and His Messenger and be disobeyed by those who disobey God and His Messenger 'so that whoever perishes might perish by a clear sign, and by a clear sign he might live

[27r] who lived' (8:42). The second alternative is to have someone who would order us to install and acknowledge him, and to impose on us his obedience, especially when he knows how much envy and hatred we have between ourselves, and how much malice, slander, enmity and hypocrisy we harbour, and how short [we are] from doing our duty of figuring out who the right imam is. If they reply: We prefer God and His Messenger's instalment, because their choice is better and more suitable for our beginning and end; and because God's choice would result in putting an end to our despotism, discord and coercion in worship, then we say to them: Why then, did God and His Messenger not do what was good for your beginning and end? Do you think that God and His Messenger wanted you to perish and to be corrupt and disunited? Have you come to the conclusion that God and His Messenger did not do unto you what was better for you, neither in this life

[27v] nor in the life after as you claim, and that they wanted to make you perish and decay, and to cause disunity among you just as you are in the present? With this you would testify against God and His Messenger (God's blessings be on him). This being the case, they would not be responsible for you naming the imam, nor for you misinterpreting the statutes concerning what is lawful and unlawful, as such matters, in your opinion, are not clear enough. In fact, your problem with the imamate is similar to your problem with legal statutes, such as religious interpretation and lawful and unlawful matters, as if it slipped your mind that such matters are strictly Qur'ānic and bear no doubt.

Hence, to those people and to those who claimed that the Prophet (God's blessings be on him), by inviting Abū Bakr to lead the prayer, induced them to make him imam, we say: Tell us, was it possible that the Prophet (God's blessings be on him) would appoint someone as imam who led the people to prayer, when there was among them someone better, more knowledgeable of the Qur'ān, more cognizant of the lawful and the unlawful and more versed in

[28r] administration and politics? If they say: It is not permissible to have someone lead them to prayer when there is one who is better among them, more knowledgeable of the Qur'ān, more cognizant of what is lawful and unlawful, and more versed in administration and what is needed in worldly and religious affairs, we say to them: This is contrary to what you have agreed upon and contrary to what you heard about the Prophet (God's blessings be on him) that he made prayer permissible behind anyone, be he righteous or not. Such a fact is clear proof that 'Amr b. al-'Āṣ, 'Abd al-Raḥmān b. 'Awf, Usāma b. Zayd, 'Alī b. Abī Ṭālib, 'Attāb b. Usayd, Ibn Umm Maktūm, Abū Majdūda and all those who led the prayer at the time of the Prophet (God's blessings be on him) and who did so by his order, were better than Abū Bakr and 'Umar. This is because, unlike the latter, the Prophet (God's blessings be on him) formally ordered them to lead the prayer. If they say: Indeed, the Prophet may invite someone to lead the prayer even though there would be among the people someone better than such a person, more knowledgeable of the Qur'ān and more cognizant of the lawful and the unlawful, we ask those people: What

[28v] argument then did you have to prove Abū Bakr's excellence

over all human beings so that you dared to nominate him for a position that the Prophet himself (God's blessings be on him), did not
dare to decide upon except 'by the leave of his Lord' (34:12, 7:58)? As
God gave him such a leave, it was only possible for him to install the
best, the most cognizant of the lawful and the unlawful and the most
versed in administration and politics. This is because the wise man
does not impose on the people obedience of anyone when they are
more obedient than he is, nor does he order them to follow someone
who is less knowledgeable of God's religion than they are, nor does
he make them in need of someone who is in need of them. It may be
permissible, according to you, for a man to lead the prayer, even if he
belongs to the common people, but how did you make him who led
the prayer, an example analogous to the imam who has no likeness
among you or equal? One should then say to such people:

[29r] Tell us, was it possible for the Prophet (God's blessings be on
him) to ask someone to lead you to prayer who was less than you in
excellence, learning, precedence in embracing Islam, knowledge of
the Qur'ān, cognizance of God and knowledge of the lawful and the
unlawful? If they say no, it was not possible, and such a deed could
never be done, then we tell them: Your answer indicates that 'Amr
b. al-'Āṣ, 'Alī b. Abī Ṭālib, Usāma b. Zayd, 'Abd al-Raḥmān b. 'Awf,
'Attāb b. Usayd, Ibn Umm Maktūm and Abū Majdūda were better
than Abū Bakr and 'Umar since the Messenger of God (God's blessings be on him) had invested them either with authority over Abū
Bakr and 'Umar, or invited them to lead the prayer. Your reply also
indicates that Ṣuhayb was considered to be the most esteemed in the
nation by 'Umar b. al-Khaṭṭāb, as he asked him to lead the prayer
over his cadaver and also invited him to lead all the people to prayer.
Furthermore, such a reply of yours would indicate that Abū Ṭalḥa
was also considered superior

[29v] during 'Umar b. al-Khaṭṭāb's reign since 'Umar made him
rule over everyone's life, thoughts and persons, including 'Alī b.
Abī Ṭālib's, 'Uthmān b. 'Affān's, al-Zubayr's, Talḥa's, Sa'd's, 'Abd
al-Rahmān's and others. All this occurred in the presence of the
Muhājirūn and the *Anṣār*. On the other hand, if those people would
say yes, it was possible for the Prophet (God's blessings be on him) to
ask someone to lead the people to prayer, even though he would be
less than they are in excellence, knowledge of the Qur'ān and cogni-

zance of the lawful and the unlawful, then we say to them: If this was possible for the Messenger of God (God's blessings be on him), then how would you explain your belief in the excellence of Abū Bakr and 'Umar over others? Especially when your argument was shown to be invalid since it was confined to the fact that he led the prayers, and leading the prayers, according to you, has now fallen short of being a sound proof, either of excellence or of learning,

[30r] or in precedence to embracing Islam, or to the knowledge of what is lawful and what is unlawful? This is if we accept the truth of your statement that the Prophet (God's blessings be on him) really did ask Abū Bakr to lead the prayer, and you know that not everyone agrees with you on that. This is because, as you have mentioned, Bilāl came to him on behalf of 'A'isha asking him to do so. We have seen that such a story does not stand without proof and evidence, for the majority of the people state that when the Prophet (God's blessings be on him) was told how people reacted when they heard of Abū Bakr's leading the prayer, he got so angry that he said to 'Ā'isha, 'Oh you! Maidens of Joseph!' He showed an unprecedented rage against such a misguided and ill-advised act, turned Abū Bakr away from the *qibla* and removed him from the place where the people had put him. Such an act is clear evidence of his utter rejection of the idea that the position of prayer leader

[30v] can be filled by the masses and the average person and that it is not fit for the elite. How then did you make what is appropriate for the masses from among you and not the elite, a position to be given to one who has no equal or parallel? Even if it were certain that the Prophet (God's blessings be on him) invited Abū Bakr to lead the prayer, such a position did by no means make him worthy of the imamate either in excellence or in knowledge or in deed. Did the Prophet (God's blessings be on him) not invite others who were inferior in excellence, learning, cognizance in the Qur'ān and knowledge of what is lawful and what is unlawful than those who were praying? It was utterly impossible for the Messenger of God (God's blessings be on him) to appoint as his successor anyone except he who is most knowledgeable, most excellent, most deserving to be his vicegerent and the most capable of undertaking the responsibility for prayer and for religious and worldly affairs. Such a person should act the same as the Prophet and should follow his

example. Only then would he be his true legatee and successor.

[31r] The unlawfulness of appointing an inferior to the imamate
Then one should say to them: Is it, in your opinion, possible for
the Prophet (God's blessings be on him) to appoint as his successor someone who is not the best and most knowledgeable in matters
concerning the lawful and unlawful, and the religious precepts
and stipulations? If they say yes, it is possible for him to appoint
an incompetent inferior person instead of an efficient superior one,
then we say to them: Therefore, there is no reason for you to give
Abū Bakr preference over anyone else, since the Prophet (God's
blessings be on him) does not mind, in your opinion, appointing
someone who is one hundred times inferior to Abū Bakr and even
inferior to all of you. In fact, what merit should one have in a position which can be held by anyone? On the other hand, if they say it is
not possible for the Prophet (God's blessings be on him) to appoint a
person if there is among the people someone better than he in excellence, knowledge of the lawful and the unlawful and of the affairs of
their life and the afterlife that they are in need of,
[31v] then we say to them: This is the difference between leading the
prayer and being the imam and all its difficulties of administration
and the problems of being vicegerent. So why did you deny this right
to the Messenger of God (God's blessings be on him) and appoint as
his successor someone who was not the most learned from among
you nor the best in excellence and knowledge of the Qur'ān, nor
the best in observing religious precepts and statutes nor in discern-
ing between the lawful and the unlawful; or was it because, in your
opinion, the Messenger of God (God's blessings be on him) is not
the best of you in learning, excellence, knowledge of the Qur'ān and
cognizance in lawful and unlawful matters? In fact, his successor
must be like him and equivalent to him, and must be among you
as his lieutenant. Or, did the Prophet have no one like him and no
equal? Why then did you make someone who has no equal comparable to someone who does [have equals]?

Then to those people one should say: Tell us, is it then possible
that you could have, after the Messenger (God's blessings be on him),
a ruler who would be in his heart a hypocrite? If they say yes,
[32r] then we can tell them: What need do you have for giving pref-

erence to a successor of the Prophet (God's blessings be on him) if the imamate could be occupied by someone who conceals hypocrisy? Accordingly, such a position would be held by the worst people. If they say this is not permissible, then we say to them: Is it permissible then that you can choose someone who conceals hypocrisy and shows belief or who shows belief and conceals unbelief? If they say no, this is not permissible to us, we tell them: Do you know then what is hidden when the Messenger of God (God's blessings be on him) did not? It took the Messenger (God's blessings be on him) a long time before God made him know their hypocrisy and unbelief. If they reply by saying yes, it is possible for us to know and to choose by our own volition someone who shows belief and conceals unbelief and hypocrisy, then we say to them: Can this,

[32v] in your opinion, be applied to God and His Messenger? If they say yes it can, then we tell them: Do you mean that God and His Messenger do not know as much as you do? If they say no, this cannot be, for God and His Messenger do not choose for the Muslims a ruler who guides their religious affairs except he who has no equal or likeness, whose external character is as his inner one and his innermost reality is as his apparent one. This is because God is omniscient. Nothing escapes Him. Out of His omniscience He chooses the one who shall have authority over mankind. Then we say to them: Who ordered you to choose, while you are unable to discern the right person who is right for the religion and for being in authority over the Muslims, the one who is God's evidence among mankind? God says: 'Advance not before God and His Messenger; and fear God, God is All-Hearing, All-Knowing' (49:1).

One should say to those people: Tell us, what was the story behind the instalment

[33r] of the imam and the imposition of his obedience upon you? Was it before or after his instalment? Did you have him installed by formal appointment or by selection? If it was by formal appointment, then who was he? If it was by selection, what imposed his obedience upon you? Who was commissioned to install and put him in charge? Was this the doing of all your people or some of them? Or was it the doing of others known by their names, or the doing of the people of his country and not of other countries? Or was it the doing of a certain number of men who were of considerable influence?

If it was the doing of all your people, then who was controlling them, knowing their differences and disparities? If it was the doing of others who were known by their names and lineages, then who were they and where were they? If it was the doing of the people of a certain country, then is it permissible for others, or only to them? If it was the doing of a certain number of men, then how many are those men? Was their number an even number or an odd one? If it was

[33v] an even number, we say: Could it be an odd one? If they say it could not, we say to them: Who did make it odd or even? Could that number be added to or could it be subtracted from? If they say yes, you could subtract one from it, then we tell them: In the same manner you could subtract another one too. What is good for one is good for two, and for three, and so on, until the whole number would be reduced to one.

Likewise, who ascribes the instalment of the imam to a particular person? If the matter was ascribed to a particular person, then what you said: 'We suppose this, say that and we did that', would be false. If, on the other hand, you make such a person worthier of installing the imam than another, you would likewise be wrong. For what is the difference between a particular person and another? The same applies also to the question of whether

[34r] all your people are responsible, or some of them, or the people of a certain country, or certain people who are known by their appropriate names and their lineages, or a certain number of individuals who, when their number is complete, would install the imam, or a particular person – rather than all the people – who would install the imam either by appointment or by choice. In fact, whatever method you choose or way you select, you inevitably should get evidence for what you believe based on a proof from God and His Messenger. But can you get any such proof or evidence, and does what you see keep you from your corrupted belief, and make you go back from doing injustice to God and His Messenger? Is there, in what has been already said, any evidence to 'a people that have knowledge' (2:230)?

Then one should tell them: Tell us what the cause was for God and His Messenger

[34v] to install an imam and impose his rule? If they say it was his consideration for mankind, so that they would worship God

through their obedience to God and His Messenger and the obedience of those who are supposed to be obeyed by His command, then
we tell them: Why then is it that He does not consider them now in
the same way He used to, nor does He give them a chance to worship
Him as before? What prevents Him from considering them in a
favourable way? Do you think He was, at the time, looking at them
more favourably than before? What made them forsake the precept
of obeying the appointed imam? If the imam who came after the
Prophet was installed by appointment then we may see the invalidity
of such an appointment. If, on the other hand, he was installed by
election by the *umma*, that is, the Muslim community, then election
would be equally invalid, and consequently

[35r] worship would come to an end, religious precepts would be
dropped as well, and all things would end up with God's disobedience, infringement and surpassing His command and statutes.

To those people one should therefore say: Are we not unanimously
in agreement that the imamate is subject to one of three things: First,
the imam is appointed by God, Who has prescribed mankind to
obedience and ordered them to follow his verdicts and submit to his
commands. In such a case, legislation concerning murder, adultery,
property and matters of legal authority would be solely assigned to
him by God; no one else would have a hand over him or with him.
This is because he who would have a hand over him would be superior to him, and he who would share any authority with him would
be his counterpart. Had there been among the people any who is
superior to the one in authority among them, then the latter would
be inferior, and the people's present life as well as their afterlife would
be corrupt. This is because God does not take the inferior as evidence
against the superior, nor the ignorant

[35v] against the learned, nor the undeserving against the deserving, nor the unbeliever against the believer.

Second, had there been among the people a counterpart to
the imam, they would not be in need of either one of them. This
is because the rule of the calumniator on mankind is not secure,
especially if they do not acknowledge his superiority to them, either
in religious or worldly matters. Such a calumniator would be just
like the first without any authenticity. If one of them would be superior to a people, he would necessarily be better than they are in

excellence, in knowledge of religion, and cognizance in politics and administration. This is because they would be asked to obey him and forsake his opposition and to accept his orders. The fact that an imam is installed by God is a divine sentence and an enjoinment on the people to be devoted and obedient to him. He who obeys him would be obeying God and His Messenger, and he who disobeys him would be disobeying God and His Messenger, 'so that whosoever perished might perish by a clear sign, and by a clear sign

[36r] he might live who lived' (8:42). If they would acknowledge such a calumniator, then they would acknowledge that they all have disobeyed God and His Messenger, because they would thus be sharing with the imam legislation concerning murder, adultery and property. They would also acknowledge that they have opposed him in all these causes during his lifetime and after his demise. The opposition of the equitable imam whose obedience is prescribed on everyone is the same as the opposition of the Messenger of God (God's blessings be on him). Hence, this *umma* shall definitely perish if it treads the path of judging things without clear evidence and sound proofs and if it passes judgements that only rely on mere opinion, and testifies against God in declaring wrongly what is lawful or unlawful, as if they never heard the saying of God (Exalted He is) 'And do not say, as to what your tongues falsely describe, "This is lawful, and this is forbidden," so that you may forge against God falsehood' (16:116), and His saying 'Whoso forges has ever failed' (20:61), and His saying 'And pursue not that thou hast no knowledge of; the hearing

[36v] the sight, the heart – all of those shall be questioned of' (17:36) and His saying 'and say not as to God but the truth' (4:171), and his saying 'The judgement is God's alone' (6:57, 12:40), And His saying 'Judgement belongs to God, the All-High, the All-Great' (40:12).

Third, the imam would be installed to rule us and ordered to administer us, while we would not be ordered to obey him, nor would we be forbidden to oppose and disobey him. On the contrary, we could have a hand over him or share authority with him, and verify his sentences, *fatwa*s and verdicts, so that we might carry out what we would think was right and oppose what we would think as wrong. This way, obedience to the imam would not be imposed on us, nor would his opposition and disobedience be prohibited. Such an imam would not be prescribed on the people. This can never be allowed by God, Who has chosen the imam for His religion so that he may be His evidence to all beings, arbitrate among mankind and be decisive

[37r] between the rightful and the wrong doers. Why would mankind need an imam whose obedience is not enjoined, whose opposition and disobedience are not prohibited, who is not trustworthy and who does not undertake the affairs of this life and the life after except in the manner you have described? What is then the difference between the shepherd and the flock? If this were truly the case then the saying of God (Exalted be He), 'Obey God and obey the Messenger and those in authority among you' (4:59), would be of no meaning, nor would there be any meaning to His saying 'If you should quarrel on anything, refer it to God' (4:59). As a matter of fact, each one of the two would say: I will reveal the same as God has revealed.

Then one should say to those people: Tell us, do you testify that the Messenger of God (God's blessings be on him) has appointed as vicegerent a particular man whose name and lineage are known to you and make him worthy of being his true successor? Or do you testify that he has forsaken

[37v] and abandoned you – here your testimony is necessary – and that he has not appointed in his place a successor whom you know by name and descent. If he did not install and appoint anyone, then forsake your opposition and hostility to the imam. In this case, both we and you would have a good example in God's Messenger. If the Messenger of God did install someone, then stop mentioning the proof you have for installing the person that you chose, such as fairness, preference to others, leading the prayer and the like. Likewise, stop mentioning Abū Bakr's saying: 'Now, the Muslims have asked me, requesting that I may be vicegerent over them,' and 'I have been put in charge of you, yet I am not the best among you.' Instead, do testify that you have been wrong and disobedient to God and His Messenger by forsaking and turning away from the imam who was installed over you, and by contesting against him and denying him a right that God did not give except

[38r] to him.

Your mere argument for installing a man who has not been installed by God and His Messenger is clear proof of your refusal to accept the imam whom God and His Messenger appointed over you. This is in spite of the fact that you have consented that God has never forgotten you nor has His Messenger left you without appointing someone that you can lean upon. This is utter justice by God and His Messenger. Yet, you went back to defaming the Messenger of God (God's blessing be on him) and discrediting God (Glory be to Him) by accusing Him of forsaking, neglecting and abandoning you. Whatever alternative you chose, you neither had evidence of being right, nor an excuse by God or His Messenger for your installing the man you had installed. This is because you did what you did neither by God's command nor by His Messenger's.

Who is the imam of this epoch?

Then, one should say to them: Tell us, did the appointment of the imam in this time take place according to the command of God and His Messenger's commands,

[38v] and should obedience be incumbent on someone in particular? If they say yes, and then they name a particular person, we say to them: Who then imposed his obedience? And when did God and His Messenger order the people to obey him? Furthermore, what is he characterised by? Is he pious or unrighteous? If they say that he is pious, then he should be the best and most excellent of mankind. If they say that he is unrighteous, they should forsake his allegiance and refuse his right to the imamate. This is because God does not acknowledge any right to the unrighteous over the righteous or to the inferior over the superior.

To such people one should say: What is more righteous both for you and us: Is it to accept Abū Bakr's saying and judgement when he disagreed with 'Umar and those who agree with 'Umar from the *Muhājirūn* and the *Anṣār* and the friends of the Prophet (God's blessings be on him), or the saying of 'Umar and those who we mentioned? If they say: We only accept Abū Bakr's saying,

[39r] he alone was right, then we would tell them: You see? Had Abū Bakr come to you, alone, and testified on only one *dirham*, would you accept his testimony? If they say yes, then they would be out of the consensus of the *umma* and against the provisions of the Book and the Prophet's Traditions. If they say: We do not accept one man's opinion and we do not approve of his testimony, then we

ask them: If 'Umar would come, accompanied by all the *Muhājirūn* and *Anṣār* who were on his side, and testify against that man on the *dirham*, would you then accept their testimony? If they say yes, then we would say: Here is 'Umar with all his partisans and all those who believe in him, disagreeing with Abū Bakr concerning his jurisdictions, *fatwa*s and verdicts. They declared him at fault and testified against him, that his jurisdictions were wrong. In spite of that you still consider him to be sanctified, although you know that his ruling against what was sent down

[39v] by God results in blasphemy, sinfulness and injustice. If, according to you, this man was really an imam whose obedience is prescribed on you, then his jurisdiction and *fatwa*s should be obeyed and his verdicts accepted. This is because he would be appointed by God who made his obedience incumbent on mankind, his sayings observed and his verdicts compliant with God, and God would not allow anyone to have authority over his, nor share any authority with him especially in matters of murder, adultery, properties and legal commands.

On the contrary, that man was opposed by the people. They decreed against his decrees, legislated differently from what he did, and stated what was contrary to his statements. Such a man, like all his followers, should have known that he was neither the true imam, nor deserving of such a position. They also should have known that his obedience was not made incumbent by God nor his allegiances enjoined or his opposition and disobedience proscribed, especially when they also knew

[40r] and testified that he ruled unjustly and contrary to God's revelation. That is why they opposed him. Their opposition was out of their free will and was a proof of their true belief in him. Actually, the fact that they did not renounce him was either because of their belief that such an act of his did not discredit him or because they were certain that he was the true imam, and consequently was most excellent, deserving and truthful in his claim, and that he was the most knowledgeable in matters of religious and worldly affairs. He was the one who judged rightfully according to God's revelations. If he was opposed, it was only because those who opposed him had deviated from certitude and real knowledge and went into confusion. They were, therefore, perplexed and dissolute because of their

disagreement on who should be the imam of excellence and justice.

If they claimed that they rightfully chose Abū Bakr, then we would tell them that they should have condemned Abū Bakr for being erroneous and going astray. He infringed on the statutes of God

[40v] and passed judgements contrary to what God had sent down. Had Abū Bakr been rightful in his deeds, you should have reproached 'Umar and his followers for being disobedient to God and opposing the imam of justice and excellence. Or do you claim that you have not been responsible for what you have done? Would we also be not responsible if we were not obedient to the imam of justice and excellence whose obedience is made incumbent? In a like manner, would we not be responsible if we were at variance with the assembly of believers, or if we were to pass judgements on what God had sent down, or if we were to infringe on the statutes of God?

In fact, for the people of analogy, disagreement and unanimity are one and the same, as are obedience and disobedience, as are belief and unbelief. This is according to your understanding. Otherwise, you must call upon each faction to observe its own precepts, then tell us which of the two factions was right and which was wrong, and what should they expect from God to

[41r] requite them with, and which of them the people should be guided by, and which they should oppose. Furthermore, you should tell us what punishment should be inflicted on the faction at fault, and what reward should be granted to the rightful one. Then, produce your proof that what you mentioned was true. 'There is no power except in God' (18:39) 'The All-High, The All-Glorious' (2:255; 42:4).

Then one should ask them: Tell us, have you really seen a man speaking evil of Abū Bakr and 'Umar? If they say yes, we say: Such a man should be either denying their investiture by God and His Messenger in power and sovereignty – for he found no divine evidence and proof for his denial, or believing in their imamate. Yet he disobeyed them in matters of murder, adultery, property and legal command, and receded from obeying their legislation, held views other than theirs and yielded to

[41v] the opposite of their convictions. In fact, this is of great discredit to them, because there are no interspaces appropriate for

them between what is lawful and what is unlawful, knowing that the goal of mankind in their quest for God is to apprehend the lawful and the unlawful. No other status can they ever find in between to get into.

Hence, we say, concerning the so-called consensus of the *umma* on these two imams, that the proof for their authority was confined only to the extent mentioned above (i.e. leading the prayer). Nothing was actually related that the Messenger of God (God's blessing be on him) had invested them with authority nor was there any consensus by the *umma* on them recently. If there was any consensus on them of any kind by the *umma*, it was out of personal opinion and not out of a formal decree by the Messenger of God (God's blessing be on him). In fact, this consensus by the *umma* means that they are only entitled to such a position. The actual consensus was, instead, that the imamate, or rather the *umma*, is oppositional on this subject and such a claim is

[42r] fallacious due to such disparity during our time as has been mentioned.

Then one should ask them: Tell us, did God (Exalted be He) not spare us the trouble of deduction, inference, personal judgement and analogy by decreeing His commandments and making them incumbent on us in His Book? Did He not author them, in essence and attribute, yet they could not be validated or come true, or be of value, or be practically perfect, except by an imam? Their answer should surely be yes. Then we say to them: Why is it that nothing can be valid or come true or be particularly perfect except by an imam? Is it not because the imam spares the *umma* the trouble of deduction, inference, personal judgement and analogy? Is the imam not in charge of the whole religion and in authority over all the Muslims? Is he not the evidence of the Lord of all beings?

Divine enjoinment of the imamate is as necessary as divine enjoinment of the pillars of Islam

Then one should say to them: Tell us, is it acceptable according to you, that prayer,

[42v] almsgiving and the like be enjoined by God (Exalted be He) by way of deduction and seeking without necessarily decreeing them in His Book? As a result of their saying, no, we say: Why then, such

a matter, which things cannot be set right except through it, cannot but be decreed from above? This is because it is only through this matter that things can be deduced, correlated and sought. It follows that these things must also be decreed from above.

Here one should say to them: Has the Messenger not received an order from God to have such matters carried out after him? Their answer must certainly be yes. Then one should say to them: Why, then, did you state that the imam, who was responsible for carrying out these matters, was not necessarily appointed, knowing that the Messenger was ordered that these matters be carried out after him? If someone would say that the Prophet (God's blessing be on him) did not decree all the commandments, for example, he did not set forth in detail the exact amount of *dirhams* to be given in alms, though he stated that for every two hundred *dirhams*, five *dirhams* should be paid, likewise, although he did not point to the very person of the imam,

[43r] he stated that since the Prophet was a righteous and superior person he demanded that the imam should necessarily be a clear proof of the Prophet's righteousness and superiority. He was not necessarily required to name a particular person for that position. This is similar to the Prophet's enjoining giving alms, without prescribing, in any of his Traditions, a particular amount. It did not need the *umma* to agree unanimously on a Tradition of his or to disagree. They will not find for this matter a way other than that way.

Then they would be told: Tell us, after all this, whether it was necessary for the Muslims to have all these matters prescribed on them without it being prescribed on the Messenger of God (God's blessing be on him) to decree them (however he himself was prescribed on them by divine decree)? If they reply: Not all stipulations formally decreed, we reply: This is a false pretention. We shall discuss this matter in due time, God willing.

In fact, no one denies that the pillars, such as prayer, almsgiving, pilgrimage,

[43v] striving in God's way and fasting of Ramaḍān are pillars that are verily prescribed by God (Glory be to Him) to His Messenger (peace be upon him). The Messenger has prescribed them in turn and enjoined us to observe them during and after his time. Therefore,

why do you not consider yourself also bound to observe what the Messenger decreed on the subject of the imam who succeeds him? Why do you admit that he was ordered to prescribe the pillars and insist on their observation after him, whereas you do not consider our standpoint concerning the necessity of the imamate to be more valid than yours? Did He not enjoin the Messenger (peace be on him) to decree such a matter? I cannot find any difference between the two enjoinments, that is, that of the pillars and that of the imam's appointment, although you insisted on the invalidity of the second, as you claimed that the Messenger (God's blessing be on him) did not appoint a particular imam, and that he did not ordain such an appointment as a commandment. Hence your claim, that

[44r] what you did mention should be that which should be followed, is false due to its inconsistency.

Then one should say to them: Tell us, did the Messenger order those who were abroad to observe these commandments? The answer must be yes. Then they will be asked: And [what] if among his orders was an order to install an imam, and 'Alī was the one who witnessed the Messenger of God (God's blessing be on him) when he was ordering the people to install an imam in a country after he would go back to it? If they admitted to that, would they not be contradicting their views concerning the imamate? If, on the other hand, they would claim that they were not supposed to install an imam because there was no obligation on their part to install an imam, then they would also be contradicting their previous standpoint even though their claim that such an order by the Messenger of God (God's blessing be on him) was not binding, since the Messenger of God was still alive,

[44v] a fact that rendered the appointment of an imam not necessary. Then one can say to them: You did not relinquish those who claimed that the imposing of the imamate after the Messenger (God's blessing be on him) did not prove the necessity of having an imam, as was the case during the presence of the Messenger of God (God's blessing be on him). In fact, it is not logically valid that the Messenger would pass away without appointing someone to take his place in the *umma*. This was a duty he had to do, as we have mentioned at the beginning. It is not possible for him to evade his duty. Evading his duty means his failure to consider

the needs of the *umma*. Such an act leads to neglecting his fellow men. This would lead to their failure in performing their religious obligations. Therefore, the appointment of the imam is a must, as it was a must in God's religion to have the Messenger appointed from above. This can be compared to the Messenger's appointment of the commander in chief of those believers at war away from their homes. They could not be left to their own discretion in choosing their commander, for fear

[45r] of discord and dissidence. The same thing would be applied to the Messenger's troops and expeditions. This could be avoided by his appointment of one particular man over the others. This was what he did at the Battle of Mu'tah where he appointed one of his Companions as a commander of the two armies as the two commanders met. The Messenger's appointing one commander over the two armies was a proof of the invalidity of relinquishing the appointment of his successor, that is, the imam of his *umma*. In fact, a real *umma* can never be the result of any corruption, nor can it be based on any deviation.

Lack of consensus on a text does not annul the text as such

If they say: Had the question of the appointment of the imam been as you stated, then the Messenger would have decreed it, and had he decreed it, then the *umma* would have reported it. Since the *umma* did not report it, then one could not say that the Messenger did not decree it. To such an argument one should reply: this is a different issue. We rather wanted of you only

[45v] to give us proof of the validity of what you have mentioned instead of that of the necessity of the imamate. In fact, we opposed you in what we said to you earlier, so that it may be clear to you that you have no proof whatsoever that supports your point of view concerning the commandment of allegiance, nor do you have any evidence confirming your belief. Because had your viewpoint been valid, the Messenger (God's blessing be on him) would have decreed it. In fact, he has decreed such a commandment and a part of the *umma* has confirmed it. On the other hand, it has not been reported that the other part of the *umma* said otherwise. In fact, if they have said otherwise, it would not be a true account. This is because it would be a mere denial, in spite of the many evidences confirming

its being decreed by him, together with his appointing his governors and commissioning the meritorious people. If someone argues that such deeds were not reported and, therefore, were not decreed, then the reply would be that such arguments of yours were clear evidence of the fact that what I have said is the truth rather than the evidence of those who reported that it

[46r] was a decree. Actually the fact that their analogy was right was another proof of the falsity of those who maintained such an argument and who burdened themselves with what was not allowed by God. Furthermore, we have denied their reaching a consensus even though most of what was mentioned was refuted at the beginning of this work. In fact, whatever consensus the Christians came to about their believing in the divinity of Christ it was not enough to prove that he did not decree that he was human. In the same manner, those who say that Christ was human by only believing in the untruthfulness of his being God and the necessity of his being human, would be using an invalid argument. They would be thus merely relinquishing the faith, which they should believe in, by only disbelieving forcefully in the faith that took hold of them previously. Such people would be using the same logic of those who fully refused what Christ had really decreed, namely that he was human. The same thing would happen to the majority of the people of our *umma*, if they maintain

[46v] their false belief, which is contrary to what the Messenger (God's blessing be on him) had decreed; their doing so cannot, however, constitute a clear proof that the Messenger did not decree. It would be similar to the logic adopted by most of the Christians who denied the fact that Christ was not human though he did not put it in writing. If, on the other hand, someone would say that even though the Christians deify Christ, they do not refuse to quote him when he said he was human, while we do not find anyone in all our *umma* who ever said that the Messenger had really appointed anyone as imam, our reply would be: Such an argument does in fact confirm what we have said. This is because if it were possible for the Christians to oppose what was really stated by Christ (peace be on him) in one way or another, it would not be a surprise to see that those who are similar to them and of the same nature oppose what was decreed to them. The very fact that they had the same mentality

[47r] makes them believe that he did not decree anything of that sort. If they say: Had the Prophet appointed any person, they would all have reported it, even if they violated his will by allegorically interpreting it as they wanted. This is what the Christians did with Christ; although he clearly stated he was human, they allegorically interpreted his statement. To this false supposition one should reply: Was it not true that Christ affirmed the coming of Muhammad by naming him in person? Why then did the Christians, in spite of their great numbers, not report it? Instead they undermined it entirely. What is surprising indeed is to see those among the Muslims who refused to report what the Prophet (God's blessing be on him) had decreed concerning the appointment of that man. This is because the Muslims' doing was different from that of the Christians; the Christians admitted Christ's saying, though they interpreted it allegorically, while the Muslims denied the Prophet's appointment of an imam in its entirety.

If, on the other hand, they say: Although the Christians did not admit that Christ had mentioned Muhammad by name, they did relate indeed what pointed to his prophecy,
[47v] then we reply: This is because we wanted to refute your argument, namely that you consider your refusal of the Prophet's appointment as proof that he did not appoint any one. So we quoted a *hadīth* which was as genuine as its transmitters and those who reported it. The *umma*, even if it did not in its entirety report that the Prophet (God's blessing be on him) did appoint a certain person, did in fact report what points to this person's imamate. This could be compared to what the Christians related about Christ pointing out the prophecy of Muhammad, even though they did not mention the fact that Christ did appoint him to be his successor in presiding over the era to come.

As for those who claimed that in the Book of God (Exalted be He) and the Traditions of the Prophet of God (God's blessing be on him) whose authenticity is agreed upon, there was a way out from people's afflictions and through which they related the sayings of God, we reply: Such matters have been based on what God (Exalted be He) said. All of these can be found in the Book and the Traditions whether people know this or not. Everything other than these two sources

[48r]   are of no avail.

In fact, had the Traditions been only those whose authenticity was agreed upon, they would be reduced in value and become inadequate. We do not take into account the consensus of one particular faction. This is because though it may be possible for man to deviate from truth and get into a state of ignorance, it is impossible for this to happen to the Book of God and the Traditions of His Prophet. God (Exalted be He) says in His Book, 'We have neglected nothing in the Book' (6:38). Also says He (Exalted be He), 'Today I have perfected your religion for you and I have completed my blessing upon you, and I have approved Islam for your religion' (5:3). In these verses of God there is indeed a clear proof and a forbiddance of any foolish pretention on God. Distrust in the Book of God (Exalted be He) and analogy in God's provisions are in no way to be practised, nor to be warranted. Nothing is permissible except what God has permitted us to do. God says, 'Who judges not according to what God has sent down

[48v]   they are the unbelievers' (5:44), the ungrateful and the dissolute. This, in fact, is a divine order for us to execute and to do what he has chosen for us in addition to what He has decreed us to do, knowing that He even forbade His Prophet (God's blessing be on him) to act against the provisions and verdicts He had decreed. He says: 'Had he invented against Us any sayings, We would have seized him by the right hand, then We would surely have cut his life-vein' (69:44–46). This is a threat directed to the Prophet so that he may avoid falling into such misdeeds, even though he has been (God's blessing be on him) the best in justice, the clearest in mind, the closest to righteousness and the farthest from neglect. The others are more prone to fall into such a danger and, therefore, more deserving to be threatened by God than the Prophet who is worthier of God's mercy than those who are closer to fault, more liable to be at variance, more prone to make mistakes

[49r]   and more distant from righteousness. Such a saying of theirs means indeed that what is prescribed in the Book of God (Exalted be He) and in the Traditions of the Prophet (God's blessing be on him) is neither sufficient nor adequate to meet the needs of mankind. For this reason they claim that He entrusted them, in most of their affairs, to confusing subjective opinions and destructive whims.

The Traditions are the second source to be followed after the Book
As for their saying: Since we have not found in the Book of God nor
in the Messenger's Traditions anything about the appointment of
the imam, we do not intend to change God's will (Exalted be He). We
will thus refer this issue to the authority of our learned men, so that
they would discuss it with each other and pass their independent
judgements. To such people we say: Although we already confirmed
that in the Book and the Traditions everything is clearly elucidated,
you neglected this fact by saying: 'We have not found anything in
them'; you thus contradicted what has been confirmed, then you
changed your minds to confirm what you have already rejected,
namely that the Book and the Traditions have everything, by saying:
[49v] 'We will refer this issue to the authority of our learned men,
so that they would discuss it and pass their independent judgements.'
We say to them: In fact, you have affirmed the existence of what
you denied. The very fact of admitting the existence of learned men,
signifies your affirmation that such an issue is found in the Book of
God and the Traditions. This is unless you meant that the source of
knowledge for these men is other than the Book and the Traditions
– making them stray from the right path and fall into heresy. If they
say: Had this issue been mentioned in the Book and the Traditions
we would not have dismissed it from these two main sources, even
if it was only insinuated. To such an argument we reply: The very
fact that you dismissed this issue from the Book and the Traditions
means that it was mentioned there. This is because God did not
allow His Messenger (God's blessing be on him) to pass a judgement on anything that is not decreed in his Book regarding what
was commanded or condemned. Even though the Messenger knows
best how to use examples and analogies, God prohibited him from it,
and prevented him from passing any judgement unless it was based
on God's revelation.

Then, we ask such people: On what basis did you think it was
incumbent on those learned men to
[50r] speculate and delve into such issues and to deliberate on provisions when God has prohibited His Messenger (God's blessing be on
him) from this, as we said above? This is also according to what was
related from the past nations about their delusion through personal
judgement. In this respect, God reproached and reprehended them

by saying: 'And they say, what is within the bellies of these cattle' (6:139) until He said, 'Say: Has God given you leave, or do you forge against God' (10:59). Did anybody, other than those people, give any opinion or analogy? Did their rejection mean anything except their insistence on what is not found in the Book and Traditions? Furthermore, who has been the cause for sending down the saying of God (Glory be to Him): 'Today I have perfected your religion for you, and I have completed My blessing upon you and I have approved Islam for your religion' (5:3) and his saying (Exalted be He): 'We have neglected nothing in the Book' (6:38), and His saying: 'That whosoever perished

[50v] might perish by a clear sign, and by a clear sign he might live who lived' (8:42), and also who has claimed that God issued His commandments and verdicts only for those of feeble and factious minds, and who has said that for this reason He suggested that 'Alī be deposed, lest they become disunited and forsake God's commanding them to be always in concord? If they offered as pretext the saying of God (Exalted be He): 'And take counsel with them in the affair' (3:159), one should say to them: You should take counsel with them only in matters related to a way you are taking or a destination you are heading for, or the like, and not in religious and legal matters. In fact, in such religious and legal matters, one can never find any reason of taking counsel. The Prophet (God's blessing be on him) never took counsel with anyone about an ordinance of God, nor in a Tradition of his. If those people offered as pretext the Tradition that Mu'ādh b. Jabal related when he had been asked by the Prophet (God's blessing be on him): 'On what basis do you pass your judgement?' He replied, 'On the Book of God'. The Prophet said, 'And if you do not

[51r] find anything in His Book?' He said, 'On the *sunna* of the Messenger of God (God's blessing be on him).' The Prophet said, 'And if you do not find it in the *sunna*?' He said, 'Then I formulate an independent judgement.' The Prophet said, 'Praise be to God, he acted in accordance with the saying of the Prophet (God's blessing be on him).' As for us we say: We had previously told you about the authenticity of the Traditions that dealt with different anecdotes. This authenticity of this anecdote is not proven, as we did find many members of the *umma* who rejected it, because it is inconsistent with

the Book due to its fallacious interpretations that contradict with the Book and the *sunna*. It is contrary to what God said about the perfection and completion with which God described his Book. Such false Traditions prescribe what is absolutely contrary to the word of God. Rather, the Tradition that is sanctioned by the *umma* is his saying (God's blessings and peace be on him): 'Any *ḥadīth* which is in line with the word of God (Exalted and Glorified be He) is mine [51v] and any *ḥadīth* that contradicts the Book of God is never uttered by me.' This is evidence that the *ḥadīth* mentioned before is a false one; it contradicts the Qur'ān, and sanctions what God prohibited and reproached people for. Even if we were to say that it was authentic and proven to be really uttered by the Messenger of God (God's blessing be on him), even if this were true, it must have meant something different from what you thought. His saying: 'And if I do not find anything in the verses of God (Exalted be He) nor in the *sunna* of his Messenger, then I would formulate an independent judgement,' should have meant that he acknowledges the fact that it must really be found in them, just like anyone would know that something is actually in the Book even though he doesn't find it there due to his ignorance. The Book, in fact, knows more than such a person knows. If someone is not aware that something is found in the Book or the Traditions, it does not follow that it is not there. Hence, his saying: 'I would formulate an independent judgement' would mean 'I would learn what I was ignorant of, act [52r] according to what I learned and be wary of forgetfulness.' For this reason, God (Blessed and Exalted be He) said to his Prophet (God's blessing be on him): 'And judge between them according to what God has sent down' (5:49). He also said: 'So that thou mayest judge between the people by that God has shown them' (4:105). This judgement was not by analogy nor was it by personal opinion. By this He rather meant: Judge between them by what God has taught you. This means that God has commanded him to judge by what God has sent down. In the case of hunting, for example, the ransom inflicted by two fair judges is usually the same as the number of cattle killed. One, however, should not understand, by the word 'same', that this can be applied to other issues and allow personal judgements and analogies. Our reply, therefore, would be: Although God (Exalted be He) has decreed that the ransom in hunting should be the same as the number of cattle, the word 'same', is too clear to be interpreted. It does not require any disagreement in opinion nor is it liable to analogy. So, what made you think that God allowed analogy and personal judgement in such issues? What is certain here is that God has

[52v] explained the meaning of the word 'same' and taught him that the word 'same' should be put into effect. Hence, one cannot find in the verse any evidence of using analogy and personal judgement. If one says: Because mankind cannot do without knowing the meaning of the word 'same' in the issue of hunting and the meaning of other similar events, and because there are no decrees about such things in the Book and the *sunna*, then analogy and personal opinion should necessarily be used. To such a person one should say: What made you believe that there are no provisions for such issues in the Book and the *sunna*? If he claims that he and the majority of the *umma* are ignorant and, therefore, are in need of using analogy and personal opinion, we reply: How can you say that the reason for not having any provisions decreed is your ignorance and, therefore, analogy and personal opinion are necessary? You should rather have said

[53r] that because of your ignorance, analogy and personal opinion should be prohibited. In fact, your ignorance is proof that it should indeed be mentioned in the Scriptures, and that someone who is knowledgeable should be in charge, and act on behalf of the Messenger over the *umma*. If someone says: Why can we not have analogy and personal judgement? We tell him: The answer is that all of us, you, we and the rest of the *umma* have unanimously agreed that all basic principles, such as prayer, almsgiving, pilgrimage, fasting, striving in God's way and the like, can never be realised by analogy and personal judgement. If this is the case and all things are put within their real sense, that is, if they are really considered to be God's verdicts and decrees, then they should never be ratified through analogy and personal opinion.

[53v] They should rather be established through the Scriptures. Likewise, all fundamental principles should be divinely decreed. If he says: Why have you associated those provisions that are similar to the fundamental principles with the fundamental principles themselves? Is that why they should be invalidated only through the

Scriptures? And why do you not consider them like the lawful and the unlawful? By considering lawful what is similar to the lawful and unlawful what is similar to the unlawful? To such a question we reply: We do not consider them as such for the following reasons:

First, God did not permit us to consider things lawful or unlawful by ourselves. He declared things to be such through His own verdicts that He prescribed. In fact, He dealt with the obscure issues by giving various judgements. For example, the menstruating woman should fast during Ramaḍān though He rid her of praying. He prescribed the various conditions pertaining to the fast of Ramaḍān and to prayer that should be performed by those who intentionally fail to observe them on time. Likewise, He prescribed the cases when breaking the fast is allowed

[54r] while travelling. It is allowed during travel provided it is compensated later on, whereas missing prayer is not allowed. However, He did not prescribe how one should compensate for what He had given leave of. Another example is the case of *ahl al-dhimma* (free non-Muslim subjects) where in some instances He exempted them from paying tribute, while He did not do the same in cases of murder. Other examples are fighting the Arab pagans until they declared Islam, accepting tributes from Jews and Christians, and dealing with free men and slaves though they are congruent both in person and existence. Pronounced verdicts differ depending on whether the cases in question are similar in all or some aspects. If the cases in question are similar in all their aspects, then the verdicts would be the same. Hence, you do not need to rely on analogy. If, on the other hand, the cases are different in some aspects,

[54v] then we should ask why do you pass your verdict according to the aspects that are similar and not according to those that are different? If he says it is because most of the aspects were similar and only a few were not, then we should tell him: Can the similarities be more than those between the free men and the slaves or between the Muslims and *ahl al-dhimma*? If he claims that they can, he would be telling lies. If he does not, then the different verdicts of God (Glorious be He) concerning these similarities would be proof that these divine verdicts could be based neither on the few similarities nor on the few differences. If, on the other hand, he says: Had verdicts about all cases been mentioned in the Scriptures, the Messenger of God

[55r] (God's blessing be on him) would have told his Companions about them. Had he mentioned them to his Companions, they would have conveyed them to us. Since the Prophet did not convey them to the people, it follows that they were not revealed to him. This is because had they been mentioned in the Scripture, there would have been one of two possibilities: either they were concealed from everyone and this means denying the Prophet the task of teaching because of the great number of those who were sent to teach, or that he conveyed them to some people rather than to all mankind; and this would mean accusing the Prophet of partiality in religion and of egoism, thus denying prophethood.

Concealing revealed scriptures does not invalidate them

Our view concerning such a matter is the following: It is not required from everyone to know all the cases. Not every person bears to know that much, nor is he responsible for knowing them. People are instinctively forgetful of the part, let alone of the whole. Had they not been so, they would be hindered from their living and

[55v] other things. Had they been exacted to do so, they would have been required to do more than they were capable of. It is not possible, therefore, for mankind but to have someone to implement God's teachings. This is because man is neither responsible for nor capable of guiding himself. Not everyone knows by nature what he can endure. However, it is not possible that everyone is ignorant of being in need of someone who would teach people what they should do, as it was impossible for the Messenger of God (God's blessing be on him) to reach every person in the world; yet everyone is bound to be reached. Hence our conviction is that the Messenger of God (God's blessing be on him) has decided lucidly what to do about such matters that take place after him. Therefore, one can never say that the Prophet (God's blessing be on him) by doing what he did, that is, by informing some rather than all of his *umma*, was partial. The fact that

[56r] he was attesting utterances on current matters in front of some of his Companions while most were not present, so that those who were present knew those utterances while others did not, does not mean that he was prejudiced. We already mentioned that the very need of the people to know the various utterances and occurrences

necessitates the existence of someone who knows what others do not, and who can endure what others cannot. This is because not everyone can have too much knowledge, due to man's weakness and shortcomings. Such a person should be different in character from everyone else. He cannot be ignorant like others, nor can he be liable to mistakes or to major sins; or else such a person would be denied knowledge, or rather, people would take him down to their level of ignorance that kept them from knowledge in the first place. If someone

[56v] says: The fact that some of his Companions who were present with him conveyed his utterances, while the majority of his Companions were away, does not exempt the Prophet from being partial. This is because those who were present acted as tutors to those who were absent. To such a person we reply: The way the Prophet would deny his alleged partiality in conveying his utterances to one rather than to all of his Companions is to appoint that one as a tutor and master who conveys the knowledge of the current matters at the time they are needed. As for those who say that it is not fair that one should pass judgement unless he already knows that truth goes with what he believes in, and not simply to rule on matters he knows nothing about, to such people we say: You only think that the utmost knowledge one can reach is right judgement through analogy, and the utmost right judgement is what is based on speculation and personal opinion. We already showed enough evidence for the inadequacy of such beliefs. He who relies on such matters should necessarily be passing judgement on issues he does not know. A righteous judge is one who is ordered to pass judgement on issues he knows, and who is prohibited to pass judgement on issues

[57r] he does not know. This is because he is ordered to refrain from basing his judgements on opinion and analogy. Truth lies in what we already explained and elaborated on. We end our discussion by praising God, the Lord of all beings.

As the Messenger is divinely appointed so are those in authority after him

Then they said that God (Glorious be He) said: 'If they had referred it to the Messenger and those in authority among them those of them whose task it is to investigate would have known the matter' (4:83). Those who are in authority among us are the learned among us. God (Exalted and Blessed be He) said: 'Obey God and obey the Messenger and those in authority among you' (4:59). The greatest act in our religion that God has imposed on the Muslims is the appointment of an imam over them. It is one of those matters that, though it was not named as such, was counted from among the qualities that were mentioned by us. Hence, we say: The important question behind the issue of the imamate lies on the person of the imam whom God ordered us to refer to and to obey. After taking refuge in him we are promised to be given knowledge of what we have to delve into, this is according to what God (Exalted be He) said. This is in line with your interpretation of His words.

[57v] The evidence of what we have just said is that God (may He be praised) ordered us to obey Him only after He had made us know Him, and to obey His Messenger only after He made him known to us in the Scriptures. Likewise, He ordered us to obey those in authority among us after He made them known to us in His Book by pointing them out, just as He pointed out the Messenger of God (God's blessing be on him). This is because when God made His obedience conditional to our obeying His Messenger (God's blessing be on him), He did this only through His designation as such. In the same manner He made our obedience to His Messenger conditional to our obedience to those in authority. Therefore, it was confirmed that our obedience to His Messenger can only be realised by our obedience to those in authority among us. This was decreed in the Scriptures, just like our obedience to His Messenger (God's blessing be on him) was decreed. Had it been possible for him to order us to obey those in authority and be loyal to them without decreeing His order, then it would be possible for Him to order us to obey the Messenger without having it decreed. Likewise, had it been possible for Him to entrust us

[58r] with choosing those in authority whose obedience is consociate with the obedience of His Messenger, then it would be possible for us to choose His Messenger (God's blessing be on him) as such. Similarly, by ordering us to obey the Prophet (God's blessing be on him), God proved to us that it was impossible for the Prophet to fall into vice, or ignorance or error. As was His ordering us to obey the

imam, it was the same as His ordering us to obey the Prophet (God's blessing be on him). One, of course, should exclude those matters that were mentioned in the Qur'ān and the Traditions, namely that no one would claim to be the Prophet's associate in prophecy, apostleship or revelation. The fact being thus, the imam should, therefore, be just as we have described. He cannot be designated by way of personal opinion or by choice. Such means cannot be applied to him, nor is it through such ways that he can be chosen. These are only applied to others. Those who believe they can be applied to the imam do not know the meaning of God's saying: 'If they had referred it to the Messenger

[58v] and those in authority among them, those of them whose task it is to investigate would have known the matter' (4:83). This is a promise from God to us that if we refer what we do not know to the Messenger he will make it known to us. Likewise, when we refer it to those in authority they would make it known to us. Our knowledge of it, whether it is from the Messenger of God (God's blessing be on him) or from those in authority among us would surely be decreed in the Scriptures. It would by no means be by personal opinion and analogy. Had the learned among you been those in authority among you and had our reply to them been only by opinion and analogy, then they would not disagree with us. If this was possible, then we would be reaching the truth. But would that not be asking the ignorant to distinguish between themselves and those who know? However, God knows their shortcoming. He feels pity for them. Their accepting everyone

[59r] is a fact which leads to a contradiction that is dispraised by God.

Suppose that such matters were sanctioned. Then when two people disagree on a certain issue, under which provision should they be judged? If they would be judged according to one of two provisions, then what would be your position? If someone said that this judgement was pronounced in accordance with some wise man's point of view, then one would say to them: Why did you not judge according to the other provision which was the point of view of another wise man? If, on the other hand, the judgement pronounced was in accordance with both viewpoints, then you would be doing what is impossible. If those two people were judged according to the other point of view, then the judge would be told to give proof of why he did so. As a result, you would be faced with two alternatives: either you rely on both viewpoints or you rely on one of them. But this is more fallacious. It is due to corruption in judgement and analogy. Both judgements would by no means be those of God (Exalted be He).

[59v] God (Glory be to Him) said: 'If it had been from other than God surely they would have found in it much inconsistency' (4:82). This leads us to say: Those in authority among us are the knowledgeable among us. They are our imams and the Prophet's vicegerents over us. They are the ark of Noah. He who boards it is saved.[11] God has ordered us to follow them and to acquire knowledge from them. He forbade us from following those who came before them. Our Prophet Muḥammad (God's blessing be on him) told us that they would not depart from his Book until they come to him together at the Basin and that as long as we cling to them we will never go astray.

The difference between the Prophet and the imam

If he says: You have thus made them equal to the Prophet (God's blessing be on him), for you have claimed that they could be known only by appointment from above, just like the Prophet, and that this cannot be accepted, then we reply: What we have said about them does by no means make them equal to the Messenger. They are different from him (God's blessing be on him) in many respects: First, by the fact that they are denied revelation. Second, by the superiority of the Prophet (God's blessing be on him) over them. [60r] Third, abrogation of Qur'ānic verses at the time of the Prophet

---

11. This refers to the Tradition 'The example of my family among you is that of Noah's ark; Whoever boards it is saved; whoever does not drowns and falls.' Al-Qāḍī al-Nuʿmān mentions this Tradition twice in his book *Daʿāʾim al Islām* (vol. 1, pp. 35 and 99). However, the two instances are slightly different among the scholars of Traditions; al-Khaṭīb al-Tabrīzī mentions it in his *Mishkāt al-maṣābīḥ*, specifying Aḥmad b. Ḥanbal as his source. But the Tradition is not mentioned in Ibn Ḥanbal's *Masnad*. All the Sunni scholars, however, consider its chain of narrators as weak. See al-Khaṭīb al-Tabrīzī, *Mishkāt al-maṣābīḥ* (vol. 3, p. 265), Nūr al-Dīn al-Haythamī, *Majmaʿ al zawāʾid wa manbaʿ al fawāʾid* (vol. 9, p. 168), and Abu'l Fawāris, *al-Risāla fiʾl imāma*, ed. and tr. Makarem as *Political Doctrine*, pp. 30, 42 and 84 (n. 122).

(God's blessing be on him) was permissible, whereas it was prohibited during their times. Had equality with the Prophet been requisite for us it would be the same for you. This is because you are required to obey the imam, if he acts equitably, just as you are required to obey the Messenger (God's blessing be on him). Did you not regard lawful the shedding of the blood of those who disobeyed him and invaded those who opposed him? If someone says: Let us suppose that what you have mentioned were correct, namely that there is a successor who is actually appointed from above, that there must be a vicegerent – unless the *umma* is affected by some hindering causes that you mentioned – and that he is knowledgeable of all the needs of the *umma*, and that he is safeguarded from any wrongdoing, what would assure us that he is 'Alī b. Abī Ṭālib and not some other Muslim?

The necessity that 'Alī b. Abī Ṭālib is the imam

To such a person one should say: Suppose that this were to happen and such a person was the appointed one

[60v] and suppose everyone, from either Quraysh or other tribes, could consider himself to be the one appointed. The *umma* would never consent to any one of those people to be the appointed person. This is because none would have the qualities required. Only one person would be excluded, 'Alī b. Abī Ṭālib. Not one of the whole *umma* would disagree that he possesses such qualities. On the contrary, some of the notables of the Companions expounded on such qualities that he had and spoke highly of him. This being the case, it was only 'Alī (peace be on him) who was the appointed one. Had it not been him there would not be anyone appointed from the *umma*; we have already shown the invalidity of having anyone else. Therefore, the only one worthy of being a vicegerent is he. Also, it was proven that no one from among the *umma* other than 'Alī b. Abī Ṭālib (peace be on him) was infallible or knowledgeable of the needs of the *umma*. No one from the *umma* thought otherwise. Moreover, we have proven that he who is not as such cannot be an imam.

[61r] One should say: Had God (may His name be blessed) ordained that the imam should be appointed by his equals, then He would be denying the religious necessity of the imamate. This is evident in His saying: 'And call in to witness two men of equity from among your-

selves' (65:2). Although He did not call the men of equity by name or indicate them in person, He made us know what equity was. So when we know that equity exists in someone we must acknowledge him and accept his witness. Such is the way in which we should act with those in authority among us. They are our men of knowledge, the bearers of our religion and the managers of our political affairs. We say to those who object: You have connected and compared between inconsistent and divergent issues. You have claimed that the principle of the imamate is not decreed in the religious texts and that it should be dealt with by independent judgement. Basing your point of view on such premises, you claimed that it is similar to other issues in religion such as that mentioned in God's saying: 'And call in to witness two men of equity from among yourselves' (65:2), comparing such issues

[61v] with a sacred text venerated by all the *umma*, where God ordered man to call into witness equity among mankind, and interpreting this divine command to suit your point of view about the imamate. It would be as if you were trying to say that God has decreed that the imam should be chosen by the *umma*. You were not able to reach this aim of yours except by trespassing your limits and then saying, after seeing justice occurring by God's name: This person is equitable, so call him in to witness. If this were sufficient then calling him to witness would be decreed in Scripture. If they say yes, then the *umma* would deem him as such, and Scripture would be disregarded. If, on the other hand, he says that such a case is in Scripture then he would obviously fall into error. In fact, he is already in error, because he relied on something other than Scripture. To such a person one could say concerning this issue: God (Glorious and Exalted be He) did not decree in his Book that knowledge is necessary. This is obviously known by nature and by God's acts. There is no need to decree it from above. Equity is an obvious issue. It can be known either

[62r] by mere observation or through public account. Hence, it is necessary to distinguish between this and other matters. A simple distinction – like between night and day, hot and cold, beautiful and ugly, agreeable and putrid – is not enough. Such phenomena, unlike more crucial matters, such as that of the imamate, are known by instinct. They do not need analogy or judgement or logical evidence

that may be different from what we have already mentioned. This is because the imamate, according to you, would be established through the opinions and analogies of jurists and subjected to their examination and probing until they choose, in their judgement, the best in both knowledge and character, and the most appropriate for it. Such inquiry depends on the extent of equity among the members of the *umma*, not to forget the various shortcomings they have regarding their view of equity.

[62v] This was in fact taken into account by the Messenger (God's blessing be on Him) who said: 'No witnessing can be accepted from a suspect or an accused or a liar.' This confirms the meaning of equity as well as strengthens our conviction, unless someone goes on in his speculations to add guidance to the meaning of equity, then it would be worthy of considering the issue at large. Such a person would be in need of the right name of the imam-to-be. Regarding your understanding of this institution, we say: Why do you base the imamate on the logic of equity of witnesses? Is it because you consider it a branch of equity or not? If you consider it a branch, you would be obviously at fault. Then we ask you the following questions: Did you not claim that the imamate was the basic principle of equity? If you admit that it is a basic principle in itself and that equity of witnesses is another basic principle, you would be at fault as well, since you would be comparing two independent principles with each other. Would it not be more correct to compare two things that share the least similarities between each other?

[63r] There is no way but to say yes. Then one should tell those people: The position of the imam then is similar to that of the Messenger. They resemble each other more than the position of the equitable witness resembles that of the Messenger (God's blessing be on him), which is a plain falsity. This is because the role of the imam is similar to that of the Messenger, in combating the enemy, dividing the spoils, defending the oppressed, serving pilgrimage, uniting the *umma*, imposing the law and the like. Similarity between the two positions extends also to God ordering the people to obey those in authority and to refer to them. Moreover, the reason that the position of the imam is more like that of the Messenger than the position of the equitable witness is the fact that the position of the imam, like that of the Messenger, is not established through coun-

selling. Therefore, it is invalid to compare the imam with the equitable witnesses. In reply, they may say [that] speculation is used in case
of prayer, enjoined by God. If someone happens to be
[63v] travelling he may reduce the period of prayer, and if he
encounters a cloudy day he cannot exactly define the time for
prayers. Speculation is also needed in case of almsgiving; how can
one distinguish between the poor, the needy and the self-sufficient
in God's saying: 'The freewill offerings are for the poor and needy ...'
(9:60). This is also used in case of striving in God's way; which illness
prevents the sick man from striving when God says: 'There is no fault
in the sick' (48:17)? Speculations can also be found in matters related
to legal punishment of children who have just reached puberty, or
in matters of pilgrimage related to stoning the devil and the weight
of the stones to be thrown by a child. Speculation is used as well in
imposing the appropriate punishment of intended murders and in
the case of observing a commandment which was not defined by
God (may His mention be Exalted) due to it being known by logic.
Hence, we say: Can we differentiate between prayers while staying
in one place
[64r] and reduce their number while travelling, or the period of
prayer on a cloudy day, or the alms to be received or those to be
given? Are those commandments not decreed in the Book of God,
and the way you chose the imam through speculation? If the answer
is yes, then the *umma* would deny him, as he would not be able to
find it decreed in Scripture. If, on the other hand, he would admit
that it was in the Scripture – a matter which is correct – then he
would be at fault because of his comparing what is in the Scripture
with what is not. In fact, the traveller does not need to speculate
whether he is travelling or not, nor is he in need of thinking whether
he should therefore reduce his prayer period, since this has been
clearly mentioned in the *sunna*. The dispute over reducing the
period of prayer is solved in the *sunna*, not because the traveller may
reduce the period of prayer by using
[64v] speculation, for this is too simple not to be known by every
inborn Muslim. This also applies in cases of fasting and breaking the
fast by witnessing the crescent, as well as in the case of giving alms,
as to how many young camels are due for almsgiving and so on and
so forth. It applies as well for cases of determining the poor and the

needy. It is, therefore, necessarily for the *umma* to acknowledge the apparent conditions and, therefore, it is incumbent on the judges to judge the apparent deeds of the suspect and pass their fair judgements. As for those who are away, they should be nurtured by the *sunna* and should know that they are not in need for their personal judgements, except in matters that need to be known through direct seeing or hearing. As for those whom God decreed to be exempted from striving due to sickness, their case is proven by direct observation. Their outward appearance would be sufficient evidence. Their sickness, however, may

[65r] be of a kind that does not show, so they would be reported as not deserving to be exempted. Their case would thus be referred to the person himself who knows his condition better than anyone else. God (Glory be to Him) does not require anyone to know what is hidden. If a sick man needed to know his real sickness, he would need to know about the science of health. Likewise, he is not required to be versed in medicine to know whether he is ill or not. Had he been required to possess such knowledge, then he would be liable to error and, consequently, he would be unaware of his illness, even though he would be noted for his knowledge. Had this been possible

[65v] it would then be possible that a man must necessarily be versed in theoretical knowledge to know whether he is satiated or hungry, or whether he is talking or silent, married or single or whether he is sated or thirsty. Had this been possible, then such a person would not even be able to know whether he was still united in marriage when he was not, or whether he was not any more united in marriage when he still was. This is definitely contradictory to the usual run of things. The same applies to the question of children reaching puberty. It need not be theoretically proven when it is physically evident. So it is with the case of stoning the devil [in Mina], a religious rite enjoined by God Whose Prophet defined the number and size of pebbles to be thrown. Deciding which pebbles to be used only needs the sense of sight, for it was decreed for simplification that the pebble should neither be smaller than an individual piece of stone nor should it be bigger. The same is applied to punishment

[66r] decreed and defined by God. He made us know the difference between murder on purpose and murder by mistake, as well as between a skull fracture and a fracture reaching the brain, and

between a stab reaching the inside of the head and a fracture reaching the membrane covering the periosteum. The penalty for each of these acts does not need any personal opinion or analogy. If any dispute would arise concerning murder on purpose or by mistake, or concerning the kinds of fracture that were inflicted, it would not need to be settled by speculation; rather it should be referred to those in authority, so that the perpetrator would know the extent of his crime, be it murder or fracture, and know the penalty assigned to such an act. All these things are, in fact, by God's grace, a clear evidence of the wrongness of those who claim that judgements should be subject to theoretical speculation. Had these things been excluded from being decreed in Scripture, then he who believes thus should exclude himself

[66v] from being the right person. He would be just like the one who excludes the night from darkness or the day from light. If he would use this as an analogy, then he would come to the conclusion that the imam cannot but be appointed; just like the commandments, they cannot but be decreed.

The necessity of the Messenger's appointing an imam to succeed after him

If someone were to ask: Did the Messenger of God (God's blessing be on him) nominate anyone as his successor? The answer would be, yes, as he also sanctioned the witnessing of the just. In fact, there was a general consensus of the *umma* that this nominee was the vicegerent of the Messenger of God (God's blessing be on him). He also understood the meaning of vicegerent differently from the way we had mentioned, that is, not as appointment from above.

He likewise considered the witnessing of the just as necessary, but not as appointed from above as well. Hence, he stated that the just who were to witness should be those whom we acknowledge to witness in accordance with the command of God and His Messenger (God's blessing be on him). Also, he pointed out that the vicegerent should be one of those who were righteous

[67r] and superior. Therefore, if we were to have an imam we should find out who possesses such qualities so that we consider him as imam. In reply to the above we say: Although we have already said enough about this question, we can add that the Messenger of God

(God's blessing be on him) has explained to us the meaning of equity and approved the testimony of the equitable. Anyone we find having such qualities we accordingly acknowledge his equity. Likewise, he explained to us the meaning of superiority and righteousness. Anyone we find with such qualities, we acknowledge them in him. But this cannot be applied to the imam. In such a case, a clear proof is needed for us that the Messenger of God (God's blessing be on him) and God's Book have stated plainly: 'He whom you find to be superior take him as imam.' This is different from his saying: 'He whom you find to be equitable, take him as witness.' But, we will never find such a statement.

As for the claim that such a person is the vicegerent [67v] of the Messenger of God (God's blessing be on him) by the unanimous consensus of the *umma*, it is an invalid claim, in that the *umma*'s so-called consensus would be made baseless. We have explained earlier how invalid the unanimous agreement of opinion is. This is, in fact, clear proof of the invalidity of the consensus of those who base their argument on such a premise. No valid proof can be based on such an argument. What we have clarified is sufficient for such purpose. To God we offer our utmost praise.

Who decides on the appointment of the imam?

To those who support such a claim we say: Who decides on the imamate? Is it all the people or only a particular group of residents of a certain country? If they say: Those who decide on the imamate are the Muslim learned men, then we tell them: All of them without exception or a certain group of them? If they say: Some of the learned men who cannot possibly come to a consensus on a false matter and that there is not exact number. Another argument can be raised here about informing [68r] those who live in remote countries without mentioning them in particular. Those people need to be informed about such an issue, or else the election of an imam by a certain number of the *umma* rather than by all of them would be a violation regarding those in remote countries. This is our viewpoint as well as that of others. Moreover, if a group of learned men unanimously agree that among them there is someone superior and thus they agree to install him as Caliph without taking the *umma*'s approval, to those people we

say: Tell us about those whose act you have validated and considered it authoritative, then you regarded their consensus conclusive
by reason of considering their act authoritative; are they a group of
people who have agreed among themselves to carry out their decision in unison? If the answer is yes, then they would have contradicted the *sunna*, because

[68v] those people, even if they were many, are not acquitted from
seeking accord. The Tradition whose authenticity no one has any
doubt of is the one whose transmitters are those who were promoters of accord. Such a Tradition should be free from any evidence
against truth. If any group of people cannot narrate Traditions
that are genuine evidence of truth, then any consensus they claim
to have would not be valid. No Tradition, however, can be genuine
unless it is concordant with the description of a true Tradition given
above. Such people would then be building their system on unsound
grounds. If someone claims that this group of people are trustworthy, even if they fail to rely on an authoritative Tradition, they would
be merely relying on such false Traditions, an evidence of their being
wrong. This is if they fail to propagate accord. Basing their argument
on false foundations, those people

[68v] {claimed to be an authority. In reply we say: those people
were wrong because the argument they used was deficient in several
respects. What they did was in fact a proof against them, because
it was a proof of being of no avail. They were copying each other.
Each was treading in the steps of the other, they all believed in the
Tradition their predecessors had transmitted, until they were sure
of its authenticity and took it accordingly as evidence for the validity of their viewpoint. What they were supposed to do instead was
to reject any personal opinion transmitted by blind followers, or by
ignorant people following those who were considered to be more
learned or by people of a low status imitating others of higher status.
Such an act, however, is not permissible in analogy. To be a source
of legislation, analogy should not allow any duplication either by the
public or by the elite, nor by the majority or by the minority. It rather
should be based on deliberation and discussion whereby any blind
duplication is naturally rejected. In fact, blind duplication of opinions is necessarily against any free interchange of views. This was
enough evidence that those people's understanding of analogy and

way of thinking were unsound. To such people one must say: It is not enough to rely on Traditions

[68v] whatsoever. Even the Christians and other unbelievers did not do so. Tell us, would any bishop, no matter how glorified he was, or any monk, no matter how pious he was, or any philosopher, no matter how knowledgeable he was, remain as such if their sayings did not promote concord? The answer would certainly be no. Then one should ask: Would it be lawful if those people rely on such Traditions in building their religious beliefs? Was it not proven that their most erroneous and blasphemous belief in Christ (peace be on him) was untrue, even though it reached consensus as being a true belief? By using such people's methods and stories about Jonah, Lot, Mark and John you could not strengthen any of your arguments. If that person you asked says the Christians are unbelievers, whereas the *umma* is not, then we reply: Did their unbelief prevent them from considering their views as final because they did not reach any consensus? If he admits that, then we say to him: If you rely on those people, whom you claimed to be trustworthy, because of their consensus on the validity of their view, or because of their reliance on their opinion, in fact, it was proven that their misjudgement and delusive conviction were due to their false claim that what they believed in and deduced was right. To such people one should say: Is it not possible perhaps that some people would say that

[68v] a given city is the greatest city they have seen? But this does not deny that some other city that they never saw could be greater. The answer to such a remark would definitely be that it is true. The same remark may apply to the *umma*. Would it be not possible that the *umma* unanimously agree that a given person is the best among those whom they know? But this also does not deny that some other person who is unknown to them would possibly be more knowledgeable and superior. Would it be right if they appoint as imam the one whom they considered the best among those they know instead of the one who is superior? Is this permissible?} [12] In reply to this we say: If

[69r] you deem it permissible to choose the person who is inferior in excellence, then he would in turn choose as his aides those who would be inferior and let go of those who would be superior in reli-

---

12. The text between the braces appears only in manuscript B.

gion. Also we say: On the other hand if, due to your neglect, care-less attitude and heedlessness, you would choose instead the one you do not know – and the other may be superior – then you would necessarily be admitting his being inferior. In addition, you would be acting as if you insist on denying him any excuse for not being able to have enough promoters for his cause. Such, in fact, is a claim you should avoid making, namely that the true imam is the one who should be chosen, for the simple reason that the pulpits of all the regions call for him and the learned of the *umma* promote his desig-nation. Such an argument can never be true. To support the infe-rior is clearly practised though, and the falsity of the imamate of the unrighteous is now proven by what we mentioned. Therefore, it is absolutely necessary that the superior should be installed by the one [69v] before him. Thus it would be impossible for him to fall into error, or favouritism, or to be distrusted by the *umma*.

This is why one should confront those people by saying: Tell us about those groups of people who have unanimously concurred that disagreement among them is legitimate, so that some of them could promote a certain man to the position of the imamate while some others could promote another. If they assert that this may be possi-ble, provided that they should justify their viewpoint against the others, then our answer would be: What would the proof be that one of the two parties was right? If they say the consensus of that party, then we reply: What about the consensus of the other party? Would it not be proof as well? If they say: The consensus of the people of the other party can never be, in that case, a proof for their being right; on the contrary, it would be a proof that they were wrong. Then we tell them: On what grounds did you rely on consensus when you admitted that only one of the two parties was proven to be [70r] right and you should, therefore, assent? Then one should tell them: What kind of false consensus is that which can be opposed by another false consensus arrived at by an equal, or even a larger, number, of opposing individuals who belong to the same commu-nity whose integrity makes it necessary not to let the bad things in it overcome the good things? How can such a community agree on disagreement and then claim that by consensus right can be attained when both parties base their arguments on the same Tradition? Then to those people one should say: Is it possible, when some of this community agrees that someone is superior and has more merit, and wins all arguments through consensus, is it possible for them not to relinquish their indifference and neglect? Is it possible that such a group would be led to overlook the one who is superior, while another group of the same community would be led to oppose him in spite of their knowledge of his merit that was the result of his excellence or his popularity, while a third group would rise to support him

[70v] because of his superiority, and to choose him instead of another? If they claim that this is possible, they would be ruling out all ignorance from all and every one of them, thanks to this man's superiority and natural discernment. This, however, is contradictory to the very objective of the imamate, as well as to the necessity of deliberation, speculation and deduction. In fact, an act that is reached through natural discernment does not need any deliberation, nor does it need any speculation or deduction to be realised. Do you need any of these to realise the light of the day or the darkness of the night? If he, nevertheless, insists on using such methods, one should tell him: These can only be used in religious matters as a means to establish a sound proof against ignorance. Otherwise they would dare to claim, relating from some eye-witness, that they saw the Mosque of Damascus although they have never seen in it. They would argue with each other, relying on information derived from some who had seen it and some who never did. Hence they disputed. Some affirm that the Mosque

[71r] is adorned. Some are sure of it being adorned, and some insist on it without having the slightest idea about it, and some deny its being adorned and have no knowledge about it whatsoever. However, they all pretend that they have really seen it while fully sound in soul and body.

Now, if people would admit such pretences, they would be relying on illusion, and accordingly they would be going astray. On the other hand, if they would deny them, they would be mixing personal opinion with fact and thus what would be based on personal opinion would be negated by the scriptural text mentioned.

Then to such people one should say: Tell us about such a group of people. Is it possible that their opinions contradict each other and the scriptural sources they quote be inconsistent? Is it possible that each of their various factions claims before its followers to be right? Is it possible that no consensus among them could ever be reached, so that when they convene, those among them who have been in the wrong know where they were at fault? And thus consensus would finally be attained among them to be a decisive proof?

If those people would agree with such presumptions, then we tell them: Is it possible that those who have won, to relate contradictory information, such as the faction relating that the Caliph fasted on Sunday

[71v] and another that on Sunday he broke the fast? So, the liars would finally know that they were lying. If someone says: This is possible, due to the fact that some thousand people or even more are liable to forget. Therefore, it could easily happen that half of the people could be in doubt about the exact days of fast-breaking and al-Aḍḥā.

Such an assumption, however, is utterly unreasonable. In fact, it is due to the failure to distinguish between fact and personal opinion. Hence, every analogy founded on such premises is false. So to such a person one must say: What is your proof that when a certain group of people who believe in the necessity of the imamate (in fact, the whole *umma* must believe so), should, if capable, support the newly appointed imam? If this imam were installed in accordance with the Book of God and the *sunna* of the Messenger of God (God's blessings be on him) as well as with the consensus of all the Muslims, would he be a legitimate imam? Or, in case we do not find any scriptural justification

[72r] for his appointment, we resort to allegorically interpreting the Book of God, would his instalment be legal? In fact, we have already proven the invalidity of this interpretation and failed to find any of the Traditions transmitted from the Messenger of God (God's blessings be on him) supporting his instalment. On the contrary we have seen that all the deeds of the Messenger of God (God's blessings be on him) have shown the opposite. This is because he invested this matter to no one, not even to his close circles or to anyone in a small town, nor to any of the climes of the earth, nor to the *umma*. Besides, no one had claimed that the Messenger of God (God's blessings be on him) had even ordered such a thing. If, on the other hand, it was claimed that the instalment was by the consensus of the Muslims,

then this would be obviously invalid, as the *umma* had disagreed on this matter, to the extent that some of the *umma* had charged those who had claimed such a matter to be unbelievers and blasphemers. Hence, if any group of people, whether they were many or few, believed in such a matter, then this group would be condemned for not observing the inviolability of the *umma*'s consensus. This would be similar to the question of the creation of the Qur'ān

[72v] and the denial of God's corporality. Such a group should be necessarily confronted with their error. If someone says that it is the *fuqahā'* who install him, then we should pose the following question: Does the *faqīh* have to reach a certain degree of knowledge to be called as such so that he who reaches that degree will be called a *faqīh*, and he who fails to reach it will not? To this question he must have replied: There is no definite degree, neither for us nor for the *umma* nor for any other nation in the world. If a person cannot be a *faqīh* unless he knows all the religion – and this, according to them, is not even attained by the one they claim to be their imam, or by anyone else, neither in the times of the Prophet (God's blessings be on him) nor after him, except for one and only *faqīh* – and this is impossible; for how can it be possible when God (Exalted be He) has said: 'Was it not a sign for them, that it is known to the learned of the Children of Israel' (26:197), a verse of the Qur'ān is sufficient proof. Is this not evidence

[73r] that if the learned among the Muslims recognise the superiority of the superior, then this is proof for his imamate? He who knows the fundamental principles written down in the Book and Traditions is therefore a *faqīh*. If he happens to lack some knowledge, but not enough to render him ignorant, then the knowledge he retains would be enough for him to be considered among the learned. No one can reach all religious knowledge or else he would be equal in knowledge to the Prophet (God's blessings be on him). Had anyone been so, then his appeal to God (Exalted be He) to increase him in knowledge would be as if he appeals to Him to be given the Prophet's knowledge (God's blessings and peace be on him). He who is so would not be worthy of being a learned man. Consequently, he would not have the merit of the imamate. In reply to the aforementioned argument we say: We never claimed that the imamate implied *fiqh*. Even if a *faqīh* does not know all knowledge he continues to be so, given that the

knowledge is enough to free him from ignorance: Hence we say that
a given person
[73v] is more learned than another who is considered to be a *faqīh*
in the *umma*. Nevertheless, this was not what we asked about. What
we asked about was the *fuqahā'* who were to choose the imam. Did
they have a definite responsibility like the followers of Malik and
those of Abū Ḥanīfa and Ibn Abī Laylā, and others? Actually, they
should be either from among those whom we mentioned above or
not. If someone asserts that they belong to one of these factions,
we reply: Who made the *fuqahā'* of this faction better suited than
those of that faction, so as to have the right to choose the imam? If
there is no sound reason, then the followers of all these factions will
have nothing to do except argue with each other about who has the
correct point of view and who is more pertinent in his belief. The
result would be either that one faction would be entitled to choose
the imam, or the *fuqahā'* of all the factions would convene to install
the imam they agreed upon.
[74r] With either of these results they must return to the idea of
consensus which was proven to be contrary to fact. The reasons
for such impracticality of consensus are the following: The great
number of factions, the wide range of provinces, the variations of
beliefs, and the enmity among the members of the *umma* and their
constant accusation of each other of unbelief. Considering either
one of these two alternatives, one is forced to bring into question,
as he did before, the following: What is the proof that the Book and
the Traditions can provide us support of such an argument, namely
which of these factions should be worthy of choosing the imam and
which of them should be allowed legally to do so? The answer to
both questions should definitely be nothing but mere conjecture. In
reply to all these points we say: It has been said by the learned of the
Children of Israel[13] what confirms the advent of the Prophet. Such
confirmation was a decisive argument against them, and consequently a decisive argument for the imamate of our imam. One can
deduce from such a verse, therefore, that both the prophecy
[74v] of the Prophet (God's blessings and peace be on him) and
the imamate of an imam are ordained. The people have no right to
choose either of them or to determine the imam by analogy. Our

13. See Qur'ān 26:197.

learned men all agree that the imamate is determined by appointment from God's Messenger (God's blessings be on him), then from
the vicegerent of God's Messenger. This belief is clear evidence of
the invalidity of all other points of view. However, the fact that the
vicegerent of the Messenger of God (God's blessings be on him)
knows the needs of the *umma* does not mean that he should be on
equal footing with him. Likewise, the fact that many have read the
Qur'ān and have learned it by heart does not make them equal to
the Prophet in learning. The Companions guarding the Qur'ān in
their hearts by memorising it are by no means equal to the Prophet's
guarding it in his heart, which God sent down to him (God's blessings be on him). This does not mean, however, that knowledge, other
than knowledge of what was revealed by God,
[75r] of the marvels and wonders of God and with which God did
not acquaint His Messenger (God's blessings be on him), was not
made known to others as well. Furthermore, by receiving the knowledge of what was revealed to him and by being called to ask God to
increase him in knowledge, the Prophet was in reality asking God
to increase him in learning what was revealed to him and in understanding what he had learned. One person may learn the Qur'ān
by heart just as well as another. Although both of them may fail to
comprehend it well, it may be easier for one to recite it better than
the other. On the other hand, it is a fact that Ḥudhayfa, [who was
noted] at the time [for his knowledge of the Qur'ān], is by no means
equal to the Prophet who was given the Qur'ān through Gabriel. In a
similar manner, some learned men chose to compare this with someone who is leading the prayer in a certain feast. He repeats what the
Prophet used to say, namely: 'Guide us in the straight path' (1:6) or
'forgive us'. Such a man cannot be compared to the Prophet because
the Prophet knew for sure that he was already guided and forgiven.
    Back to the question of consensus, we say: If the *fuqahā'*
[75v] of all the religious factions, such as the Mu'tazila, the Khawārij,
the Ḥashwiyya, the Shi'a, and others, as well as the followers of
Mālik, Abū Ḥanīfa and others, do not assemble in one body which
would settle their differences and which would be fit for designating
an imam, they would not be worthy of being called *fuqahā'*. On the
contrary, those different factions have been always at odds on such
complicated questions as that of the imamate. What they should do

instead is to put an end to their disagreements that are hindering their leaders from agreeing on an imam. In contrast to this, we see that every one of those leaders is promoting himself when he is not even recognised to be worthy of being called a *faqīh*, for the simple reason that not one of these leaders acknowledges the other. Since no religious faction accepts the beliefs and creed of the other factions [76r] because such disparity among those denominations and their leaders is prevailing, it follows that no consensus of the *umma* can be attained and thus no faction is acknowledged by the others to be on the right track. Hence, no leader of those leaders is unanimously acknowledged to be a *faqīh*, let alone to be an imam. On the contrary, every one of them charges the others with innovation and of going astray, whereas the one who should be chosen for the leadership of the *umma* is the one whose justice and knowledge are unanimously accepted. However, being divided into different denominations that agree neither on any one of them nor on anyone else from any other denomination, the *umma* never consented to anyone being the imam. Not one of those denominations was able to give a decisive proof that one single leader of its leaders or one group of its groups is worthy of such a position. Every denomination has equalled the others in claiming that their men are more knowledgeable and learned than the men of the opponent denominations. This being so, it became certain, therefore, that no one has known for sure that he is a *faqīh* by consensus.

That is why we say: When someone has all the characteristics of an imam, the *umma* must disregard everyone but him just as it has selected the Prophet (God's blessings be on him) [76v] over Maslama, and for performing prayer over relinquishing it, and so it is with almsgiving and all other commandments, for they are decreed upon us in the Scripture.

Here, we say: When people are assured that a man is the right imam, they must admit that both his absence and his presence are the same. This is when they are certain that He is the imam and he has been appointed by the previous imam, just as they had been required to confess the prophethood of the Prophet (God's blessings be on him). Since they were not to use any personal opinion or analogy, they were not to acknowledge an imam whose appointment was neither decreed in the Book nor mentioned by the Messenger, who had prohibited the acknowledgement of anyone who has not been decreed upon. He who is not decreed upon by the Book and the Messenger cannot be spared from the bias of personal opinion and judgement.

Hence we say to those people: Tell us, did the *fuqahāʾ* force you to install someone with qualities shared by no one? Did they enjoin you to consider him faultless unlike anyone else?

[77r] If they reply: We have been enjoined to declare allegiance to the one whose qualities are supposedly better than all people known for their superiority and knowledge, this person should be referred to in the Book of God (Exalted be He) and the Traditions of the Prophet (God's blessings and peace be on him). His distinguishing qualities should not be limited to a certain definite lineage. This is because the qualities of excellence in knowledge, deed and speech can also be found elsewhere. A person of such qualities, when installed in such a position, would be an asset to mankind, for he would not ask them to do except what is within their capabilities.

To such people we should, therefore, say: Imagine if they were commanded by the man that you described. He would have no partisans, nor would he have a solid lineage or a known homeland to back him. Can they but be marched upon by rival countries or nations? If they can be satisfied with a man of merit from their own country, why then were they told to have the best when the best may be found

[77v] elsewhere? He did not say the best in a given country nor in a given tribe. If this was not right then there would not be an alternative for you but to fully explore this or that country until your search reaches Samarkand and al-Andalus and other countries. If you had another motive we would tell you: Who gave you this motive so that you left yourself short of the right one? What made that country in your opinion more deserving than the others so that it would not be necessary for you to search all the countries and summon all the *fuqahāʾ* of the *umma* in order to select from them representatives who can choose from among themselves the proper imam? What made you ignore the *fuqahāʾ* of the various countries in spite of this knowledge? What made you deprive them from participating in such a task which is their very duty, as was mentioned before? Where is the consensus of the *fuqahāʾ* when such a duty is restricted to the

fuqahā' of one country only? How can the *fuqahā'* perform
[78r] the duty of choosing the best in knowledge and piety? However, the impossibility of such congress of *fuqahā'* is clear evidence that God did not ask His creatures nor afflict them with it. He does not ask His creatures to do that which is outside their capabilities. For example, He did not impose the commandments of prayer or almsgiving except after He defined and specified them, nor did He assign a Messenger except after He prescribed who he is in person. Likewise, He did not afflict mankind with His Messenger's demise except after He made it clear who should be his vicegerent and legatee. He then put mankind to the test of the legatee's avowal after He made them know him by His very appointment of him. Thus, the mere abstention of the Book of God and the recognised Traditions of His Messenger from asking to look for the imam in the four corners of the earth, in addition to the impossibility of attaining the knowledge of the imam by such a procedure,
[78v] are clear evidence that the person of the imam is prescribed in Scripture as we have mentioned at the beginning. If someone would say: They may know the superior person and the extent of his superiority and in what ways he is superior by means of oral account. Hence, they can distinguish between his superior qualities and those of the one they already have known in person. By doing so they would not need to resort to speculation or to search in the land. Such is the way that the people of deliberation who would be present should follow when they have to know the person who is superior over the others. Therefore, the final decision on the person of the imam must not be made except after knowing for sure who the best is. Hence, it is not necessary to know the chosen one in person. In the same way the people of deliberation are selected. Hence it is not necessary to wait to know the nominee in person to decide whether or not he is superior over the other nominees. Such a decision can, therefore, be arrived at only in such a way. If, on the other hand, they would not agree
[79r] by having someone among them say, 'This is the right person', while others say, 'That is the right person', our answer would be: If one of the two parties would be at fault and the other would be right, the party at fault should, therefore, yield to those who are right. God (Exalted be He) gave those who are right the upper hand. It is proof

and evidence that those who are at fault do not have. But, if none of the two parties can prove that its nominee is the right person, then both parties would be wrong, and both nominees should thus be dropped, since neither of them was proven to be the right man. The case being so, we ask those people: What will happen if both parties disagree? Here we must bear in mind that such an issue should be in line with the Messenger of God (God's blessings be on him) and the consensus of the *umma*. By resorting in their judgement to either the Scriptures or to allegorical interpretation, there is nothing there that would support their claim. In fact, both parties would resort to the same thing. Hence both parties would fail to attain any positive result. Likewise, if they claim they are supported by instructions of the Messenger

[79v] they would find themselves even further from the truth. If they claim the consensus of the *umma* they would obviously fail, due to their disagreement. If the case was so, they should realise that their debate about the imamate is false whether or not they came to an agreement, and that which is false should not be pursued. Hence, in accordance with all the arguments stated above concerning the imamate and the issues related to it and to the authority of the imam, it is incumbent on everyone to know that such a subject has been forced upon them. This is because it has been proven to be mere innovation. By conceding to such innovation they prove to be out of compliance with God's commandments.

Hence, one should say to them: Could the imam be unacquainted with some of your needs? If so, then he could possibly be unacquainted with all your needs. With such a fact they could not disagree. He who is ignorant

[80r] can never be of merit. If he is deficient then he is a man of inequity. Such people were defamed by the prophets (God's blessings be on them) though they did not designate them by their wrongdoings and define them as men of inequity. We have already told you that no one is permitted to install in such an office anyone but the best from among the ones with merit. He who asks such a question should be told: Do you see what will happen if you sanction the idea that the imam could be lacking some knowledge? Can such a man teach anything other than ignorance? If he seems to avoid displaying his own ignorance he cannot prevent others from displaying their

false teachings. Even if he sheds light on our own blunders, he would stone a sinful woman. This is only one example among many others. Even though such mistakes are seldom seen, others may be more knowledgeable no matter how much this person may know. If someone says: This is true – and it is – we say to him

[80v] in the like manner, it is likely that another who is more knowledgeable may be more of a worshipper than he, unless such a position makes him disgraceful. Such a person who may be a better worshipper is likely more self-denying, except if his ego makes him covet worldly things. He may be more pious, unless that leads him to irreverence. By the same token he may be more courageous in his striving in God's way, unless he forsakes such striving and flees from battle. He also may be more knowledgeable of the Qur'ān unless his conceit leads him to be ignorant of it. If this were possible then such a person may have more merit than the first. If someone says: Although it may be possible for such a person to improve in one of these qualities, he cannot possibly improve in all of them. He thus cannot be superior over the one who is already superior in all these qualities. So, if such a man is found, the first would be

[81r] of less merit and consequently he would not be worthy of the imamate. If, on the other hand, the first man excels in one quality and is equal to the other in all other qualities or more than equal, then he would not be less worthy. To such a question one should reply: Such an argument can be used as well by the opposing side as follows: If the qualities can vary in excellence and can become either superior or inferior, it follows that all the qualities depend one on the other; therefore, the imam's qualities would be forever fluctuating, which means that if the imam would be noted in jurisprudence he may become inferior in relation to someone who is more knowledgeable. Thus he would be inadequate in comparison to the one who is better in that particular field. This is invalid because the imamate of an inadequate person is invalid. Had the imamate of someone inadequate in jurisprudence been valid, then the imamate of a person inadequate in other fields would be valid as well. Those who believe in the validity of the imamate of a person superior in jurisprudence

[81v] are, therefore, erroneous. This is because all inadequacies in the qualities are the result of the lack of practical application. He who is inadequate in jurisprudence is thus not free from neglect in

this field. Hence if the imamate of the person inadequate in all fields is invalid, it follows that the imamate of the person inadequate in some fields is invalid as well.

Then one should tell these people: What do you say about the one who opposes such a conclusion? They definitely would answer: The imam should be the most knowledgeable in jurisprudence, without necessarily being the best and with most merit among the people. This opinion is based on the fact that the need for jurisprudence is the most urgent need. This is because all the commandments are based on jurisprudence and are practised accordingly, whereas their need for the imam's rectitude and piety is restricted to the fact that he should be far from committing a great sin so that he would not be misunderstood.

[82r] The *umma* only requires the imam to be trustworthy, whereas people cannot dispense with the imam being the most knowledge-able in jurisprudence. Had the imam been short of knowledge in some field of jurisprudence he would be harmful to them. He would inflict upon them misfortune due to his foolishness. Hence the people should strive to avoid any harm resulting from such an imam.

As for the saying mentioned above, namely: 'We have warned you against installing anyone except the worthiest of the worthy,' we reply as follows: Such warning implies that the imam should be the most knowledgeable in jurisprudence as well. You should know that no one among the believers, whether weak or strong in his belief, has not been made to learn how to pray and what renders prayer invalid. If these rules were not properly stated, no one would have the chance of knowing that doing something correctly entails knowing what must not be done. Nothing can be declared lawful unless it is proven not to be unlawful by God in His Book and the Traditions of the Prophet (God's blessings be on him).

[82v] Man should be distinctly informed of what is prohibited, in such a way that he would be responsible. He who knows clearly such prohibitions, yet he commits them, shall be considered sinful. He who does not find a proof in the Holy Book and the Traditions cannot be held responsible. Accordingly, we say: God (Exalted be He) does not enjoin deep knowledge on anyone. This is because knowl-edge is an undertaking which by nature is not within the power of everyone. It was enjoined on the believers to know things that lead to

their welfare, together with other things necessary for their spiritual welfare, such as fasting in Ramaḍān, praying five times a day, doing the pilgrimage and almsgiving, which can neither be ignored, nor can they not be taught. Other than these matters, it is not within the power of anyone to know the very meaning of revealed truths. Such knowledge was not enjoined by God on all the Muslims as such. Knowing their need for such truths and their inability to bear such knowledge, God has ordered instead the successors and legatees of His Prophet to guide the Muslims to such truths,

[83r] taking into consideration their dire need. Hence we say: Unlike one who is knowledgeable, an ignorant person is not held responsible. He who is not held responsible, whether versed in religion or not, is not counted among those who know. If he does not know, he cannot be given any assignment, nor can his sanction and prescription be acknowledged. They say: But the one in charge of the Muslims may miss some of God's stipulations. In case this happens, he may then consult and look into what is written in the Book and the Traditions. If he still fails to know, after such consultation, then he would be deemed recalcitrant. In reply to this we say: It is not permissible for such a person to fail to know any divine command. No matter how much he resorts to consultations and analogy, such a person can never be an imam. This is because such failings are evidence

[83v] no matter how much consultation and analogies he makes. In fact, such consultations and analogies were not sanctioned by the Messenger (God's blessings be on him) nor were they contained in the Holy Book. If it were possible for the imam to miss such truths it would be possible for him not to know them. If it were possible not to know them, then religion would be imperfect, but God (Glory be to him) has told us in His Book that religion was perfected. Since it was perfected, and analogy and personal judgement and opinion were proven to be invalid, then the perfection of religion means that the vicegerent of God's Prophet should necessarily know all the sacred commandments of religion revealed to God's creation. Nothing that is liable to happen should, therefore, be beyond the scope of knowledge of the imam. This is the evidence of his imamate. If it were possible for him to be ignorant of something of this sort, then he should not be a guardian; rather, he should be guarded. He would

not teach; rather, he should be taught. It is impossible for the imam
to disobey any

[**84r**] commandment the *umma* is in dire need of obeying, neither
should he be liable to deserve any legal punishment; this is not
permissible to a person who is in the *umma* as the Prophet (God's
blessings be on him) was. In reply they say: Should he not be in this
respect considered like a governor appointed by the Prophet to be in
charge of a certain distant province on his behalf? To realise good
judgement, such a governor adjudicates according to jurisdictions
that were set forth and made known by the Prophet and given to that
governor. To be able to realise justice, the governor resorts to valid
deduction and consultations with the learned who hope to receive
help and guidance from God (Glory be to Him), as God does not
require mankind to do anything beyond their abilities. In reply to
such an argument we say: Why have you considered the imam in
his task like governors of provinces? Is it because the Prophet (God's
blessings be on him) allowed one of them

[**84v**] either to pass a judgement or to consult others? What if it
happened that he did not allow the governors of provinces to do so,
knowing that you consider the imam to be on the same footing as
these governors, even when his knowledge is dependent on that of
the Messenger of God (God's blessings be on him)? It is, therefore,
not plausible that the Messenger would pass away before he would
pass such knowledge to the imam. It would be illogical as well that
the imam resort instead to the written Tradition of the Prophet just
as the governors do. Likewise, it is illogical that the imam would
resort to outside consultations, personal judgement and deductive
opinions. In fact, this is even interdicted to the governors of provisions. This is in line with your saying: 'Lo! It is only in the Book of
God (Exalted be He) and the Traditions of His Messenger (God's
blessings be on him) that you can find the perfection of religion.
In them there is all what the Muslims need.' Had God (may He be
Blessed and Glorified) entrusted us to analogy and consultation

[**85r**] in legal judgements the Holy Book and the Traditions would
not be perfect. He who strives for truth, God would condition him
to it. He who does not strive for truth uses his personal opinion in
God's religion and fabricates unfounded judgements for which no
sanction was made by God. I swear, God has never asked the imam

to pass any judgement concerning His revelations. He has never asked him to do what he could not. He has taught him that and stated it in His Scriptures. So praise be to God for His blessings and His mercy. In reply to their falsification one should ask them: Is it conceivable that the imam errs in his analogy? They say: If he errs he would be recalcitrant, whereas he was ordered to be righteous. Such is what the imam admits, because he has erred, and has proven such an error. To such a statement of theirs one should reply: Tell us, how can we know that he has erred and disobeyed? If they say: It has been proven by the learned, then we say: What proof? Were they

[85v] at variance with each other, some were with him and some were not? What if an event happened to the Muslims and every party was claiming to be right? What if a decision should be taken on the spot? If they say: In such a case they would have to discuss the matter; then if one would say: They did, but every party held fast to its own point of view, even though some of the parties were wrong. Such is the way of those who have depended on analogy since more than one hundred years ago. The various opinions did nothing more than make each party stubbornly hold on to its own standpoint. If some party would say: Our opinion should assume command, the others would say: Why? Such an opinion is recalcitrant, how can the Muslims not renounce it, and how can they accept to be ruled by recalcitrance? If they are answered: Then the opinion of the men of learning who oppose such an opinion should be adopted. To such an argument we reply: How can the latter opinion be more correct than the former one?

[86r] How can the previous opinion be abrogated by a different one? What about all those who were collaborating with it? If they answer: When the truth is sought, the All-Good facilitates the opinion appropriate for apprehending the event in question. To those people we say: What is the evidence that God (Glorified and Exalted be He) lets a verdict of His be based on speculation? If analogy could not be proven to be the right means for correct judgement or it was wrongly implemented – as we mentioned earlier – then justice would be reached by forsaking analogy and invalidating what the unjust have stated. This is because power is only in God's hands. To such a statement they reply: Since you have said that there is no alternative to having a just imam who would know how to manage

our problems, our answer would be: Such an imam is the Messenger of God (God's blessings be on him). He has left behind a sacred Book and his Traditions in which he has clarified everything. Such sacred Writ is

[86v] there in our midst. All the people and all the religious factions have agreed on that. We have seen that a governor of a province does not have to know all what the Prophet knows. Rather, he has to resort to the Messenger of God (God's blessings be on him), that is, the Book of God and the Traditions of His Messenger (God's blessings be on him), and not to analogy, personal opinion and common deliberations. Likewise, when analogy is necessary one has to resort to the one in charge of the imamate as stated in the Book of God and cited by the Messenger of God (God's blessings be on him) in his Traditions. In like manner, the governors of provinces, after the Messenger of God (God's blessings be on him) has plainly indicated the truth to the one who would be in charge after him, should refrain from referring to analogy and common deliberation. Had it been accepted to have as ruler someone who does not know the revealed truths of our religion, even if he were a governor of a province, then it would be accepted that we would be ruled by someone who is not

[87r] the best among us. What is accepted in relation to a governor must be accepted in relation to the imam. This standpoint of theirs is indeed a contradiction of their belief in the imamate of the best in the *umma*.

To such an argument we reply: The Messenger of God (God's blessings be on him) is the imam of imams. Such is the belief of all religious factions whether it was related by them or not. It is well understood among them that both the Book and the Traditions are concordant with each other. This is mentioned in the Prophet's Tradition. These two sources are the refuge of the imam, as we have mentioned earlier. Hence analogy can never possibly be a substitute. Moreover, God (Exalted be He) has forbidden its observance in His Book, as we mentioned earlier.

Also they say, and you approved, that the imam is not necessarily infallible. To such a statement we reply: Do you claim that the governors appointed by the Prophet (God's blessings be on him) were as such? And that all those he appointed were like you described, nor was it known that they did not err or yield to

[87v] temptation, while God has ordained people not to follow anyone unless they know that he is right, and that he was to be their cynosure after the Messenger of God (God's blessings be on him)? They should not assist him in erring. As for us we say: If you have a proof that the imam may not be necessarily infallible, just like the governors of provinces, then the requirement you have previously imposed that he should be the best would fail, just as the governors of provinces are. Hence they should be told: Even if you consider the imam to be analogous to a provincial governor, it was only by virtue of his appointment by the Messenger (God's blessings be on him) that he occupied his position. The Messenger never asked them to choose their imam, nor did he entrust the people of the province to choose their governor. If someone among them would say: If you impose this person on me I would impose that person on you. In fact, just as the provincial governor is not appointed from above,

[88r] so should the imam not necessarily be appointed. Since the provincial governor is not to be appointed, the imam should, therefore, not be appointed. To such an argument we reply: If we admit that this was true, then we would be following your previous analogy and opinion, whereas the position of the imam should rather be analogous with that of the Messenger (God's blessings be on him), not with that of the province governor. As God did not entrust us with selecting our Messenger and installing him, but designated him by name, so did He with the one who would be in the place of the Messenger. If God safeguarded our prominence by sending us a messenger and thus sparing us from sin and from perishing through recalcitrance, as well as from being exposed to change and diversion, he did the same when it came to his successor

[88v] and heir. This is because we are in need of his legatee just as we were of him (God's blessings be on him).

Hence we say: God (Blessed and Exalted be He) has imposed on the people the obedience of their imam. He told them that the imam's authority over them is right, like that of the Messenger before him. He saved them by assuring them that he would never lead them to error, as he was invested by His Messenger who ordered them, through the Holy Book as well as the Traditions, to obey him just as they did with the Messenger (God's blessings and peace be on him). In reply they said: If you say it is forbidden that a man be brought to

the imamate by election, while the Messenger of God (God's blessings be on him) used to appoint someone as governor of a province
and that governor used to choose a lieutenant to rule over a remote
region of the same province, if it is permissible for him to choose on
account of the man's just and righteous qualifications by depending
on the credits of that man and the recommendation of others, based
on such criteria put

[89r] by the Prophet, in the same token, the *umma*, in choosing the
appropriate person, should use the same criteria of righteousness.
Nevertheless, the people should not be concerned with either the
apparent or with the inner significance of the imam's infallibility.
The believers should rather be concerned, as the imam ordained,
with the substantiation of belief among them, especially because
some of them do not take some of their deeds into consideration.
Have you ever seen the imam entrusting the Muslims with their
affairs without appointing someone to be in charge of them? In the
like manner you should know that the Prophet (God's blessings be
on him) or his vicegerent never leave the task of appointing an imam
to the Muslim public. Rather, he appoints him after he chooses
him from them. We never denied such a kind of choice. Rather, we
rejected the people's carelessness and their investing

[89v] themselves with such authority, since they had no sound proof
that this authority is inadequate. In fact, you already reiterated your
comparing the imam with the witness of equity[14] with your saying:
Likewise, it is lawful that we choose the imam according to the same
quality of righteousness. To this statement one should reply: Do you
believe that the Messenger (God's blessings and peace be on him)
has enjoined you to install a righteous governor as he enjoined you
to witness a righteous man of equity? If he says yes, then he would
be proving that he is a liar. If he says: I judged the imam by analogy
with the witness, then we tell him: Therefore, make it legal that the
imam can be short of reading the Qur'ān or short of being a *faqīh*.
Although this is permissible with relation to the witness, it is not
in relation to the imam, as he must, unlike the witness and all the
believers, be infallible. We have stated above

[90r] that the imam cannot be but infallible, his inside as his

---

14. In reference to the Qur'ānic verse 'And call in to witness two men
of equity from among yourselves' (65:2).

outside. His position is more like that of the Messenger than it is like the witness of equity. A thing is comparable with what it resembles most.

The imam's blood relation to the Messenger

It is not logical to say that no one can be an imam unless he has a blood relation to the Messenger of God (God's blessings be on him). One can have a stronger blood relation to the Messenger than another without necessarily being superior. Hence, the one who is more related would not merit the imamate more than the other. In reply, they say to us: If the uncle does not merit the imam, would the uncle's son or the son of the uncle's son merit that position or another more distant relative, even if he is not from Hāshim, but from Quraysh, or even as far as Muḍar or Nizār if you sanctioned it in case there is

[90v] no one whose blood relation to the Prophet could be found? If someone would ask about the extent a person could reach in his lineage so that he could be an imam, then could the brother be more deserving or would things become more confusing, as it was when the imam was chosen even though he belonged to another sect? In such a case our answer would be: If the imamate is from outside the closest of kin, then that does not make it free from all blood relations – as you have done in validating it for the one who did not satisfy any criteria, neither in knowledge nor in any blood relation. The limit of kinship from which the imam must belong is not that he is the paternal cousin's son, nor of a closer or more distant kin. It is rather a relation that people agree upon and recognise its subjects as being relatives. Nevertheless, although blood relation is

[91r] one of the basic elements in determining who the imam should be, it has to be sustained by excellence and probity. If a brother or relative of the imam, be they sons or others, deserve the position equally in kinship, then the rightful imam among them would be the one who has been either invested by a testament or distinguished by godliness or by a virtue which the other counterparts do not have, be they his equals or even closer in kinship to the previous imam. These are the principles that should be followed; unless the person concerned belongs truly to the hegemony, then he would necessarily be the one pointed to by the previous imam's testament and, there-

fore, should be the one inserted. If someone says: If kinship without excellence is provided? Then it would cease to be a necessary condition for the imamate. Excellence would then be the only condition [91v] that people would never deserve the imamate without. If excellence is the criterion most distinctive of the imamate, then he who embodies it is the one who deserves the imamate the most, whether he is a relative or not.

Then one should ask those people: Tell us about knowledge. Is it from among the attributes that characterise the imamate? If they say yes, then one should ask: Can a knowledgeable person be invested with the imamate if he is not God-fearing? If the answer is no, he cannot, then one should reply: If knowledge is the quality which makes a person deserve the imamate, must we not appoint to it the knowledgeable person who is not God-fearing? If, on the other hand, godliness is the quality which makes a person deserve the imamate – for it is possible to have a learned man who is not God-fearing – then would he not deserve the imamate? But, indeed, a godly man does deserve it, whether [92r] he is a learned man or not. Someone would argue that knowledge alone cannot be a requirement for imamate unless it is associated with godliness. Only with both qualities together can a person deserve to be the imam. If a person is both godly and knowledgeable then he deserves to be the imam. This, however, does not necessitate that a man of learning is excluded from the other qualities of the imamate. If he is found not deserving, then one has to find the reason why by referring to the Book of God. This is because the imamate is its perfection, especially when it is enhanced by other qualities.

They also asked: Who was the imam during the call of the Prophet (God's blessings and peace be on him) who received the Word after Jesus (peace be on him)? They asked as well: How can one depict from all related news that which was said about the imam without being defined by name? To such a question we reply: Just as we knew about the Prophet (God's blessings be on him) without his being defined by name.

[92v] Further, how can one know about the imam during his lifetime and nothing can be known about him after his death? In case of Jesus (peace be on him) we know that he had a legatee who succeeded

him. His legacy continued through a legatee who acted as a proof of his call until the advent of the Prophet (God's blessings be on him). Though we did not know such a legatee by name or person, he was evidence that no man can be installed unless he appoints a vicegerent who would succeed him. The fact that we do not know him does not mean that we are necessarily ignorant of the fact that he knew that many of us did not know which one of them was the actual imam. Our ignorance, however, should not result in denying them. In this respect we say that the one who came after Jesus (peace be on him) was either close or distant from him, without being necessarily descended from his mother or related to her (this is peculiar

[93r] to Jesus (peace be on him) since he was fatherless). However, in the imamate, due to his close relation, the imam's immediate paternal cousin may possibly become an imam if he is the imam's closest relative, provided no one in the *umma* would be closer to the previous imam. Such a condition, however, is not incumbent in respect to the one who comes after Jesus, or any other prophet or any act related to sending down prophets and relatives or to abrogation of religious laws. Such acts are lawfully permissible, unlike those associated with the Prophet's blood relation (God's blessing and peace be on him). This is due to the discontinuance of divine messages and the predominance of tyrants and the imams' going underground and the emergence of their lieutenants as façade leaders. Such issues were sufficient to make things too intricate.

[93v] This is why the imamate was restricted to the Prophet's progeny. Such restriction was in itself proof of his mortal nature, a fact which is considered the foremost of all truths including the appointment of the most knowledgeable, pious and trustworthy heir, as well as evasion of the judgement of low-class people. So praise be to God.

Also they said: It is known that events that happened in the past were known through the transmission of news, the authority of which was agreed upon according to the mentality of the people of the different provinces and of other factors, such as their ideas concerning countries and sovereigns. On such premises people bared their faith in the call of the Prophet. Hence it was known that when the Prophet (God's blessings and peace be on him) passed away, people chose Abū Bakr as his vicegerent. All of them unanimously agreed that the Prophet (God's blessings be on him) did not

install him. Rather, he was installed according to their opinion,
[94r] and the Muslims when they installed him were under the
impression that he was the best of them. By installing him they were
convinced that they were following the Prophet's commandments
(God's blessing and peace be on him) that he was the best of the best.
They were also convinced that their doing was in accordance with
God's knowledge and command, and had they been left alone they
would have deviated from the right path. They were confident that
God and His Messenger had entrusted him with the imamate on
such a basis. Such was always the Prophet's Tradition with regard
to the believers, if you remember. Hence, he who believed in God
and His Messenger was called a believer, and the one chosen by the
believers was called an imam, a ruler in God's name and the name of
His Messenger (God's blessing and peace be on him). The believers
accept such divine appellation and other similar ones.

To such people we reply: What is your proof that all the Muslims
did this and that no one was considered better than Abū Bakr and
that they were not mistaken in choosing him and that they did not
go astray? What is your proof that such an act was not imposed on
them, either forcefully or voluntarily? Had
[94v] they recognised what we had already said, they surely would
have agreed on what we had said before. Here we say: Those who
invested him with the imamate have committed a religious innovation which deviated them from the right path. God and His
Messenger never appointed him to any position whatsoever. Those
people wrongly surmised that he was appointed. They likened his
so-called appointment with the Qur'ān calling a believer anyone
related to the believers.

Our reply to such a generalisation would be: Did God not rule
that everyone who testifies the oneness of God and acts accordingly,
that he be called a believer, without naming anyone in particular?
If they reply yes, we say: Did He name the one chosen by the people
as imam, even without designating him as such? Further, did the
Messenger of God (God's blessing and peace be on him) find anyone
fit for the imamate as he said: 'He who finds someone superior in
righteousness and knowledge then he would be the imam?' This is
what was meant by the saying of God (High and Glorified be He):
'those in truth are the believers?' (8:4). If they argue in such a way

then they would be clearly deceitful. They would be denying the saying of the Messenger of God (God's blessing and peace on him) [95r] 'He who has such and such a quality take him as imam and make him a leader.' Since these qualities are found among the believers, one should look at the believers with an eye of discernment, not only in respect to the imamate, but also in respect to other fields. This is why we raise the subject once more to say that those who were put in authority by anyone other than the Messenger of God (God's blessing be on him) and who ruled by virtue of unanimous but false judgement were ruling in sin, just as were those who invested them with such an office. This is because they disobeyed the Messenger (God's blessing and peace be on him) by putting in office someone who was not sanctioned by God. In fact, they all agreed on ratifying personal opinion and analogy of some of the Companions of Muḥammad (God's blessing and peace be on him). They said: Formulating personal opinion can be legal. Then they used to remain passive [95v] until they were sure that what they had said was right, for it is contrary to Islam to say anything they are not sure of. In reply we tell them: What is the proof that one must seek permission to use one's opinion in matters related to God's religion? Is it a commandment mentioned in the Book of God (may His name be Blessed) or is it an obvious Tradition of the Messenger of God (God's blessing be on him)? If they act contrary to it, as we mentioned earlier, then they would be ordained to follow the commandments mentioned above; if, on the other hand, they abide by the consensus of the Companions of Muḥammad (peace be on him), namely that personal judgement is permissible, then they would be required to give a proof for the occurrence of such a consensus. If they act according to the will of the majority, then they would be asked about what is meant by majority and minority, as was mentioned before. In this respect they would be asked: What proof do you offer that the majority has the right to sanction independent judgement? If the religion of the Muslims forbids people to say what they do not know, and if independent judgement on matters that are not known [96r] to be right is forbidden (as there is no proof of its validity), then anyone who validates such judgement would be wrong, presumptuous and straying from the right path. Such a claim would be clear evidence that his belief in the imamate of Abū Bakr was wrong. This is because his claim would have been relying on false premises, as would be the selection of Abū Bakr's, based on the pretence that he was the best. The fact that such people chose him and believed in his excellence and superiority was in itself wrong, for they were supposed to know what makes a person good, especially because they were from the *Muhājirūn* and the *Anṣār*, whom God (Glorified and Exalted be He) had described in his Book and adjudged their going to heaven as He said in the *sūra* of Barāʾa: 'And the Outstrippers, the first of the *Muhājirūn* and the *Anṣār*, as those who followed them in good-doing' to the end of the verse (9:100).

[96v] How is it possible not to be protected by God from error when God described them as such? However, when a statement is pronounced about a certain people, it is the public who are meant by it and not the upper class. God (Glorified and Exalted be He) said: 'If they desire to set things right, God will compose their differences' (4:35). Who is better suited for desiring righteousness than those who were described by God as such? In this respect we say: The common narratives about peaceful arrangements among people are proof that the issues subject to agreement do not even exist. One of these issues is Abū Bakr's right to the imamate, as it is contrary to what the Messenger of God (God's blessings be on him) has desired, as well as to what the *umma* has consented upon, or even the majority of the *umma* have claimed that the Messenger did appoint him. In fact they were telling lies when they claimed the *umma*'s consensus; their claim that he was the best was invalid. In fact, there was no agreement among them on this matter. Some sanctioned his imamate because they believed in the right of the inferior to be imam.

[97r] Others categorically rejected his right to the imamate and accused his partisans of falling into error.

In fact, we already distinguished between two kinds of consensus: consensus of opinion and consensus on the Traditions. In this respect we have stated the following: Had it been lawful to accept the opinion of those who have been called men of learning because they were traditionally accepted as such, then we would be acknowledging the opinion of inequitable people. Such people would be inequitable whether their opinion was made on their own or under duress. In both ways their opinion would obviously be invalid. As for God saying: 'And the Outstrippers, the first of the *Muhājirūn* and the *Anṣār*' (9:100), epithets which God has commended them with, they are, we firmly believe, virtues for those who have not relinquished them. God (Glorified and Exalted be He) said: 'And do not make your own works vain' (47:33). He also said: 'Then whosoever breaks his oath breaks it but to his own hurt' (48:10). He blamed all those mentioned above by saying

[97v] 'you thought thoughts about God' (33:10). If you say that he reprimanded a special group of people, we say: He also commended a group of people. Most of them had been vanquished in more than one place and fled from staying with the Messenger (God's blessing be on him). Negativity has befallen them without them knowing. They have certainly relinquished their allegiance to God. How great would they have been had they not defiled the good deeds they previously realised? How would it be if those who were praised would not merit any dispraise and those who were dispraised would not become worthy of rightfulness? God dispraised those who associated others with God; then when those among them conceded to belief, dispraise was no longer appropriate and they became worthy of commendation. Likewise, those who were praised for their good deeds but did not continue in their good deeds were dispraised. If someone says: God never dispraised anyone except those whom He knew would not believe

[98r] even though God's dispraise was addressed to the public in general, the fact that the praise addressed the public does not mean that not one of them committed an error, and does not also mean that errors were never committed. The fact that people dispraised each other is in itself an error. This does not mean that 'Uthman and his murderers, or that 'Alī and those who fought him were right in their dispute. This did not make one of the two contending parties right, nor did it render the traitors sincere. One of the two sides was entitled to be dispraised. It follows that the very presence of dissemblers, the doubtful, the hypocritical and the vanquished among the people is evidence that praise, which was addressed to the people, did not cover every one in the mishaps that occurred. All this means that ... those who were previously praised are not worthy of being taken as a proof of their righteousness

[98v] and worthy of being true. If the Book of God and the

Traditions were suitable for them, the rejected impostor would be accepted. He would be a witness, before his partisans, of the great scale of blasphemy, deception and dissoluteness. In this respect we say: If two arbiters wanted any reform, God would condition them to it. This is in case they wanted reform by obeying God's commands and relinquishing what He had prohibited. This applies also to those other than the two arbiters, as well as to those who want what is right by following God's command. Those people are conditioned by God to succeed. To these arguments we reply: Those whom you mentioned did not want any reform, for they were plain innovators. They acted against the will of God. They promoted those whom God had demoted, and eclipsed the good deeds that their predecessors had done.

[99r] Their bad deeds were evidence of their sly hypocrisy that added to their straying from the right path. You cannot prove that their electing Abū Bakr was based on verses in the Book or on any Tradition of the Messenger (God's blessing and peace be on him). The fact that there was someone comforting them when they embraced Islam and followed its tenets did not reduce the gravity of their recalcitrance, nor did their conduct improve when the people ceased their praise. On the contrary, they conspired together to keep on straying away from the right path, except those among them who were secured by God. The *umma* did not oppose them, neither in their behaviour nor in their insistence, nor in their love of the earthly life. What we have said is more than enough.

As for us we say the following: We have already described the situation of the imamate, and we have pointed out that consultation among people reached such a corrupt state. Therefore there was no alternative other than having an imam and that

[99v] the imamate, which we have confirmed, excluded all people whether they were related to the Prophet or not. In fact, the *umma* reached a consensus that no one was appointed as imam from above, for no one was born infallible except the Prophet. Even the Prophet was not unanimously agreed upon. Others claimed to merit prophet-hood and fabricated rumours to support their claims, hoping that they would be installed. However, we already have proven the necessity of having an imam. So if it was argued that everyone who was not qualified may or may not be an imam, and at the same time that

no one can be an imam because no one possessed the qualities that an imam should have

[100r] by consensus, hence, no one should be worthy of being an imam except the one we have mentioned. At such point then, the one we already pointed out would be the imam. As for the pretender, who had no evidence of being worthy of the imamate, the right to be an imam would not be given to him nor would he be able to prove such right.

Hence we say to those who claimed that al-ʿAbbās (God's mercy be on him) had been legated to the imamate, that we have not known anybody to have ever claimed that he was legated, in spite of the fact that a group of people do believe that had the imamate been established by way of consultation he would be entitled to it; and thus they would consider those who would choose another to be wrong. Such a claim was based on the right of inheritance. Their point of weakness, however, is similar to what we have already mentioned, namely that piety and goodness are not enough. As for inheritance we say: Had he been entitled to the imamate because of inheritance, then all inheriting offsprings would also be entitled, so that

[100v] the uncle would be more entitled to the imamate than the children of the daughter. Our saying that if there is a son then the uncle does not inherit is obviously due to the fact that such inheritance leads to another progeny. He who claims that would be committing an error and invalidating the imamate as such. We never saw or heard such a claim except from those who hear violent hatred against the partisans of the family of Muḥammad (God's blessing be on him). Anyone who adopts or claims such a thing cannot reach any truth nor does he undo any falsity without proving and testifying his point of view, as we mentioned before. We also said that a proof of the truth of ʿAlī's imamate (may God glorify his face) is the Tradition of the Pond of Khumm whose authenticity is unanimously agreed upon. Yet, a group of the people objected, claiming that the consensus on a Tradition cannot be honoured unless it deals with subjects similar to the number of times of prayer and the amount of

[101r] alms one must give or the number of stones one must cast during the pilgrimage or the number of times of circling around the Kaʿba, whereas Traditions dealing with fundamental and special issues cannot be relied upon. Uncountable sayings similar to that

of the Pond of Khumm or even more widely known can be cited, such as the Tradition of the ten who were promised Paradise, namely al-Ṣiddīq, al-Fārūq, and so on, or the Tradition about the people of Paradise calling upon God, or even a more widely known one: The saying of 'Alī (peace be on him), namely, that the best of this *umma* after the Prophet are Abū Bakr and 'Umar. Such sayings are unreliable. In reply we say: Those who rely on such an argument are wrong. Such sayings can by no means be compared to the Tradition of Khumm. As it is obvious to all, whether old or young, this Tradition is of the same kind as those sayings that tell us about the number of prayers and the like; no one in the *umma* has any doubt

[101v] of its authenticity, as it was transmitted in an unprecedented way. It was never reported that any one of the *umma*, to whatever faction he belongs, has rejected it or has avoided any part of it, even though they did not take it as evidence as it did not raise their interests as much as those Traditions that dealt with the number of prayers or those that dealt with God's commandments concerning almsgiving, pilgrimage and the like. Unlike those sorts of Traditions, this Tradition does not draw the interest of the people like those which dealt with the number of prayers per day. On the contrary, this Tradition did not raise in them any vainglory as those that deal with the number of prayers and the like. Such Traditions render their narrators who have reported them from the Messenger of God (God's blessing be on him) to be transmitted by others without any derogation whatsoever. There are many Traditions of this kind that were transmitted from the Messenger of God (God's blessing be on him). One of them was his conversation with the wolf, and his talking with the arm

[102r] and the like, or the Tradition about satiating many people from a small lamb. All these Traditions did not constitute a subject of enhancement like the Tradition dealing with the number of prayers per day, which is the concern of all, whether knowledgeable or ignorant. In fact, many people did go to the Pond of Khumm, but under a false pretext. Their instigation of such Traditions that show the Muslims how to observe their rites were used as evidence in themselves. As for the evidence of the Prophet's true message (God's blessing and peace be on him), it was in the proofs he gave at the Pond of Khumm and other instances; such proofs were at the

basis of prayer. This is because God's commandments were derived from that of prayer in different times of the day and night. The fact of being imposed at different times of the day and night caused the people to be more interested in knowing the different times for prayer that they had to perform, more than knowing the amount of alms they had to give. People were more in need to know, for example, that noon prayer consists of four prostrations than to know that they have to pay five *dirhams* as alms for each two hundred *dirhams*. Likewise,

[102v] the ignorant public is more interested in knowing that for two hundred *dirhams* one has to pay five *dirhams* than to know that during the days following the Day of Sacrifice one has to stay in Minā slaughtering animals, then stay in Arafat in the afternoon, then visit the House on such and such day, or to know that he ought to fast ten days in case he does not find any animal to sacrifice. Such things have been mentioned in the Book as well as in the Traditions. Their observance is a proof of the true believers whose belief is rectified by observing the commandment of prayer which is only realised by the number of prayers per day. Hence Tradition has regulated this pillar by the number of prayers. No Imāmī faction has said anything contrary to this, nor is there any Tradition abrogating such a commandment. The same applies in the case of the Tradition about the Pond of Khumm. No one of the *umma* has denied it nor has it been related that

[103r] the Messenger of God (God's blessing be on him and his family) said anything contrary to it, nor has it been related that anyone has denied it. All that happened was that those who objected to its contents tried in vain to alter its true meaning to fit their corrupt points of view. They resorted to certain Traditions which were related by a single man, such as the Tradition of al-'Ashīra related by Sa'īd b. Zayd. However, some of the *umma* have rejected such a Tradition under the pretext that a kin of his who was considered a man of learning narrated that on one occasion 'Alī accused him of lying when narrating a *ḥadīth*. He said to him: I testify before God that you have lied to the Messenger of God (God's blessing and peace be on him). It was also related that he said to him: 'You testified for me and I now testify for you'. Likewise, the master of the middle-aged men of Paradise, as related by one partisan of a certain

faction of the *umma* who was a man of learning as well,
[103v] have rejected this Tradition and accused its transmitter of lying. The same thing happened with the Tradition spoken by 'Alī (may his face be honoured and God's blessing be on him): 'The best of the *umma* after their Prophet is ...' However, he reportedly spoke of other Traditions that contradicted the former one, such as those in which he charged them with injustice, calling attention to his superiority, meritorious deeds and veracity. Did all these Traditions not resemble that of the Pond of Khumm, which all the learned men of the *umma* knew about? Not a single group of the *umma* displayed any negativity towards it. How can they reject it? So how could any of them who know be dubious about it? How could they claim that the *umma* had unanimously agreed to give allegiance to Abū Bakr and leave 'Alī behind? How could he join them later by giving allegiance to him? Further, how could they claim Abū Bakr's superiority by relying on the incident of the Cave of Ḥirā'? How could they rely on such cases and at the same time depend on consultation when they steered the five members of the committee
[104r] to choose one of them, resulting in 'Alī being ousted. He only acquired it the fourth time when three of the members sided with him and two of them sided against him while one refused to pay him allegiance. In fact, they kept fighting him until they resorted to the committee where they decided to oust him by the consent of two of them when one of the two was chosen. Had it been not for the ignorance of the ignorant, how then would it be possible after all that happened that such a position be merited by al-Ṣiddīq and al-Fārūq? In reply we say: Concerning the Tradition which was unanimously agreed upon as proof of the right of Abū Bakr, 'Umar and the consultation committee, we say: Those people did go astray because of what they had done. They disobeyed the Messenger. It was proven through the Traditions of the Prophet that such allegiance was against the command of God and His Messenger (God's blessing and peace be on him). Furthermore, their deeds
[104v] were self-contradictory. This is because at the beginning they claimed that the Messenger of God (God's blessing be on him) empowered them to choose as their imam the best among them. We have no doubt that the Messenger of God (God's blessing and peace be on him) knew who the best was. Even if we suppose that

the Messenger of God (God's blessing and peace be on him) had refrained from installing the fittest because he thought it was most appropriate not to do so, it would in no respect mean that Abū Bakr's nomination of 'Umar would be the best he could do. Hence, Abū Bakr's nomination of 'Umar would signify one of two things. Either that the Messenger of God (God's blessing and peace be on him), unlike Abū Bakr, had been ignorant of who was the best after him or that the Messenger of God (God's blessing be on him) had refrained from installing the most appropriate even when he knew that it was the best thing to do, as if he thought that the mere fact of refraining from installing the best was the best course of action. Both alternatives were degrading from whoever believed in either one of them. Also, by appointing a consultation committee, 'Umar

[105r] committed the same error, for nothing could be found in the Book of God or in Traditions of His Messenger to support it. In fact Abū Bakr could not prove that what he did was ratified by the majority of the people, or that such a majority could convince 'Alī (God's blessing and peace be on him) to withdraw. This being confirmed, it was established that they were in error. We have already proven, at the beginning of this book, that it is invalid to establish the imamate by way of consultation and analogy. As for their claim that 'Alī (May God honour his face and bless him) joined the people in their manoeuvre was a matter far from the truth. If it were truly confirmed that he actually did, even though he testified to their wrongdoing, and that it was his rightful claim, he would have done it out of dissimulation which was granted to him. As for their claim that

[105v] he had waived it in favour of someone else through the consultation committee, it is a false claim. In fact, he disclosed their faults and made the way to their salvation clear. He guided them to the right path and explained the invalidity of their claim. When they refused his guidance, his enthusiasm subsided and eventually he forsook them. If you say the one who gave allegiance to him was inadequate in knowledge, then they would be following his steps in ignorance. In reply we say: Those in the consultation committee who opposed him could not revoke his right to the imamate, nor could they prove that he was entitled to it. Also, his disagreement with the people of falsehood does not corrupt justice. On the contrary,

it increases their falsehood and leads the truthful to a state of affection with the imam (God's blessings and peace be on him), and that which confirmed his imamate is what we mentioned earlier,

[106r] namely, the invalidity of the standpoint of these people, and the impossibility of the Messenger passing away without appointing someone who would succeed him. Such a successor should be of certain qualities without which the imamate would never stand. These qualities could only be found in 'Alī (God's blessings and peace on him) who possessed them by general consent of the *umma*. In fact, the basic principles of their religious creed required them to deny those who opposed his imamate and confute their demand to refer this issue to consultation. This is why he commissioned some of his servants and subjects to oppose those who doubted his imamate. He fought them and rose to strive against them the best he could. In fact he did not once spare fighting the ringleaders of injustice who came before; it was not, therefore, out of frailty that he did not fight for his right, nor was out of inability. It was, rather, out of tolerance and clemency in contrast to their injustice and their setting fire to the house of Fāṭima, his spouse

[106v] and daughter of his Prophet (God's blessings and peace on him), and introducing his defamation in their prayer, and usurping the right of his followers to the imamate. As for their saying: How, after all his doing, can he be of more merit than al-Ṣiddīq and al-Fārūq? On the contrary, this is utter ignorance and sheer blindness. Such sayings are, in our opinion, clear proof of the straying of those who said and authored such things. Concerning the merit of the imamate, as it should be in reality, it is based on the realisation of the core principles outlined by God. Among those principles are the following: struggle against the enemy, precedence in embracing Islam, reading of the Qur'ān, knowledge of the lawful and unlawful, blood relation with the Messenger, and the like. He who has such qualities the most would be more meritorious as to the imamate; he who instead has qualities leading to defeat, and who is less knowledgeable

[107r] and has doubt in the Messenger would be of less merit. An example of this is what happened on the day of Ḥudaybiya between the Messenger and Ḥudayba, when Ḥudayba was shown to be insincere. Such is an example of how one can be less meritorious in comparison to a far superior person. On the other hand, we say about those who were enchanted with ʿAlī (God's blessings be on him) that they were similar to those who degraded him. He reacted strongly against their erroneous acts, not only because they were wrong but also because of the effects of such acts on the people, especially when they took him for another and witnessed the likeness of him. This is what we also think about the idols and about the Messiah (peace on him). People were afflicted with him because of their delusion. Such delusion could have had a valid cause, though it could have been fearfully dangerous. For among his acts (peace on him) were acts with which

[107v] he pointed to his Prophethood (God's blessing and peace be on him). Some people over-estimated them to the extent that such acts led them to exaggeration. Similar acts showed the apprehension of the worshippers of the idols. Anecdotes were narrated about those worshippers who resorted to a hollow idol into which a man used to enter and talk to the people. Another anecdote was related about an idol which was installed in a house suspended between the ceiling and the floor. Inside both the ceiling and the floor they put blocks of magnet which attracted the idol with equal force. The idol was thus suspended between the floor and the ceiling. A similar story of the idolators was related about Wudd and Sawāʿ, two men known for their piety.

[108r] When they died their people were grieved. The devil came to them with two idols and said to them: These idols are their representations. Seeing the two idols as images of the two worshippers, the people grew intimate with them. The next generation started to give the idols greater esteem until they finally worshipped them. The reason for that was the superiority of the two men and the high esteem given to their representations. Our argument concerning this matter was that the people's defect was due either to the fact that they considered God's favour to be misunderstood to the extent that it turned out to be contrary to truth or to the fact that such an act was used by some impostors to cheat the masses. Hence, it was certain that a group of people fell into error concerning such a person. However, we were sure that such an error was committed for some reason: either for a good purpose

[108v] intended by God and given by the Messenger (God's blessing

and peace be on him) or by someone else, or as a sort of warning.
Had this not been the case, divine justice would not be established
and the obedience of his Messenger (God's blessing be on him) and
the servitude to his superiority would not be validated. Such servitude was obviously evident, thanks to his previous knowledge of the
Battle of the Camel when ʻAlī would be victorious, and how many
men would be killed. Also, his knowledge of the Battle of Nahrawān,
that all the enemies would perish save ten, whereas only ten of his
partisans would be killed. Another instance was his knowledge
about what would happen to Dhu'l-Thadya. All these are evidence of
his truthfulness. This was in addition to

[109r] his pulling out the rock from the well on his way to Iraq and
when a monk came to him to tell him that it was written that no one
would conquer it except a prophet or a legatee of a prophet. Another
sign was what was narrated about the sun when it went back so that
he might perform the afternoon prayer. This happened to him twice:
once during the life of the Messenger and another time after the
Prophet's demise. All these events happened to him because of the
knowledge he learned from the Messenger (God's blessing be on
him) and with the help of certain names of his most beautiful names
through which God's ordinance was realised by divine compliance
with the call of those who called him seeing such evidences.

One can know how people could have committed those errors.
However, such errors were indeed a proof of his superiority. It was
thus proven that those who opposed him were cheaters, as we have
mentioned before.

However, some may say: It is possible that some people who
opposed Islam would have told lies about him. They intentionally
were cheating those whose beliefs were weak, out of their enmity to
the religion,

[109v] especially when Islam vanquished them, To such people we
say: What you said may possibly be right, but as it denoted a meaning contrary to what the people normally excepted, it was possible
to have a false and deceitful denotation. Thus, if someone says: Why
then did the Messenger (God's blessing be on him) not exceed his
human nature, even though he had done things that only prophets
could do? We tell him: If we say that those people were mistaken in
not seeing any miracles in such deeds of his, we should not conclude

that anyone else who performs a miracle should cause others to misjudge him. As it was said about Jesus (peace be on him), that those who erroneously made exaggerated statements about him did so owing to the small number of his miracles. Although people have seen many miracles done by Moses and Ezekiel, they did not misinterpret them. With such an argument one can argue against those who misinterpreted the miracles of Jesus.

[110r] In the same way, one can argue against those who misinterpreted the Prince of Believers. As a matter of fact we disown those who exaggerated beliefs in 'Alī, or those who put him at the same level of the Messenger (God's blessing be on him). In fact, we state that 'Alī was the Prophet's brother, legatee and successor, and the heir of his knowledge. Such is his rank in our faith; it is to this rank that we call upon those who disagree with us to believe in. To such a statement, however, they reply: We have previously seen others who claimed to be the legatee of the Prophet, but we have never seen anyone among them, no matter how great he was, to have the least trace of knowledge or to have been known for his doubtless certitude or who was noted for his wise judgement and subtle knowledge of religious matters. Hence we say: No one has been worthy of being legated by the Messenger of God (God's blessing and peace on him) except he who has an obvious vestige of knowledge and a sound way out from doubt, a true understanding of good judgement and a clear explanation of religious matters, whether concrete or abstract. If the knowledge of your learned

[110v] men was deficient in this respect, it does not mean that its deficiency denies the right of those with merit, nor is the love of someone sufficient to establish his right to the imamate. We have already invalidated all stipulations based on analogy and opinion, and abrogated all knowledge derived from other than the imam by the knowledge of the imam himself. We have proved that the imam's knowledge, which people are in need of, cannot be true except if he is appointed by the previous imam.

As for that which proves the imam's imamate, it is the previous imam's allusion to him and the referral of his followers to him. We have seen above that no one can be installed as imam except one superior in knowledge and piety. We have shown that such an imam is the best after the Messenger, as we stated at the beginning of this present work, provided he was confirmed according to the legation given to him by ‘Alī (peace on him). He would thus be acting in ‘Alī's place (peace on him), just like anyone legated to that position [111r] without being affected by anyone who would not know him or who would reject his appointment. Just like the previous imam was not affected by those who objected to such appointments, even though they would have agreed that such imams were neither prophets nor were they considered equal to the Prophet in their sayings or in their knowledge. They considered such a Tradition to be in conflict with more authentic Traditions, and thus it cannot be reliable. In such a case, the imamate would, therefore, be either in line with what it was before, or ineffective. In such cases it would not matter. Someone who does not know can neither reject nor accept a Tradition nor take it as evidence for rejection or acceptance nor decide that such a Tradition is in conflict with other Traditions. To such arguments we say that he who is not a Prophet cannot be equal to the Prophet (God's blessing be on him) either in his sayings or in his deeds. This by no means contradicts the Tradition in which the Prophet excluded

[111v] prophethood. In such a Tradition, prophethood was totally left out in the comparison between the imam and the Prophet with Aaron and Moses. Likewise, blood brotherhood was excluded. In fact, the rank of Aaron to that of Moses was, unlike anyone else of his people, the rank of ministership as well as that of support. He was recognised to be the best after Moses in knowledge and excellence as well as having most merit for his throne. Hence the Messenger of God (God's blessing be on him), by comparing ‘Alī with Aaron, excluding prophethood as well as brotherly relationship from such comparison, meant that ‘Alī was compared with Aaron only in his being, from among all his people, his *wazīr*, his support and his being the closest to him in resemblance, the best after him, who is next to him in knowledge, and the most worthy

[112r] of his position. Since the imam can only be as we have described, and since the Messenger could only appoint the one whose qualities were just as we have mentioned, then the Messenger's saying should be a clear evidence that ‘Alī was the right appointee to this position. He was the designated one to carry out such a matter. Hence, we say that it was impossible for the Messenger to leave such

a special matter to chance. Had this been possible, such a position would be accessible to anyone no matter how imperfect he would be. Such an assumption would contradict all the qualities an imam should have, since no one possessed such qualities, as no one other than 'Alī could be described as perfect, and since the imam, as we have already shown, cannot but be perfect, and since this could not be applicable except to 'Alī, he was, therefore, the only one to merit this position and to be worthy of it,

[112v] as it would be impossible to have such a special matter stated by him.

They also argued that there was no agreement on 'Alī's mastery, but that there was even discord on the subject. His right to such a will of God was never consented to. In fact, those who believed in this did not reach any truth. They yielded to him obediently. Though he never intended to vanquish others by force, he was not like the others who punished by slaying those who disbelieve in them. He did not charge those who did not pay allegiance to him with blasphemy. This is because his right was well founded and evident. How many a prophet had been fought before, yet his call was never affected and how many leaders of injustice, before and after the advent of Islam, had been unhurt and spared any opposition, yet

[113r] this did not help the truthfulness of their call? Furthermore, those people who adopted such injustice did not deny 'Alī's favour to the Companions of the Prophet (God's blessing be on him) and to their men of learning and to those in authority in both their military and cultural affairs. They did not deny the fact that he knew about those who opposed the truth. They all consented on giving preference to al-Ṣiddīq and al-Fārūq over 'Alī, that they were more fit for the imamate than he was, as he was among the nominees for the *shura*. They consented that he was knowledgeable and pious and a man of superiority. This was what they consented to before he was installed as imam. After that, they disagreed among themselves on his being worthy of the imamate. Many among them fought him and did their utmost to prove that he did not merit the position. We were with them when they all agreed on his superiority. We then stood against those who fought him, taking into account the many testimonies he and his partisans gave.

[113v] In reply we say: You have acknowledged his superiority and

mentioned his merits. Your claim that the *umma* has consented to Abū Bakr and 'Umar's imamate has not been true. We never saw any consent by the *umma* that they were superior in their cognizance of jurisprudence or in their knowledge. Some people even related that they were from among the people of *'Aqaba*. Both their partisans and their enemies did know that they were incapable of carrying the precepts of the Book. Likewise, they were short of vanquishing the enemies of God. Besides, their decisions were not always in agreement with that of the Messenger of God (God's blessing be on him). This was proven by their utter absurdity, as one of them said: 'I have been put in charge of you, yet I am not the best among you' ... . While the other was known to have abrogated God's verdict by a verdict which he had passed out of ignorance and confusion contrary to that which God (Exalted be He) had sent down;

[114r] in fact, he was in all this admitting his ignorance by saying: 'everyone is more cognizant in jurisprudence than 'Umar'. This was proven to be true by what came out of him on the day of Ḥudaybiya when he rejected the command of the Messenger of God (God's blessing be on him) and renounced the provocation to God's religion, filling the people with doubt as to the goal of the Messenger of God (God's blessing be on him). On this day he could not but divulge what had remained lurking in his heart for long. They were telling lies by claiming that the people had unanimously consented to consider those two people superior to 'Alī and that the *umma* has disagreed on 'Alī's superiority, as well as on the different accounts that proved their deceit. We previously mentioned that the imamate of 'Alī (peace be on him and may God honour his face and bless him) was not validated due to their acknowledging it. Its validity was not established because some were convinced of its rightfulness. In fact, the credit of those who acknowledged him is proven by their obedience to him, and the discredit of those who rejected him was proven by their disobedience to him. We have already said enough concerning this subject, as well as having sufficiently pointed to its validity.

[114v] I swear by my life, had the imamate, as you thought it was, been based on consultation it would have ended up validating the fact that 'Alī's imamate was more valid than that of Abū Bakr. This was because it was confirmed that all but one of the people consented on swearing allegiance to him. In fact consensus could not be affected

by the objection of one person. In such a case, he who resorts to adjustment in order to settle such a dispute would in fact be infringing upon his allegiance. Their argument concerning such a matter would be based on the fact that the concluded contract should not be breached unless there would be a unanimous consensus to renounce it. Therefore, the contract arrived at by the people of consultation could never be taken as valid if it were opposed by one person or two; it should rather be ignored. Consequently, the decision arrived at by the consensus of the Companions of Muḥammad (God's blessing be on him and his family) should be the only one to be taken as proof.

[115r] In fact I do not know whether you would be contradicting your original belief: that if one violated his allegiance to Abū Bakr and refused to swear allegiance to 'Uthmān or refused to swear allegiance to 'Alī, then one would be condemned to death. Following this argument, Mu'awiya's imamate would not be disputed. This is not in our case the line of reasoning that leads to our belief in the rightfulness of 'Alī's imamate. What we wanted to say is that fighting 'Alī was wrong. His being in authority provides the right guidance for both sides. To such a statement they reply: What about the imamate of al-Ṣiddīq and al-Fārūq? The *umma* did unanimously consent on them and they were installed as imams, and they stayed on the right path until they died as pious and superior as they were before.

[115v] Thus they won the contentment of all the Muslims. No one, during their reign, was murdered, whereas during 'Alī's reign (peace be on him) people were so much at variance with him that many of them were killed, and consequently many were certain of his wrongdoing and convinced that he should not be installed as imam. As for us, we were cognizant of his courage, his forwardness, his fearless heart and dreadless combats during the lifetime of the Prophet (God's blessing be on him), who never invited Abū Bakr, 'Umar and the like to take part in any combat. Thus we say: You have invalidated your claim that consensus was reached in their favour. In fact they ascended to authority that God forbade them to ascend to. They disobeyed the Holy Book and the *sunna* of the Prophet (God's blessing be on him and his family). They stopped the *khums* fifth-part paying and many other commandments out of hatred. It was enough for us to realise

[116r] the falsity of your claim in more than one instance. Abū Bakr, for example, disagreed with ʿAlī in his rule. We have already mentioned to you that according to us ʿAlī's imamate (peace be on him) was not established because of your agreement so that it would be abrogated by your disagreement. We already mentioned why his imamate was confirmed. ... In fact, the principles of our faith and those of our opponents lead us to stick to the point which made us confirm his imamate. Had his imamate not been confirmed, such things would be meaningless. As for his forwardness and his fear-lessness in combat, they were matters which no one could deny, though you claimed that others were noted for their fearlessness in combat and the like. Such things could not be overlooked. For the *umma* has unanimously agreed

[116v] that God (Glory be to Him) had urged everyone to strive against his enemies and that the Messenger (God's blessing and peace be on him) in some of his wars, was in front of his army. God never distinguished between any of the Muslims in war nor did He favour any one of them above the others in delegating him to the task of commanding the war. No one in the *umma* ignores such auspices. No one in the *umma* considers those who devoted their hearts to be like those who spared their lives, or those who knew nothing of the art of combat. So how could it be possible for him to appoint ʿAmr b. al-ʿĀṣ when he spared war for his life and never tried even once to indulge in combat? Far be it from being related to him! Actually, he used to run away from combat owing to his knowledge of their defeat, due to his fear of enfeebling Islam. He would not know what would result from their involvement, or else why did he not entrust them with any important task, for which task is greater than combatting the enemy? Can they undertake

[117r] retracing combat? So how strange it is for any one who has the slightest reach of mind to commit such a mistake, unless his heart is overwhelmed by desertion of God. They argued that the Prophet (God's blessing and peace be on him) put Abū Bakr in charge of pilgrimage, and sent ʿAlī to read his message to the public, thinking that it was the governor's custom to have his subordinate read his message. In reply to those people we say: Such arguments of yours lead you in fact to nullify the importance of Abū Bakr's presiding over the pilgrimage which was confirmed by the Traditions. However,

when Abū Bakr was on his way at the head of the pilgrimage, the angel Gabriel appeared to the Messenger of God (God's blessing be on him) and said to him: 'O Muḥammad, God orders you not to have anyone do your task except you or a man of your blood.' So the Prophet sent 'Alī after him, and made him return; and 'Alī continued his way as commander of the expedition to convey the message of his cousin. If things were as you mentioned, namely that those who were sent by the Messenger (God's blessing be on him)

[117v] would be superior, 'Amr b. al-'Āṣ would also be superior, as would be Usāma. Since such was the case it would be untenable that 'Umar was put in authority over them and that the Messenger passed away while both Abū Bakr and 'Umar were under Usāma's command (some said that 'Umar alone was under the command of Usāma). As for 'Alī, he was put in command over both Abū Bakr and 'Umar so many times. However, many in the *umma* said that he knew the divine secrets and that he used to give to everyone his due right. They also claimed that some of his Companions and partisans claimed that he was a prophet and even a god, while others clung to the Prophet's *ḥadīth* that says: 'There is no prophet after me'. Also, that he did not legate anyone mentioned above to succeed him. To those slanderers we reply: You have acted unjustly against those you claim to have said that he knew the divine secrets, because divine secrets are only known

[118r] by God. However, we say: 'Alī's superiority is proven by the fact that the Messenger (God's blessing and peace be on him) had taught him and told him about the existence of a number of things. 'Alī used to mention these things, and then they would come true. Each time he mentioned them he used to say that the Messenger of God (God's blessing be on him) had told him about it. 'Alī used to say: 'I swear by God; I never told lies, nor did anyone accuse me of doing so.' As for the claim of those who said that he was a prophet or that he was a god, we testify that those who claimed that were unbelievers and polytheists; though we never heard such people, we utterly rid ourselves of them. In fact, there was an extreme sect who held 'Umar with a similar belief. They told lies about the Messenger of God (God's blessings be on him), accusing him of saying: 'When the chastisement of the Battle of Badr was sent down, no one was exempted from it except 'Umar',

[118v] and to have said, "Umar is the lamp of the people of heaven in which the prophets reside.' Other sayings falsely attributed to him go as follows: "Umar wrote to the Nile which conquered Egypt on his behalf.' Another one relates that 'Umar saw the mast of a ship while he was in Nahāwand. It was also related that he saw a poet reciting before the Prophet (God's blessings be on him). When 'Umar entered, the Prophet ordered the poet to stop; when 'Umar left, the Prophet ordered him to resume. When the Prophet was asked why he did that, he replied that 'Umar did not like what was untrue. Another saying goes as follows: 'Every time revelation was delayed from me I was afraid that I was replaced by 'Umar.' Many such sayings were also related. As for the *ḥadīth*: 'There is no prophet after me,' and that he was accused of not legating any successor we say: What does this have to do with that? This is something mentioned in the Holy Book and was mentioned by the Prophet (God's blessings be on him) and consented to by the *umma*. God (Exalted be He) said 'and the seal of the Prophets' (33:40), and the Prophet (God's blessings be on him) said: 'There is no prophet to come after me.' In fact, the Prophet's will

[119r] was a matter that was subject to disagreement among the *umma*. We did not know of anyone who related that the Messenger (God's blessings be on him) did not appoint a legatee. No narrator has narrated such accounts. Had anyone given such a negative account he would be like that person who testified that some person did not free his slave. Such a person could not be called a witness. Then they asked us: Tell us about the Prophet (God's blessings and peace be on him). Did he appoint a successor by his own accord or through a revelation which was sent down to him? Those who say that God (Exalted be He) had taught him how he would choose and conditioned him and spared him any error and protected him from any possible mistake, then ordered him to choose and install the one he had chosen – and thus he was safeguarded from any error, whether he was informed by God of the appointee's name or not. Then they said about the legatee that was appointed by that imam, was he designated by that imam's accord

[119v] or by divine revelation? Had he been designated by a revelation from God, and by the Prophet, he would be considered a prophet designated by the Prophet (God's blessings be on him). Then they

said: If it was claimed that the Prophet had designated him, the same can be said about the second imam and the third, till the Day of Judgement. On the other hand, if the designation was done by the imam's opinion, everyone would be able to count the names of the imams until the Day of Judgement. To such a conclusion of theirs, one would reply: If this argument were valid, every appointee would be like any governor of a province, and every such governor would be considered like an imam. If the Prophet would fail to nominate him, he would be therefore on the same footing as the imam. This is because, as we have previously said, the imam does not receive revelation. Revelation is a privilege that is only confined to the prophets (peace be on them). Therefore, it may be that the Prophet made the imam know every imam

[120r] till Judgement Day, and made him able to name every one of them. Likewise, it may be that he did not do that, but that the imam after him would appoint the best among his family, especially because the previous imam would have taught him how to make the right choice. As we have previously mentioned, the imam cannot but be conditioned by God and, safeguarded from error, divinely chosen to grasp His knowledge. He, therefore, taught him and appointed him as imam after him. If he had appointed an imam after him, it did not mean that he appointed the provincial governors, nor even that he appointed the senior governors of the state. Likewise, it did not mean that he appointed the officers of the senior government, nor the commanders in charge of the army nor the commanders of the right and left wings nor the flag bearers. They said: And they asked us

[120v] did the imam accept such a stand by the Prophet or not? By asking such a question they argued as follows: If we say he did not accept it from the Prophet (God's blessings be on him), then they would have admitted that the imam was not obeying the Prophet (peace be on him). On the other hand, if they said that he did accept it from the Prophet (God's blessings be on him), then the imam would have accepted such a stand by the Prophet, but would have criticised us for saying the same thing about him. The result would be that the imam would have accepted such a stand by the Prophet (God's blessings be on him). If, on the other hand, they claimed that the Prophet had designated by name the governors of the provinces

until Judgement Day, the reply would be that this was the same as
the witness had testified, namely that the imam vested in them the
authority of the Prophet until the Day of Resurrection. In reply they
say: Authority may be established without necessitating the enemy's
participation in ruling and without having falsehood prevail. To
such an argument we reply that the imam would not act except in
accordance with the will of the Prophet (God's blessings be on him
and his family). We already admitted the possibility that the Prophet
had told him the names, or that he had

[121r] ordered him to choose those who would be in authority after
him. Therefore, if the Prophet had designated the imam by name, it
would be in accordance with his order of designating the imam, and
if he had ordered him to choose he would be doing so in accordance
with his own diction as well. If he would be giving the knowledge
he would then be giving it to someone who could bear it. In both
cases, he would be giving his knowledge to a person who would be
obedient to God and, therefore, he would be safeguarded from error.
It would thus be incumbent on all the citizens to declare their allegiance to the appointed imam. In either way, the imam could not
have been in this position due to his own free will. He should be
ordered to such a position, either by being appointed by name or
by being chosen from above because of his competence. He should,
therefore, be knowledgeable, and safeguarded from error by God.
The imam was asked about that, after he explained what was meant
by the Prophet's saying: 'The Prophet is worthier than they are to
themselves', he refuted

[121v] their argument. The Messenger does not utter anything
supposed to be a precept without being understood in its real meaning, whether he said it in the form of a Tradition or in the form of
a preachment. Those who hear those utterances are to know the
Prophet's intentions and their meanings. This is in line with the
Messenger's Tradition: 'The believers are tied with friendships, one
to the other.' Another obvious meaning of the word *mawlā* is that of
cousin, and since 'Alī was obviously the cousin of the Prophet, it was
absurd that the Prophet would tell his audience this well-known fact.
So the meaning he intended to express was that God made it incumbent on His Messenger to express, namely that 'Alī (peace be on him)
was their *mawlā* in the sense that he was in authority over them and

that they became obligated to pay allegiance and obedience to him and that he should impose on them his rule inverted on him by the Divine and written down in the Holy Book and according to which they would not forsake their obedience to God

[122r] and His Messenger (God's blessings be on him). They argued by claiming that the choosing of the imam goes to the jurists. We mentioned previously, however, that jurists were in disagreement with each other concerning this question. Since they were in disagreement, how could it then be that such a question be in their hands, when their so-called jurists of contending religious factions were in charge of choosing the imam and were at the same time void of knowledge and recognition and unworthy even of being called jurists since each of the faction did not recognise the others? Each faction's belief is rejected by the others of heresy and falsehood. Not one of them could, therefore, be rightfully called a jurist or could choose the imam. For the imam should in principle have the consensus of all the *umma*. Every jurist must believe, therefore, in his justice, his knowledge and his excellence, whereas the *umma* never reached such a consensus, or agreed on

[122v] anyone in particular. The consensus of the partisans of one faction on a person or on a group of people does not give them the right to impose their will. For every faction claims to possess an equal consensus through its particular jurists. In fact, no jurist has the right to be considered as such since he is not recognised by others. Therefore, no one of them has the right to install an imam unless such an imam meets the conditions decreed in the Holy Book. In fact, we have not found the Messenger (God's blessings be on him and his family) stipulating anything of that sort. That which is not found in the Holy Book, nor decreed by the Messenger cannot be considered different from mere personal judgement and opinion. With the Will of God, we have set forward the difference between the imam and those who act as witnesses or the like. What we previously mentioned was too clear to

[123r] be mentioned again 'God is sufficient for us; an excellent Guardian is He' (3:173). He 'is your Protector – an excellent Protector, an excellent Helper' (8:40). No might is there or power except in God's, the Most High and the Most Great.

O God, bless Muḥammad and the family of Muḥammad, as

you blessed Abraham and the family of Abraham. You are 'the All-Laudable, All-Glorious' (11:73).

The transcription of this blessed copy was terminated on the twenty-eighth day of Dhu'l-Ḥijja of the year 1329. It was copied by the humble Aḥmad 'Alī son of Mulla Yūsuf 'Alī. May God forgive him and his parents by the truth vested in the pure imams (the forgiving Lord's blessing be on them). Amen.

Select Bibliography

Abu'l-Fawāris, Aḥmad b. Yaʿqūb. *al-Risāla fi'l-imāma*, ed. and tr. Sami N. Makarem as *The Political Doctrine of the Ismāʿīlīs (The Imamate)*. Delmar, NY, 1977.

Arberry, Arthur J. *The Koran Interpreted*. London, 1955.

de Blois, François. *Arabic, Persian and Gujarati Manuscripts: The Hamdani Collection in the Library of The Institute of Ismaili Studies*. London, 2011.

Brett, Michael. *The Rise of the Fatimids: The World of the Mediterranean and the Middle East in the Fourth Century of the Hijra, Tenth Century CE*. Leiden, 2001.

Cortese, Delia. *Arabic Ismaili Manuscripts: The Zāhid ʿAlī Collection in the Library of The Institute of Ismaili Studies*. London, 2003.

Dachraoui, Farhat. *Le califat Fatimide au Maghreb (296–365 H./909–975 Jc.): histoire politique et institutions*. Tunis, 1981.

—— 'al-Manṣūr Bi'llāh', *EI2*, vol. 6, pp. 434–435.

Daftary, Farhad. *The Ismāʿīlīs: Their History and Doctrines*. 2nd ed., Cambridge, 2007.

—— *Ismaili Literature: A Bibliography of Sources and Studies*. London, 2004.

The Encyclopaedia of Islam, ed. H. A. R. Gibb et al. New ed., Leiden, 1960–2004 (*EI2*).

Gacek, Adam. *Catalogue of Arabic Manuscripts in the Library of The Institute of Ismaili Studies*, vol. 1. London, 1984.

Gimaret, D. *La doctrine d'al-Ashʿarī*. Paris, 1990.

Halm, Heinz. *The Empire of the Mahdi: The Rise of the Fatimids*, tr. M. Bonner. Leiden, 1996.

al-Haythamī, Nūr al-Dīn ʿAlī b. Abī Bakr. *Majmaʿ al-zawāʾid wa manbaʿ al-fawāʾid*. Cairo, 1353/1934.

Ibish, Yūsuf. *Nuṣūs al-fikr al-siyāsī al-Islāmī*. Beirut, 1966.

Ibn Ḥammād (Ḥamādu) al-Ṣanhājī, Abū ʿAbd Allāh Muḥammad b. ʿAlī. *Akhbār mulūk Banī ʿUbayd wa siratuhum*, ed. and French trans. M. Vonderheyden as *Histoire des rois ʿObaïdides (Les califes Fatimides)*. Algiers and Paris, 1927.

Idrīs ʿImād al-Dīn b. al-Ḥasan. *ʿUyūn al-akhbār wa funūn al-āthār*, vol. 5, ed. M. Ghālib. Beirut, 1975.

—— *Uyūn al-akhbār*, vol. 5 and part of vol. 6, ed. Muḥammad al-Yaʿlāwī as *Taʾrīkh al-khulafāʾ al-Fāṭimiyyīn biʾl-Maghrib: al-qism al-khāṣṣ min Kitāb ʿuyūn al-akhbār*. Beirut, 1985.

Ivanow, Wladimir. *Ismaili Literature: A Bibliographical Survey*. Tehran, 1963.

Khaṭīb al-Tabrīzī, Abū ʿAbd Allāh Muḥammad b. ʿAbd Allāh. *Mishkāt al-maṣābīḥ*, ed. Muḥammad N. al-Albānī. Beirut, 1961.

al-Kirmānī, Ḥamīd al-Dīn Aḥmad b. ʿAbd Allāh. *al-Maṣābīḥ fī ithbāt al-imāma*, ed. and tr. Paul E. Walker as *Master of the Age: An Islamic Treatise on the Necessity of the Imamate*. London, 2007.

Madelung, Wilferd. 'Das Imamat in der frühen ismailitischen Lehre', *Der Islam*, 37 (1961), pp. 43–135, reprinted in W. Madelung, *Studies in Medieval Shiʿism*, article VII.

—— 'A Treatise on the Imamate of the Fatimid Caliph al-Manṣūr Bi-Allāh', in Chase F. Robinson, ed., *Texts, Documents and Artefacts: Islamic Studies in Honour of D.S. Richards*. Leiden, 2003, pp. 69–77.

—— 'Imāma', EI2, vol. 3, pp. 1163–1169.

—— *Studies in Medieval Shiʿism*, ed. Sabine Schmitdke. Farnham, Surrey, and Burlington, VA, 2012.

al-Maqrīzī, Taqī al-Dīn Aḥmad b. ʿAlī. *Ittiʿāẓ al-ḥunafāʾ bi-akhbār al-aʾimma al-Fāṭimiyyīn al-khulafāʾ*, ed. J. al-Shayyāl and Muḥammad Ḥilmī M. Aḥmad. Cairo, 1387–1393/1967–1973; ed. Ayman F. Sayyid. Damascus, 2010.

al-Naysābūrī, Aḥmad b. Ibrāhīm. *Kitāb ithbāt al-imāma*, ed. and tr. Arzina R. Lalani as *Degrees of Excellence: A Fatimid Treatise on Leadership in Islam*. London, 2010.

al-Nuʿmān b. Muḥammad, al-Qāḍī Abū Ḥanīfa. *Daʿāʾim al-Islām*, ed. Asaf A.A. Fyzee. Cairo, 1951–1961. English trans., Asaf A.A. Fyzee, completely revised by Ismail K. Poonawala, as *The Pillars of Islam*. New Delhi, 2002–2004.

Poonawala, Ismail K. *Biobibliography of Ismāʿīlī Literature*. Malibu, CA, 1977.

Index

تثبيت الإمامة

تثبيت الإمامة

المنسوب إلى

المنصور بالله

تحقيق
سامي مكارم

فهرس الموضوعات

تمهيد

[١ ب] 'هذا الكتاب تثبيت الإمامة تأليف الإمام الهُمام ظل رب الأنام مولانا إسمعيل المنصور بنصر الله، صلوات الله عليه وآبائه الطاهرين وأبنائه الأكرمين.'

مقدمة

'بسم الله الرحمن الرحيم، وصلى الله على رسوله محمد وآله وسلّم.'

'أما بعد'، زادك الله رغبةً في العلم ومحبة للفهم، وأوزعك شكر ما به عليك أنعم، سألْتني، أرشدك الله'، عن تثبيت إمامة أمير المؤمنين عليّ بن أبي طالب (صلوات الله عليه) واستحقاقه الأمرَ دون غيره. وسأبيّن ذلك بما لا يدفعه الخصماء وأستشهد عليه بما لا ينكره الأضداد [٢ أ] والأعداء، 'فاستعمله في الفكر'، رحمك الله، وصحة النظر فيما يوجبه العقل بالاستدلال قبل النظر في الروايات وفيما يدّعي كل فريق ممّن أثبت الإمامة وزعم أنّ' لا بد للناس من إمام.

' ساقطة في ب   ' في ب: بسم الله الرحمن الرحيم، الحمد لله رب العالمين وصلّى الله على رسوله سيدنا محمد وآله أجمعين وسلّم.   ' ساقطة في ب   ' في ب بعد الله: أمرك   ' في ب: فاستعمل الفكر   ' في ب: أنه

هل الإمامة بالرأي أم بسلطة لكم أم فريضة؟

فأول ذلك أن يُسألوا عن قولهم: لا بد للناس من إمام. فيقال لهم أذلك[1] شيء رأيتموه وأمر توهّمتموه، أم بحكمٍ منكم على عباد الله، أم فريضة لازمة؟

فإن قلتم هو فرض: فَمَن المنصوص[2] عليه منكم ومن صاحب الأمر إذا[3] كان الله سبحانه قد نص عليه وأوجب على الخلق طاعته وقرن طاعته بطاعة رسوله (صلى الله عليه وآله)؟ فإن قالوا: هو[4] أبو بكر، قلنا: فقد كذّبكم[5] أبو بكر بقوله [2 ب] إذ قال: « رضيت لكم أحد هذين[6] الرجلين، أبا عبيدة بن الجرّاح أو عمر بن الخطّاب[7]. فبايعوا أيّما شئتم »؛ ثم بقوله: « أقيلوني، أقيلوني »[8] ثم بقوله: « ليتني[9] كنت سألت رسول الله (صلع) لمن الأمر بعده؟ » وبقوله: « أما بعد، فإن المسلمين استخلفوني ورضوا بي » وبأخذه من بيت مال المسلمين أجرتَهُ في كل يومٍ درهمين. وأكذبكم أيضاً عمر 'بن الخطّاب[10] بقوله: « كانت بيعة أبي بكر فلتة، وقى الله شرها، فمن أرادكم على مثلها فاقتلوه »؛ وبقول عمر 'بن الخطّاب[11] أيضاً: « إن أترككم فقد تركّكم من هو خير مني، وإن أستخلف فقد استخلف من هو خير مني ». يريد بذلك أن رسول الله (ص) لم يستخلف أحداً، وأن [3 أ] « أبا بكر قد

وطاعته ايما شئتم

استخلفني عليكم قبل موته »؛ وبقول الأنصار: « منا أمير ومنكم أمير »، وقد رويتم عن رسول الله (صلع) (أنه قال¹): « لو كنت مستخلفاً رجلاً من غير مشورة لاستخلفت ابن مسعود ». فكيف جاز لأبي بكر أن يغيِّر النص ويزيل الفرض وينقل الشيء من الموضع الذي وضعه الله فيه. وكيف يستقيل مِن أمرٍ عَقَدَه الله (تع) ورسوله⁽²⁾ بزعمكم؟ فكيف يكون العقد من الله ورسوله لأبي بكر وأبو بكر يرى تغييره ووضعه في أبي عبيدة أو عمر بن الخطاب؟ وكيف يكون أمرٌ قد حَكَم الله به ورضيه فلتة؟ والفلتة لا تكون إلا زوالاً عن الحق في قول عمر بن الخطاب. فإن كان ذلك رأياً رأيتموه وأمراً [3 ب] توهمتموه. فكيف جاز لكم أن تظنوا بأن الله لم ينظر لخلقه ولا أغناهم عمّا لا بد لهم⁽³⁾ منه، وأنكم في ذلك أنطق⁽⁴⁾ وأنصح للأمة من الله (تع) ورسوله (ص) فيما فعلتم. ويقال لهم: أرأيتم إن كان الله أمَرَ نبيَّه (صلع) أن ينصب لكم رجلاً فلم يفعل. أليس قد خالفه⁽⁵⁾ وعصاه؟ وإن كان قد حُظِّر ذلك عليه فمن أطلق لكم ما حُظِّر على رسول الله (صلع)؟ وإن كان ذلك تحكما⁽⁶⁾ منكم على الخلق فمن أجاز لكم التحكّم عليهم حتى سفكتم دماءً حقنها الله (تع) وأوطأكم فروجاً حرَّمها الله، وأبحتم أموالاً حظَّرها، وحكمتم في دين⁽⁷⁾ الله وعلى⁽⁸⁾ عباده بما لم يأذن به الله؟ فهل على [4 أ] هذا ثواب أم فيه عندكم عقاب؟ وهل هذا جائز لكم

---

¹ ساقطة في أ   ² ساقطة في أ   ³ ساقطة في أ   ⁴ في ب: أنظر   ⁵ في
أ خالقه مرددة مرتين   ⁶ في أ وب: تحكم   ⁷ في ب: عبادين   ⁸ في ب: على

في غير الإمامة أيضاً كما جاز لكم في الإمامة؟ وإلا فمن أجاز لكم ذلك
في الإمامة وحظّر في سائر الأشياء؟

ثم(١) يقال لهم: أيُّما كان أصلح: ما فعل رسول الله (صلع) من ترك
ذلك، أو ما فعلتم من نَصْبِكُم ﴿من نصبتم﴾(٢)؟ فإن قالوا ما فعلنا، قيل لهم:
فأنتم ﴿أولى وأحق﴾(٣) بالصواب من رسول الله (صلع) في زعمكم؟

ثم(٤) يقال لهم: خبّرونا عن نصب الإمام، أمن الدين أم ليس من
الدين؟ فإن قالوا: ليس من الدين، قلنا: فما الحاجة بنا إليه؟ وإن قالوا:
من الدين، قلنا: فهل على الله بيانه وعلى رسول الله بلاغه؟ فإن قالوا
نعم، قيل: فهل أخلاّ(٥)؟ فإن قالوا لا، قيل لهم: هذا فضول منكم [٤ ب]
في دين الله وتقدُّمٌ منكم(٦) بين يَدَي الله ورسوله. أرأيتم إن كان من
الدين فتركه الله ولم يبيّنه أو الرسول فلم يبلّغه فهل تدرون، لعل كثيراً من
أمر الدين وما لا بد للمسلمين جميعاً منه لم يُنزله الله ولا بلّغَهُ رسوله؟
وإلى هذا بعينه جريتم في الفتيا في الفرائض والأحكام والحلال والحرام
والدماء والعبادات(٧)؛ فزعمتم أن الله افترض عليكم الفرائض وأمركم
بأمور ونهاكم عن أشياء لم يبيّنها في كتابه ولا على لسان رسوله حتى
اضطرّكم ذلك إلى العمل بالقياس والرأي والاستحسان. فهذا غاية الكفر
وسوء الثناء على الله ورسوله(٨).

هل تنصيب الإمام فرض أم سنة أم تكلّف؟

ويقال لهم: خبرونا عن نَصْب الإمام: أفرضٌ [٥أ] من الله أم سنّة؟ فإن كان فرضاً، فَمَن المفروض علينا منكم طاعتُه؟ فإن قالوا: أبو بكر، قيل لهم: (قد كان أبو بكر يعلم¹ أنه المفروض علينا طاعته أم كان لا يعلم؟ فإن كان يعلم، فلِمَ قال: « ليتني كنت سألت رسول الله (صلع) لِمَن الأمر بعدك؟ » ولِمَ قال: « رضيت لكم أحد هذين الرجلين، فبايعوا أيهما شئتم: أبا عبيدة بن² الجرّاح أو ³ عمر بن الخطّاب ». ولِمَ قال « أقيلوني، أقيلوني » ولِمَ قال: « أما بعد فإن المسلمين⁴ استخلفوني ورضوا بي ». ولِمَ أخذ أجرته من بيت مال المسلمين؟ ولِمَ قال عمر بن الخطاب: « كانت بيعة أبي بكر فلتة، وقى الله [المسلمين]⁵ شرّها، فمن أرادكم على مثلها فاقتلوه »، ولِمَ قالت الأنصار: « منا أمير ومنكم [٥ب] أمير ». ولِمَ قال [أبو بكر]⁶: « وُلّيتكم ولستُ بخيركم ». ولم يقل: إن الله ولّاني أموركم واسترعاني عليكم وأمرني بسياستكم وأعطاني كذا أو فعل بي كذا. على أنه قد خبّر عن نفسه بما لا يجوز على الله أن يسترعي مثله، مع قوله: « إن لي شيطاناً يعتريني، فإن رأيتموني قد غضبت⁷ عليكم فاجتنبوني. لا أمثل بأشعارهم وأبشارهم ». وكيف يجوز من الله أن يسترعي مَنْ هذه صفته، وأن يختار للدين من يرى نقصه وتغييره، ويرضى للمسلمين بغير من رضيه الله لهم مثل أبي عبيدة

---

¹ في ب: وقد كان يعلم أبو بكر ² ساقطة في أ ³ في أ: وعمر ⁴ في ب: المسلمون ⁵ ساقطة في أ وب ⁶ ناقصة في أ وب ⁷ في أ: غضبت عليكم

بن الجرّاح وعمر بن الخطّاب، ومن لا يؤمّن على أن يمثل ¹'بأشعار مؤمن وأبشاره' ومن لا يقوم بأمر المسلمين إلا دون قيامهم لأنفسهم، إذ ليس عنده [6 أ] ما يفتيهم من أمر حلالهم وحرامهم وفرائضهم وسننهم وأحكامهم وما أوجب الله²' عليهم من أمر 'دينهم ودنياهم'³. وكيف يجوز على الله تعالى أن يسترعي راعياً يوجِب طاعته على خلقه جميعاً، ولا يعلمه بذلك ولا يرشده إليه ولا يُعلم بذلك رعيته، وهو مع ذلك⁴' قد افترض عليه القيام بأمرهم وافترض عليهم السمع والطاعة له والقبول لخبره؟ فإن كان يعلم أنه الإمام المفترض الطاعة، فما دعاه إلى ما ذكرناه من هذه الأمور وما⁵' دعاه من هذه الأقاويل؟ وكيف لم يحتج على الناس جميعاً بنحو ما ذكرنا من نَصْبِ الله له وإعلامهم ما أعلمه الله ورسوله، وأن الله ورسوله قد أمره بالقيام [6 ب] بأمور الناس جميعاً وافترضا⁶' عليهم الطاعة⁷' والانقياد لحكمه والقبول لخبره. أو يكون الأمر تكلفاً ليس بفرض؟ فإن⁸' كان تكلفاً، فكيف جاز للناس أن يقولوا له يا خليفة رسول الله؟ فهل صدقوا أم كذبوا في قولهم له ذلك؟ فإن كانوا صدقوا، فما وجه الكلام الذي تقدّم من أبي بكر وغيره؟ وإن كانوا كذبوا فلِم⁹' رضي 'أبو بكر بذلك'¹⁰ وقبله ولم يُنكره ولا ردّه؟ وقد علم القوم جميعاً، بعد النظر والكشف، أنها شهادة زورٍ كاذبة 'فكيف استجاز

---

¹ في ب: بشعر مؤمن ونشره   ² في ب: الله تعالى   ³ في ب: دنياهم ودينهم   ⁴ في ب: هذا   ⁵ في ب: ولا   ⁶ في ب: وافترض   ⁷ في ب: طاعته   ⁸ في ب: فإذا ⁹ في أ: فلما   ¹⁰ في ب: أبي بكر منهم بذلك

تركهم ومقارنتهم على شهادة زورٍ[1] على رسول الله (صلع) في كل يوم
حتى هلك ومضى لسبيله؟ وما الفرق عندكم بين الشاهد بالزور [٧ أ]
والمشهود له؟ ويقال لهم: هل تدرون؟ لعلّ كثيراً مما فعلوه ومما[2] هو
دون الإمامة عندكم قد غُيِّرَ مِن[3] موضعه وأُزيل عن جهته ونُسِب إلى
غير أهله وتُرك الفرض فيه إما تعمداً على طريق الخطأ والغلط والنسيان،
إذ[4] كل ذلك جائز في أمر الإمامة وهو الفرض الأكبر الذي لا يقوم
الناس ولا يصلحون إلا به، فما ظنكم بسائر الفرائض التي دقّت على
أفهامكم وغمضت عن استخراجكم فلم تجدوا سبيلاً إلى معرفتها بقياس
ولا بنظر ولا بفكر حتى حكم بعضكم على بعض في الشيء الواحد
بمائة قضية مختلفة. ولو حُكم بألف لم يزدد من الحق إلا بعداً، لأن
النظر والقياس والاجتهاد [٧ ب] لا يهجم بهم[5] على نفس الحق عند الله،
ولا يغنيهم عن الإمام، كما لم يغنِهِم عن الرسول (صلع). أو لعلّ أكثر
الفرائض قد غُيِّرت عن مواضعها وشُبِّهت بما لا يشبهها. ولو طالت بهم
المدة لكان الرجوع عنها كالرجوع عن غيرها مما وصفنا. وإذا جاز[6]
هذا في البعض حُكم به على الكلّ، لأن حُكمَ البعض حُكمُ الكل
وحُكم الكل حُكم[7] البعض. ثم[8] يقال لهم: أتدرون؟ لعل أكثر ما
أُلزموا[9] العمل به وجعلوه فرضاً كفرض الإمام الذي نصبوه وأوجبوا على

---

[1] ساقطة في ب   [2] في ب: مما   [3] في ب: عن   [4] في ب: إن   [5] في
ب: بمستعمل   [6] في أ: أجاز   [7] ناقصة في أ   [8] في ب: و   [9] في
ب: لزموا

الخلق طاعته مما لم يأمر به الله ورسوله، إذ كان نصب الإمام عندكم
مما 'لم يأمر الله به'(١) ولا رسوله في زعمكم نصاً وكانت أمور القوم على
مثل [٨ أ] هذا تجري وبه يحكمون. ويقال لهم: أخبرونا(٢)، هل يخلو
الأمر أن يكون تكلّفاً أو فرضاً؟ فإن كان تكلفاً فما الحاجة بنا إلى تكلّف
أمرٍ كفيناه ولم يأذن الله لنا فيه ولا رسوله مع ما يؤدي إلى صاحبه من
الذم القبيح واللوم مع الجرم العظيم والوزر الجسيم، لأن التكلّف مذموم
عند الله في جميع الحالات، سيما في الأمر الذي لا يجوز فيه التكليف،
لأن فيه من الله حكماً قد سبق وأمراً قد نفذ وقضاء(٣) لا يُرَدّ ولا يُغَيَّر.
فمن فعل ذلك منا(٤) كان عاصياً لله ولرسوله. أو يكون فرضاً لازماً وأمراً
واجباً. فإن كان فرضاً، فقد فرغ الله منه وكفانا فيه المؤونة، وإن كان
غير فرضٍ سقطت عنا [٨ ب] فيه الشبهة. وإن كان في طاعة 'الله
ورسوله'(٥). مع ما يدخل على أنفسنا من الراحة العاجلة من ترك
المقايسة(٦) واجتهاد الرأي في الإحكام والفتيا وبأن هذا حلال وهذا
حرام. ونرجع إلى أن الحكم كلّه لله. وهذا هو التعبّد بعينه. ويقال لهم:
اخبرونا(٧)، لو وَلَّيتم أبا عبيدة بن الجرّاح أو عمر بن الخطّاب، أكنتم
قائلين له(٨) يا خليفة رسول الله؟ فإن كنتم قائلين له ذلك، فهل في
أنفسكم شك بأن هذا كذب لا خفاء به؟ وإن كنتم لا تقولون له ذلك(٩)

---

١ في ب: يأمر به الله   ٢ في ب: خبرونا   ٣ في ب: وقضى   ٤ في ب: ما

٥ في أ: طاعة لله ورسوله   ٦ في ب: المقائسة   ٧ في ب: خبرونا   ٨ في أ: لهم

٩ ساقطة في أ

بالتقديم. وهذا الأمر فقد أخطأه كثير من هذا الخلق بهذه الأمور التي قدَّمنا ذكرها. وقد تقدم بين يدي الله ورسوله 'وحُكمَ في دين الله وعلى عباده بما لم يأذن به الله ولا رسوله'١. [٩أ] فهل ترون فرقاً بين أن يقبض الرجل مالاً وهو يعلم أنه لا يملكه، وينكح فرجاً وهو يعلم أن الحكم فيه إلى غيره، ويريق دماً محقوناً ويعلم أن الله لم يأمره٢ بالتقدّم على الحكم في شيء من ذلك ولا جعله إليه٣، وبأن٤ يأخذ مالاً حراماً عليه أخذهُ ويطأ فرجاً محرماً عليه وطئه ويريق دماً محقوناً٥ وليس هذا كلّه من فعله لا عن أمر الله ولا عن رسوله. فسواء٦ في الحكم أخذ مالاً لنفسه أو أمر بأخذه أو وطأ فرجاً حرام عليه وطئه٧ أو أُمر بوطئه أو سفك دماً محقوناً أو أمر بسفكه. وهو في ذلك كله يعلم أنه ما أصاب جهة من جهات الحق 'عند الله'٨ ولا يشهد بذلك لنفسه ولا لنظرائه المتكلفين [٩ب] من أصحابه. لأن الخطأ يوجب الخطأ والصواب يوجب الصواب. وهو٩ صفةُ مَن قال: سأنزل مثل ما أنزل الله. ومن كان تقدمه وقيامه لا عن أمر الله وأمر رسوله فقد بان خطأه. 'وكل ما١٠ زاد في علمه شيئاً زاد ذلك في خطأه وخلافه وعصيانه لله ولرسوله.

ويقال لهم: خبرونا عن الأذان، أهو أشهر بين ظهرانيكم أم نصب الإمام؟ وفرض الوضوء والصلاة والزكاة وما أشبه ذلك من الفرائض

---

١ ساقطة في أ   ٢ في ب: يأمر   ٣ في ب: وأن   ٤ في ب: ويريق   ٥ في ب: أو   ٦ في ب: سواء   ٧ ساقطة في أ   ٨ ساقطة في أ   ٩ في ب: وهذه ١٠ في أ: وكلما

والأصول أشهر أم نصب الإمام؟ وفرض الخُمُس أوضح مع سهم المؤلفة
قلوبهم أم نصب الإمام؟ فهل ترون ذلك كلَّهُ مغيَّراً مصروفاً عن جهته
ومتروكاً لا يُعمل به؟ وما الفرق بين تغيير الإمام وتغيير [10 أ] الصلاة وتغيير
الخُمُس وسهم المؤلفة قلوبهم، وتغيير الحج والتمتع بالعمرة إلى الحج
وغير ذلك مما قد بيَّن الله فرضَه وأمر بالعمل به نصاً، ولم يختلفوا في
تنزيله وصحة فرضه ووجوبه، قد أُحِلَّ منه ما كان حراماً وحُرِّم منه ما
كان حلالاً. وذلك كلَّه مشهور عند أوائلهم وأئمتهم لا يكلمون فيه أحداً
ولا يستعملون فيه تقيّة لعلمهم أن ما قالوا من(١) شيء فهو مقبول وما
حكموا به فهو جائز، ولمَّا جاز لهم تغيير الإمامة جاز لهم تغيير ما ذكرناه
جرأةً على الله وعلى رسوله.

تعيين الرسول أحدهم للصلاة لا يعني تعيينه للإمامة

ثم يقال لهم: أخبرونا عن قولكم: رأينا رسول الله (صلع) قدَّمه للصلاة
فقدَّمناه(٢) ورضيه لهذا فرضيناه، هل لكم في ذلك إلَّا ما [10 ب] لغيركم
من قولِ مَن قال: رأينا رسول الله (صلع) قد عزله عن الصلاة ظاهراً
مكشوفاً فعزلناه ورأينا الله ورسوله قد ردّاه عن تبليغ بعض سورة من
القرآن فرَدَدْناه عن تبليغ الكلّ ورأينا رسول الله (صلع) قد حَذِره وكرهه
وأمر بإنفاذه مع صاحبه في جيش أسامة فكرهناه. فأي موضع اختيار
هذا؟ وهل لكم في ذلك إلا ما لغيركم ممن طعن عليه ورأى أن ليس هو
بإمامٍ مستحقٍ للتقدم.

---

١ في أ: منه   ٢ في أ: فقدمناه

هل الإمامة من الله لواحد دون واحد أم لمن غلب؟

ويقال لهم: خبرونا عن الإمامة، أفرض من الله لواحد دون واحد، أم لمن غلب؟ فإن كانت فرضاً في واحد ثم لا فرض بعد ذلك لواحد، فالكلام عليكم قائم بحاله؛ لأن الكلام في الأول كالكلام [11أ] في الثاني والثالث والرابع والخامس والعاشر، وكذلك أبداً وإن كانت لمن غلب عليها، فالحكم منكم بأنها لمن غلب عليها بالنص من الله ومن رسوله، أو رأي رأيتموه وتحكّم منكم على الأمة. وما وجه الكلام في الإمامة عندكم إلا على هذه الجهة: إما على جهة فرضٍ أو لطاعةِ رجلٍ بعينه تعرفونه باسمه أو لمن غلب عليها.

ولا بد لكم من مذهب تذهبون إليه في نصب الإمام وإقامته. فأي مذهب ذهبتم فلا بد أن تكون معكم بذلك حجةٌ بأن الله ورسوله أمراكم بذلك قولاً وفعلاً. فائتونا بالبيّنة على ما رأيتم من ذلك وما ادّعيتم، ﴿ولا قوة إلا بالله﴾[١] العلي العظيم.

ثم يقال لهم: ما تقولونه في حكم ما غاب عنكم [11ب] وعنا؟ أهو حكم ما شاهدتم وشاهدنا أم هو خلافه؟ فإن كان[٢] حكمُ الغائب حكمَ الشاهد، فقد نرى وترون أن الإمامة بغير النص وبغير الاختيار وفي غير موضع الاستحقاق. فهل كان الأمر قديماً إلا هكذا؟ وإنما يُستَدَلُّ بالشاهد على الغائب بصحة الدلالة. فهل في هذا بيانٌ ﴿لقوم يعقلون﴾[٣]؟

---

١ سورة الكهف (١٨) ٣٩.   ٢ ساقطة في أ.   ٣ البقرة (٢) ١٦٤:؛ الرعد (١٣) ٤:؛ النحل (١٦) ١٢:، ٦٧؛ العنكبوت (٢٩) ٣٥:؛ الروم (٣٠) ٢٤:، ٢٨؛ الجاثية (٤٥) ٥:

هل تجوز إمامة المفضول؟

ثم يقال لهم: خبرونا عن انقياد الناس للإمام في كل عصر وزمان، دليل[1] على أنه أفضل منهم وأعلمهم وأحقهم بذلك الأمر؟ وأنهم لا يصلحون ولا ينقادون إلا به وعلى يديه؟ أو حذراً من سيفه وسلطانه وتظاهره بالظالمين وإخوانهم؟ فإن كان الأمر كذلك، فإن معاوية بن أبي سفيان ويزيد [12 أ] بن معاوية ومروان بن الحكم وعبد الملك من مروان والوليد وسليمان وهشام وفلان وفلان وطغاة بني أميّة كانوا خير الخلق طراً وأفضلهم وأحقهم بمقام رسول الله (صلع). وإن كان الأمر بخلاف ذلك والقوم منقادون لمن غلب عليهم وتولى شيئاً من أمورهم، فهل كانت حجتهم قديماً في إمام العصر والزمان إلا هكذا؟ هل جرت الأمور إلا مجاريها؟ وهل كانت حجتهم في أبي بكر ونصبه وإقامته إماماً واحتجاجهم عنه إلا[2] كاحتجاج جماعتكم وحكامكم وفقهائكم وقضاتكم ومن تحتجون بقوله من عظمائكم ومحدثيكم في تفضيل من ذكرنا من بني أميّة وغيرهم إلا هكذا؟ وما الفرق بينهم؟ ولن تجدوا [12 ب] فرقاً أبداً.

دوام الإمامة

ثم يقال لهم: خبرونا عن الإمامة؛ وإن اختلفت[3] أوقاتها وأزمانها، فهل اختلف[4] حكمها عند الله وعندكم؟ فإن قالوا ليست[5] بمختلفة في

---

¹ في ب: دليلاً   ² ساقطة في أ   ³ في ب: اختلف   ⁴ في ب: اختلفت   ⁵ في ب: ليس

نفسها ولا في حكمها عند الله – لأن الله (تع)(١) لا يخالف أحكامه –
قلنا لهم: فإن كان حكم الله في الإمامة غير مختلف وكان الأمر بالنص
عندكم فأين النص الآن؟ فإن كان بالاختيار منكم، فأين الاختيار منكم
وأين موضعه؟ ومن المأمور بذلك الاختيار؟ فإن زعموا أن الله قد(٢)
خالف بين أحكامه ودفع(٣) الإمام عنهم – إذ كان لا يفرض(٤) على خلقه
طاعة من لا يطيعه ولا يتعبدهم(٥) بالطاعة لمن يعصيه ويخالف أمره
ويتعدى حدوده – قلنا فقد بطُل الإمام عندكم لا محالة [13 أ] ولا بد من
أن يكون الله أبطله وأمركم بتركه أو(٦) يكون ذلك رأياً من رأيكم. فأيّما،
خبرونا، كان أفضل؟ أكان(٧) في نصب الإمام الأول أو رأيكم اليوم في
ترك الإمام الأخير؟ ومتى جاز للناس، ﴿إن صح(٨)﴾، أن ينصبوا إماماً أو
يتركوا نصبه؟ ثم ائتونا بالبيّنة على ما تدّعون من ذلك؛ أم تزعمون أن الله
(تبارك وتعالى) قد كان بخلقه في ذلك الدهر أنظَرَ منه لهم في هذا
الدهر؟ تعالى الله عن ذلك علواً كبيرا.

هل أوصى الرسول بنصب الإمام

ويقال لهم: أخبرونا(٩) كيف كان الظن برسول الله (صلع) عندكم أنه
يوصي وأن يستخلف، أو أن لا يوصي ولا يستخلف؟ فإن قالوا: أكان
الظن به أن [13 ب] يوصي ويستخلف، قلنا لهم: ما الذي أزال حسن

---

١ في ب: تبارك وتعالى   ٢ ساقطة في ب   ٣ في ب: ورفع   ٤ في ب:
يفترض   ٥ في ب: تعبدهم   ٦ في أ: و   ٧ في ب: كان   ٨ ساقطة في ب   ٩ في
ب: خبرونا

الظن به حتى زعمتم أنه ترك الوصية والاستخلاف وهل يخلوا ذلك
عندكم من أن يكون الله قد أمره بترك الوصيّة والاستخلاف وحذّره ذلك
وحظّره عليه، فعمل من ذلك ما أمره به. وهذا نقض لِما خبّر عن ربّه؟ أو
يكون الغالب عليه الخطأ والنسيان والجهل؟ وحاشاه، لما في ذلك من
مصلحة العباد، والقصد في ذلك مخالفته وعصيانه من حيث يعلم. وقد
أجل الله قدْر نبيّه (صلع) عن أن تزلّ به قدم أو تثبت عليه حجّة. فإذا لم
نجد الأمر بما وصفناه، فما حجتكم في إقامة [14 أ] رجل تزعمون أنه
خليفة رسول الله (صلع) قد جمع خلافته ووصيته وأحلّ أمواله وضياعه،
وحكم في أهله وتراثه وأنتم(١) تشهدون عليه عند الله أنه لم يوصِ ولم
يستخلف؛ وهذا غاية الطعن منكم على نبي الله (صلع) وسوء الثناء
عليه. فهل حجتكم في حكم المحتجين عليه إلا هكذا؟ قلتم له يا
خليفة رسول الله وهو لا يدّعي ذلك لنفسه ولا يقول: ⟨إن رسول الله
استخلفني، بل يقول:⟩(٢) إن المسلمين استخلفوني ورضوا بي، ويقول:
« ولّيتكم ولست بخيركم ». ولا يقول أن الله (تع) ورسوله ولّياني
أموركم. وهو يأخذ أجرته من بيت مال المسلمين في كل يوم درهمين،
وهو مع [14 ب] هذا(٣) يقول: « إن لي شيطاناً يعتريني، فإذا رأيتموني قد
غضبت فاجتنبوني، لا أمثل بأشعاركم وأبشاركم »(٤). مع علمكم بأنه لا
يقرأ القرآن. ومن كان لا يقرأ القرآن فأجدر(٥) أن لا يعلم تأويله ولا

ناسخه ولا منسوخه ولا محكمه ولا متشابهه. وكيف يفرق بين الحلال
والحرام مَن هذه صفته. وقد رأيناكم جعلتم الناس طبقات. فلم يدخل
في طبقة يوجب له فضلاً في دين ولا دنيا. ذكرتم ان النبي (صلع) ذكر
أهل الصدق فقال أبو ذر، وذكر أهل القرآن فقال عبد الله بن مسعود
وأبي بن كعب، وذكر أهل الفرائض فقال زيد بن ثابت، وذكر أهل
القضاء [١٥ أ] فقال: علي بن أبي طالب، وذكر أهل[١] العلم بالحلال
والحرام فقال معاذ بن جبل. فكيف رضيتم بأن تنصبوا رجلاً يقوم
عندكم[٢] مقام رسول الله (صلع) يحتاج إلى الناس جميعاً في حالته ولا
يحتاج الناس إليه في شيء من حالاتهم. لقد بلغتم الغاية القصوى في
سوء الاختيار وسوء الثناء على رسول الله (صلع).

أسباب أخرى مبطلةٌ لإمامة أبي بكر وعمر

ويقال لهم: خبّرونا ما الذي يجب على الناس بعد الإقرار بإمامة أبي بكر
وعمر؟ فإن قالوا: الائتمام بهما، قلنا: والائتمام بهما هو[٣] السمع والطاعة
لهما والقبول لقولهما والانقياد لحكمهما وأن يُعتقد أن كل ما قالا به
وأفتيا [١٥ ب] وَحَكَما فهو صواب واجب وأمر لازم كلزوم الفرض. أو
يُشَكّ فيه فيُنظر لعلمهما قد أخطيا وحكما بغير الحق وبخلاف التنزيل
وما عليه المسلمون. فإن[٤] قالوا: ليس علينا ننظر عليهما ولا معهما،
وعلينا أن نقبل قولهما ونصدّق أخبارهما ولا نتجاوز حكمهما. قلنا: فمن
فعل ذلك منكم فهو آثِمٌ أو ظالم أو كافر أو فاسق. ولا شيء عليه ولا

---

[١] ساقطة في ب   [٢] في أ: عذركم   [٣] ساقطة في ب   [٤] ساقطة في أ

تبعة تُلزمه في دين أو دنيا. فإن ألزموا مَن فعل ذلك اسم «آثم أو ظالم»(١) أو
كافر أو فاسق، ألزموا ذلك جميع الصحابة، وأولهم عمر بن الخطّاب في
خلافة(٢) أبي بكر، ثم الناس جميعاً، «لأن الخلاف عليهم قد شملهم،
وإذا كان الناس جميعاً»(٣) [١٦ أ] بتلك الصفة من الإثم أو الكفر أو ما دون
ذلك، لم تثبت على أحدهم(٤) الحجة ولم تُقبل لهم شهادة أبداً»(٥). فإن
زعموا أن لنا أن ننظر عليهما ونتأمل أحكامهما ونقايسهما(٦). قلنا: فإذا
اختلفنا؟ فمن ينظر في أمورنا؟ وعند مَن نجد قنوعاً وإلى مَن نفزع مما
قد نزل بنا؟ وقول من يُلزمنا حتى لا نضل(٧) ولا نأثم ولا نفسق ولا نكفر
على موافقته على(٨) قوله(٨) ومَن يردّ علينا(٩) ما عزمنا عليه من أخذٍ وترك؟
وقد تعبدنا الله بأمرٍ غيرِ مشكلٍ ولا مختلف، إذ كان الرسول قد جاء بردِّ
كل مختلف إلى الله وإلى الرسول(١٠) وإلى صاحب الأمر. فإن رجعتم إلى
صاحب [١٦ ب] الأمر رجعتم إلى أمر غير مختلف. كما أنكم إذا رجعتم
إلى الله وإلى رسوله رجعتم إلى أمر غير مختلف. والعدد الكثير إذا
اختلفوا فجائز أن يكونوا كلهم مبطلين وليس بجائز أن يكونوا كلهم
محقّين، وجائز أن يكونوا بعضهم محقّا وبعضهم مبطلاً. وقد رأيتم الناس
جميعاً مختلفين وليس منهم أحد يزعم أن الله أمَرَهُ بالعدل ولا أطلق له
الحكم ولا جعل إليه من أمر الأمة(١١) شيئاً. وقد كان القول لرسول الله

---

¹ في أ: آثم أو ظالم أو آثم   ² في ب خلافه على³ ساقطة في ب   ⁴ في أ: أحد
لهما   ⁵ ساقطة في أ   ⁶ في ب: تقاسمهما   ⁷ في ب: نزل   ⁸ في
⁹ في أ: عن   ¹⁰ في ب: رسوله   ¹¹ في ب: الإمامة

(صلع) مطلقاً والحكم له جائزاً، وكان لا يقول على الله إلا الحق ولا
يحكم إلا بالعدل[١] ولا ينطق عن الهوى.

وقد مضى [١٧ أ] رسول الله (صلع)، فهل نصب لكم رجلاً يقوم مقامه
ويحذو مثاله؟ وأمركم بالسمع والطاعة له؟ إذ كان قد أمركم بطاعة رجلٍ
بعد النبي وأقامه مقامه وجعل ما كان 'مردوداً إلى النبي'[٢] مردوداً إليه؟ وإن
قالوا: نعم، قلنا: فمَن ذلك الرجل؟ فإن قالوا: علي، فقد أقرّوا بالكفر
بالله، إذ خالفوه بعد النص إليه ولم يرجعوا إلى رأيه ولا حكمه، ولا
رضوا بقوله؛ فإن قالوا: لم ينصب لنا رجلاً، قلنا لهم: فلم يكن لقول الله
سبحانه: ﴿يَا أَيُّهَا الَّذِينَ آمَنُوا أَطِيعُوا اللَّهَ وَأَطِيعُوا الرَّسُولَ وَأُولِي الأَمْرِ
مِنكُمْ﴾[٣] معنى ولا لقوله ﴿فَإِن تَنَازَعْتُمْ في شيءٍ فردّوه إلى الله وإلى
[١٧ ب] الرسول وإلى[٤] أُولِي الأَمر منكم﴾[٥] معنى. فمن ذلك حكمتم
بالرأي والقياس والاجتهاد والاستحسان والتقريب والظن. وقد كان ذلك
محظوراً على رسول الله (صلع). فإن زعمتم أن الله قد رفع ذلك الأمر
عنكم وأطلق لكم ما كان حظّره على رسول الله، فهلموا أنبئكم[٦] على
ما تدعون عليه من ذلك على الله ورسوله ولا تفتروا على الله

---

[١] في ب: بالحق   [٢] ساقطة في ب   [٣] النساء (٤):٥٩   [٤] ساقطة في ب
[٥] كذا في الأصل. أما الآية القرآنية فهي: ﴿فَإِنْ تَنَازَعْتُمْ فِي شَيْءٍ فَرُدُّوهُ إِلَى اللَّهِ
وَالرَّسُولِ﴾ النساء (٤):٥٩   [٦] في أ: بينتكم

الكذب(١) ﴿إِنَّ الَّذِينَ يَفْتَرُونَ عَلَى اللَّهِ الْكَذِبَ لَا يُفْلِحُونَ﴾(٢).

ويقال لهم: خبّرونا، هل أمر رسول الله (صلع) بإنفاذ جيش أسامة والذين معه؟ فإن قالوا: نعم، قلنا لهم: فكيف لم تنفّذوا وصيته في إنفاذ الجيش [١٨ أ] والذين معه وقبلتم بزعمكم وصيته في نصب الإمام؟ فخبّرونا أن لو أنفذتم الجيش على ما أمركم به رسول الله، أكنتم مطيعين أم عاصين؟ وخبّرونا، لو أطعتم الله تعالى ورسوله وأنفذتم الجيش بمن فيه ممّن أمرهم رسول الله (صلع) بالنفوذ مع أسامة، هل كانت الإمامة تحصل لأبي بكر؟ أو تزعمون(٣) أن رسول الله (صلع) لم يعلم أن الله يتوفّاه وأن الإمّة كانت تحتاج بعده إلى أبي بكر؟ أو كان علم بذلك مع علمه بأن الناس لا يقومون ولا يصلحون إلا به؟ فتركه متعمّداً وأمر بإنفاذ الجيش مع صاحبه؟ وإذا أمر الله ورسوله بإنفاذ أبي بكر [١٨ ب] وعمر في الجيش. فمن جعل ذلك إليكم، ردّهما وردّ غيرهما؟ وهل علمتم من ذلك ما جهله رسول الله (صلع)؟ 'وهل'(٤) يقدّم رسول الله (صلع) أو يؤخّر إلا بأمر ربّه؟ فهل أطعتم الله ورسوله فيما فعلتم من ردّ أسامة والذين معه؟ أوَ ما سمعتم الله يقول: ﴿وَمَنْ يَعْصِ اللَّهَ وَرَسُولَهُ فَإِنَّ لَهُ نَارَ جَهَنَّمَ خَالِدِينَ فِيهَا أَبَدَاً﴾(٥) وقوله: ﴿قُلْ أَطِيعُوا اللَّهَ وَأَطِيعُوا الرَّسُولَ﴾(٦).

---

١ إشارة إلى أول الآية ١١٦ من سورة النحل (١٦): ﴿وَلَا تَقُولُوا لِمَا تَصِفُ أَلْسِنَتُكُمُ الْكَذِبَ هَذَا حَلَالٌ وَهَذَا حَرَامٌ لِتَفْتَرُوا عَلَى اللَّهِ الْكَذِبَ إِنَّ الَّذِينَ يَفْتَرُونَ عَلَى اللَّهِ الْكَذِبَ لَا يُفْلِحُونَ﴾   ٢ النحل (١٦):١١٦   ٣ في ب: تعلمون   ٤ في ب: فهل   ٥ سورة الجن (٧٢):٢٣. في أ وب: كليهما خالدا فيها   ٦ سورة النور (٢٤):٥٤

ويقال لهم خبّرونا أيّهما[١] كان أولى برسول الله (صلع)، وقد علم أنه ميّت، أن يبدأ فيحكّم الفرض الأكبر الذي لا شيء أجلّ قدراً ولا أعظم خطراً منه عنده[٢] وما لا يصلح للناس ولا يقومون [١٩ أ] إلا به، أو يهمله ويؤخره ويتقدم فيما هو دونه فيُحكمه إحكاماً لا تَنَازُعَ فيه ولا شبهة؟ فإن قالوا: كان أولى به أن يحكّم الأكبر ثم الأصغر، قلنا: فقد فعل ما كان أولى به. قلنا: فكيف زعمتم أنه أهمل أمر الإمام مع علمه أنه لا بد للناس من إمام يقوم بأمرهم ويجمع ألفتهم ويحكم بينهم ويجلد زانيهم ويقطع [يد] سارقهم ويغزو بهم ويقسم الفيء بينهم ويعرّفهم ما جهلوا من أمر دينهم وحلالهم وحرامهم، فلم ينص عليه ولا نصّبه ولا بيّنه حتى لا يخفى مكانه على صغيرهم وكبيرهم، وهو مع هذا يأمر بإنفاذ جيش أسامة ويترك ما هو [١٩ ب] أجلّ وأعظمُ أمرٍ عنده منه، هذا[٣] مع علمه أن الإمام المفروض الطاعة يُنفذ الجيوش ويغزو بالناس ويقوم فيهم مقامه (صلع) غير مقصّر ولا متهاون بما قلّده الله ورسوله من ذلك. فإن زعمتم أنه ترك نصب الإمام، وهو ذاكر لما في[٤] نصبه من المصلحة والاتفاق، وعالمٌ بما في تركه من القبح والفساد، أو تَرَكَهُ ناسياً ومتهاوناً ومقصراً، فقد يلزمكم أن تجوّزوا النسيان بجميع الفرائض التي أمره الله بتبليغها. لأن جواز الخطأ والنسيان عليه في فريضة واحدة دليلٌ على خطأه ونسيانه لجميع الأشياء التي لا بد للناس جميعاً منها، إذ [٢٠ أ] كان الإمام لا بد

---

١ في أ: أيّما   ٢ ساقطة في أ   ٣ ساقطة في أ   ٤ ساقطة في أ

للناس جميعاً منه. فإن زعمتم أنه[١] تركه بعد الذكر له والعلم بما تركه 'ما عددنا ووصفنا'[٢] من القبح والفساد وبعد أن قد علم أن الله قد أمره بنصبه وأمر جميع الخلق بطاعته وولايته، فهذا غاية الخلاف والعصيان لله فيما أمره من إرشادكم وصلاحكم. وليس بهذا وصفه الله، بل وصفه بخلاف ذلك من الرأفة بكم والنصيحة لكم والرحمة.

وإذا ثبت أن النبي صلى الله عليه وآله أمر بإنفاذ جيش أسامة، 'وقد كان عالماً بصغير من فيه وكبيرهم'[٣] مع علمهم أجمعين[٤] بأن[٥] الله الذي أمره أن يقدم جيش أسامة وإنفاذ من فيه ليحتج عليهم بذلك عند الله تعالى لتكون الأمة شاهدة للنبي(صلع) على من أنكر ذلك منهم وردّ أمره وخالفه وعصاه. [20 ب] وهذا[٦] وهذا[٧] من كتاب الله (تع)[٧] بيّنٌ لإخفائه قوله (تع)[٨]: ﴿فَكَيْفَ إِذَا جِئْنَا مِنْ كُلِّ أُمَّةٍ بِشَهِيدٍ وَجِئْنَا بِكَ عَلَى هَؤُلَاءِ شَهِيدًا يَوْمَئِذٍ يَوَدُّ الَّذِينَ كَفَرُوا وَعَصَوُا الرَّسُولَ لَوْ تُسَوَّى بِهِمُ الْأَرْضُ وَلَا يَكْتُمُونَ اللَّهَ حَدِيثًا﴾[٩]

ثم يقال لهم: خبّرونا عن الفرائض التي ذكرها الله (تع) في كتابه وأمر بالعمل بها نصاً. ولم يختلف الناس في تنزيلها وصحة فرضها ووجوبها، مثل الحج والجهاد والحدود والقصاص والأحكام في الدماء والفروج والأموال وإنصاف المظلوم وإيتاء ذي القربى حقّه وابن السبيل

---

١ في أ: أن ٢ ساقطة في أ ٣ ساقطة في ب ٤ ساقطة في أ ٥ في ب: أن ٦ في أ: هذا ٧ ساقطة في أ ٨ ساقطة في ب ٩ سورة النساء (٤):٤١-٤٢

والمسكين. هل يدرك ذلك أو يطاق العمل به إلا بالإمام العادل [٢١ أ]
الفاضِل العالِم؟ فلِمَ قلتم إن لأبي بكر ذلك بعد شهادكم على قوله:
« ليتني كنت سألت رسول الله (صلع) لِمن الأمر بعده »، وبعد قوله:
« قد رضيتُ لكم أحد هذين الرجلين، فبايعوا أيهما شئتم: أبا عبيدة بن
الجرّاح أو عمر بن الخطّاب »، وبعد قوله: أمّا بعد، فإن المسلمين
استخلفوني ورضوا بي، وبعد[١] قوله: « أقيلوني أقيلوني! » وبعد أخذه
من بيت مال المسلمين أجرته، وبعد قول عمر: « كانت بيعة أبي بكر
فلتة، وقى الله المسلمين[٢] شرّها فمن أرادكم على مثلها فاقتلوه »، وبعد
قول عمر: « إن أستخلِف فقد استخلف من هو خير مني »، يعني أبا
بكر، « وإن أترككم [٢١ ب] فقد تركّكم من هو خير مني » يعني النبي
صلى الله عليه وآله وسلم[٣]. وبعد قول أبي بكر: « ولّيتكم ولست
بخيركم »، ولم يقل: إن الله تعالى[٤] ولأنّي أموركم وأمرني[٥]
بسياستكم. وفي قوله: « ليتني كنت سألت رسول الله (صلع): < لمن
الأمر بعدك...> » دليل على[٦] علمه وعلمكم ومعرفتكم أن[٧] الله
ورسوله لم يجعلا[٨] إليه شيئاً من أمور الناس وأن لهذا الأمر صاحباً غيره
يحكم فيه بأمر الله وأمر رسوله(صلع)، هذا مع إجماعكم على أنه لا بد
للناس من إمام. فإذا كان لا بد منه كان واجباً وإذا كان واجباً لم يجز أن

---

١ في ب: وبعده   ٢ ساقطة في ب   ٣ ساقطة في ب   ٤ ساقطة في أ   ٥ في
ب: ولا أمرني   ٦ في ب: عليه وعلي   ٧ في ب: بأن   ٨ في ب: لم
يجعل

يتولّى نصبه وإقامته إلا الله ورسوله . وأبو بكر مقرٌّ بأن الله ورسوله [٢٢ أ]
لم يقدّماه ولا نصّباه ولا أمرّاه .

ثم إن رسول الله (صلع) عقد لأسامة بن زيد عليه وعلى صاحبه ولم
يُعقَد لهما على أسامة بن زيد . فأيّهما(١) كان أحق وأولى من طريق النظر
والاختيار: من عَقَدَ له رسول الله (ص)، أو من عقد عليه وعقدتم(٢) له
ووليتموه؟ وكيف جاز لأبي بكر أن يكون أميراً على أسامة بن زيد وقد
جعل الله أسامة اميراً عليه؟ لأن رسول الله (صلع) لم يأتِ من ذلك إلا
ما(٣) أمره الله به . وكيف حلّ لكم أن تحلّوا عقداً عقده الله ورسوله
وتردّوا أمراً قد حكم الله به؟ وتزعمون أن الذي رأيتم من رد أبي بكر من
جيش أسامة ونصبه إماماً [٢٢ ب] خير من الذي رآه الله ورسوله من إنفاذه
في الجيش مع صاحبه . وما تنكرون أنّ كان قد أخطأ رسول الله (صلع)
في ترك الإمامة(٤) أو لم ينصّبه أن يكون قد أخطأ في كل شيء؛ لأن
جواز الخطأ عليه في شيء واحد دليل على جواز(٥) خطأه في كل شيء،
وأعوذ بالله من هذا القول(٦) فكيف! لم تنكروا ذلك عليه؟ ولم تركتم
مناظرته وتذكيره؟ وكيف لم تختاروا رجلاً لم يأمره رسول الله بإنفاذه في
جيش أسامة 'بن زيد'(٧) ؟ إذ كان في المسلمين من يصلح لذلك الأمر
عندكم . أوَ ما كان النبي (صلع) يعلم ما علمتم فيختاره للموضع الذي
اخترتموه له أو يخلفه فلا يأمر بإنفاذه في الجيش لِمَا [٢٣ أ] عنده من

---

١ في أ: إيما   ٢ في ب: فعقدتم   ٣ ساقطة في أ   ٤ في ب: الإمام
٥ ساقطة في ب   ٦ في أ: وكيف   ٧ ساقطة في أ

القيام والمصلحة للناس؟

وحيث[١] قد أمره مع الجيش، فلا يخلو ﴿من أن يكون قد﴾[٢] أصاب وأخطأتم أو قد أخطأ وأصبتم. ويقال لهم: خبِّرونا[٣]: هل أصبتم ما عند الله بنصبكم مَن نصَّبتم وبفعلكم ما فعلتم، أو أخطأتم؟ فإن كنتم قد أصبتم فقد أخطأ رسول الله (صلع) – وحاشاه – وإن كنتم قد[٤] أخطأتم – وذلك أولى بكم[٥]– فقد أصاب رسول الله (صلع). فكيف[٦] تركتم سنّة رسول الله (صلع) بزعمكم وأخذتم بما رأيتم؟ وكيف علمتم أن الذي فعله رسول الله (صلع) كان خطأً ومعصية وأن الذي فعلتم كان صواباً وطاعةً في إقامتكم مَن[٧] أقمتم؟ وهل تشهدون على رسول الله (صلع) بالخطأ [٢٣ ب] ولأنفسكم بالصواب؟ ولا بد لكم في[٨] ذلك من جواب.

وجوب نص الرسول على الإمام

ثم يقال لهم: خبِّرونا[٩] إذا كان نصب الإمام مرفوعاً عن رسول الله (صلع)، فمن وضعه عليكم؟ وسؤالنا لكم في الإمام كسؤالنا لكم ولإخوانكم في الفتيا والأحكام والقضايا في الحلال والحرام وما قد نهى الله ورسوله عن التقدم فيه وعليه، والقول فيه بالظن وغير الحق. وقد لعن الله الحاكم بغير ما أنزل الله (تع)، وسمّاه كافراً وظالماً وفاسقاً، وذلك

---

[١] في أ: وحين   [٢] ساقطة في ب   [٣] في أ: أخبرونا   [٤] ساقطة في ب   [٥] في ب: وكيف   [٦] في ب: وكيف   [٧] في أ: ما   [٨] في ب: من   [٩] في أ: أخبرونا

كله من دينكم وإليه تَدْعون وبه تحكمون. وقد سمعتم الله سبحانه يقول: ﴿وَلَا تَقُولُوا لِمَا تَصِفُ أَلْسِنَتُكُمُ الْكَذِبَ هَذَا حَلَالٌ وَهَذَا حَرَامٌ﴾[1] وقال ﴿إِنَّ الَّذِينَ يَفْتَرُونَ﴾ [أ 24] عَلَى اللَّهِ الْكَذِبَ لَا يُفْلِحُونَ﴾[2] وقال (تع): ﴿وَلَا تَقْفُ مَا لَيْسَ لَكَ بِهِ عِلْمٌ﴾[3]، وقال (تع): ﴿لَا تَقُولُوا عَلَى اللَّهِ إِلَّا الْحَقَّ﴾[4]، وقال ﴿قَدْ خَابَ مَنِ افْتَرَى﴾[5] ظلماً.[6] ومثل هذا كثير.

ويقال لهم: خبّرونا لِمَ تركتم الاقتداء برسول الله في ترك الإمام وإسقاط فرضه وحكمه عنكم بزعمكم؟ فإن قالوا الأمة لا تصلح إلا بالإمام[7] ولا يقوم الدين ولا يتمّ الفرض إلا به؛ وفي تركه فساد الدين وهلاك الأمة والناس أجمعين وزوال الفرض. قلنا: فإن كان رسول الله (صلع) يعلم[8] من ذلك ما علمتم وتركَهُ متعمداً، أليس هذا صفة الجائر الظالم لأمته؟ وإن كان لا يعلم من ذلك ما علمتم فهذه [ب 24] صفة الجاهل بأمر الله (ع ج) والمقصّر في دينه، فأيكم أحق وأولى بهذه الصفة، أنتم أم رسول الله (صلع)؟

ويقال للذين احتجّوا لأبي بكر بزعمهم أن بلالاً أتاهم عن أمر عائشة أن مُرُوا أبا بكر فليصلِّ بالناس. قلنا: أرأيتم لو أن الله ورسوله أوجب على

---

[1] سورة النحل (١٦):١١٦   [2] النحل (١٦):١١٦ [3] الإسراء (١٧):٣٦ [4] النساء (٤): ١٧١   [5] طه (٢٠):٦١   [6] ساقطة في أ: قد يكون الناسخ خلط بين الآية ٦١ من سورة طه والآية ١١١ من السورة نفسها التي تقول ﴿وَقَدْ خَابَ مَنْ حَمَلَ ظُلْمًا﴾ [7] في أ: بإمام   [8] في ب: قد يعلم

الخلق قبول قول عائشة، أكنتم قابلي قول بلال على عائشة؟ هذا على أن
بلالاً^(١) عندكم أعدل الخلق وأفضله. فكيف والأمر يجري عندكم
والحكم يجري منكم على أنه لو جاءت عائشة ومعها مائة من
المهاجرات المؤمنات يشهدن^(٢) في درهمين لم تجز شهادتهن حتى
يكون معهن رجلٌ عدل. ولو أن عائشة أتت [٢٥أ] قوماً فقالت لهم، إما
عن نفسها وإما عن رسول الله (صلع)، أن مُروا أبا بكر فليُصلِّ بالناس،
ما وجب عليهم قبول ذلك منها إلا بحجة.

ثم يقال لهم: أرأيتم لو أن النبي (صلع) ناداكم فأسمع صغيركم
وكبيركم أن مُروا أبا بكر فليُصلِّ بالناس وفعلتم ذلك عن أمره، ألم يكن
في خروجه يتهادى بين علي بن أبي طالب (صلع) والفضل بن عباس بن
عبد المطّلب، ورجلاه تخدّان الأرض خدّاً، حتى عزله وصرفه عن
الموضع الذي كان فيه ما يدلّ على إنكاره ما فعلتم من تقدمته^(٣)؟
فأيها^(٤) أبيَن وأظهر عندكم: ما فعله رسول الله (صلع) من عزله وصرفه
[٢٥ب] وتأخيره، أو ما فعلتم من تقديمه؟ هذا وليس الشهرة في ولايته
وتقديمه في عزله وصرفه وتأخيره من الله تعالى ورسوله. ثم قد
علمتم أنه (صلع) خرج على حالٍ لا يجب على أحدٍ من الناس أن
يخرج على مثلها من العلة والضعف. فكيف جاز لكم أن تزعموا أن
إمامته وولايته من الله^(٥) لا من الأمة جميعاً، وإنما قام بمقام يصلح

في ب: بلال   ٢ في ب: يشهدون   ٣ في ب: تقديمه   ٤ في ب: فأيما   ٥ في
أ: من الله له

عندكم للبار والفاجر، فلم يرضه الله له ولا رسوله ولا تركّكم في شبهة من أمره. فكيف رضيتموه، بزعمكم - إذ لم يرضه رسول الله (صلع)، أو لم تردّوا‎(١)‎ عزله ورده عن تبليغ الصحيفة من سورة براءة كما [٢٦ أ] رويتم عزله عن الصلاة؟ أولم ترووا أن النبي (صلع) 'لم يصلّ خلفه، وقد رويتم أنّه‎(٢)‎ صلى خلف عبد الرحمن بن عوف، وهو عندكم دونه، وأمر عتّاب بن أُسيد أن يصلي بالناس بمكة ورسول الله (صلع) مقيم بالأبطح وابن أم مكتوم وأبو مجدودة‎(٣)‎ كانا يصلّيان بالناس وخلقٌ كثير لا يُحصى عددهم. على أن التقدمة للصلاة ما صحت له ولا صحت الدعوى‎(٤)‎ بذلك أيضاً. ولو صحت ما وجب له فضل ولا علم. وكيف يوجب ذلك له وكلكم يزعم أنه لو قام للصلاة أو قدّم‎(٥)‎ غيره فصلّى بالناس لكان ذلك‎(٦)‎ جائزاً‎(٧)‎ والصلاة تامة، مع علمكم وإقراركم أن الإمامة وخلافة الرسول (صلع) لا تصلح لكم. فكيف أثبتم ما يجزي فيه [٢٦ ب] أضعفكم ديناً وإيماناً وفقهاً ورأياً وتدبيرا على ما لا يجوز إلا أفضلكم وأعلمكم فيه وأفقهكم وأبصركم بأمور الدين والدنيا. فتدبّروا ما قد شرحته تجدوه كما وصفت و﴿لَا قُوَّةَ إِلَّا بِاللَّهِ﴾‎(٨)‎ ﴿الْعَلِيُّ الْعَظِيمُ﴾‎(٩)‎

ويقال لهم: خبّرونا أيما كان أعم نفعاً وأبْيَنَ صلاحاً وأجمع للشمل

‎١‎ في ب: ترووا   ‎٢‎ ساقطة في أ   ‎٣‎ في ب: مجدورة   ‎٤‎ في أ: الدعوة   ‎٥‎ في ب: قدوم   ‎٦‎ ساقطة في أ   ‎٧‎ في ب: جائز   ‎٨‎ سورة الكهف (١٨):٣٩   ‎٩‎ سورة البقرة (٢):٢٥٥

وأبعد من الفُرقة والاختلاف وأصلح في البدء والعاقبة، أن ينصب الله[1] ورسوله إماماً فنعرفه كما نعرف آباءنا وأبناءنا فيطيعه منا من يطيع الله ورسوله ويعصيه منا من يعصي الله ورسوله ﴿لِيَهْلِكَ مَنْ هَلَكَ عَنْ بَيِّنَةٍ وَيَحْيَا مَنْ حَيَّ [٢٧ أ] عَنْ بَيِّنَةٍ﴾[2] ويأمرنا[3] بنصبه وإقامته، ويفرض علينا طاعته مع علمه بما فينا من التحاسد والتباغض والغل والطعن والتعادي والنفاق، مع العجز عن بلوغ الواجب من استخراجه. فإن قالوا: بل نصب الله لنا ورسوله لأن اختياره لنا خيرٌ من اختيارنا لأنفسنا وأصلح في البدء والعقبى فيه. وفي اختياره أيضاً لنا قَطْع التحكم والاختلاف وإلزام التعبّد.. قلنا: فلأية علّة لم يفعل الله بكم ولا رسوله ما هو خير في البدء والعقبى؟ أترون أن الله ورسوله أرادا هلاككم وفسادكم وتباعُدَ ما بينكم؟ فقد علمتم الآن يقيناً أن الله ورسوله لم يفعلا بكم ما كان خيراً لكم في عاجل [٢٧ ب] الدنيا والآخرة بزعمكم. وأنهما أرادا[4] هلاككم وفسادكم والإغراء بينكم. وهذا مذهبكم وبذلك تشهدون على الله وعلى رسوله (صلع). إذ لا حجة لهما عليكم في نصب الإمام ولا في شرح ما فُرِضَ عليكم من الحلال والحرام. إذ كان عندكم غير مشروح. والقصة عليكم في الإمام كالقصة عليكم في الفتيا في الفرائض والأحكام والحلال والحرام. وهذا ردّ القرآن مجرّد غير مشكل.

---

[1] في أ: « وأبعد من الفرقة والاختلاف وأصلح في البدء والعاقبة أن ينصب الله » مرددة مرتين   [2] الأنفال (٨): ٤٢   [3] في ب: أي يأمرنا   [4] في ب: أراد

ويقال لهم وللذين زعموا أن النبي (صلع) قدّمه للصلاة فقدمناه[1] وجعلناه إماما. خبّرونا: هل كان يجوز للنبي (صلع) أن يؤمّر[2] رجلاً يصلّي بالناس وفيهم من هو خيرٌ منه وأقرأ للقرآن وأعلم بالحلال والحرام وأبصر [٢٨ أ] بالتدبير والسياسة؟ فإن قالوا لا يجوز أن يصلي بهم رجلا وفيهم من هو خير منه وأقرأ للقرآن وأعلم بالحلال والحرام وأبصر[3] بالتدبير وما يحتاج الناس إليه من أمر الدنيا والآخرة[4]؟ قلنا لهم: فهذا خلاف ما قد سبق به إجماعكم، وخلاف ما جئتم به عن النبي (صلع) في الرخصة في الصلاة خلف كل بَرّ وفاجر. وفي قولهم هذا دليل على أن عمرو بن العاص وعبد الرحمن بن عوف وأسامة بن زيد وعلي بن أبي طالب وعتّاب بن أسيد وابن أم مكتوم وأبا مجدورة[5] وكل من صلّى بالناس في عصر النبي (صلع) بأمر النبي خير من أبي بكر وعمر، إذ كان النبي (صلع) أمرهم بالتقدّم بالصلاة نصاً. فإن قالوا: بلى، يجوز أن يقدّم النبي (صلع) رجلا يصلي بالناس وفيهم من هو خير منه وأقرأ للقرآن وأعلم بالحلال والحرام، قلنا لهم: فما [٢٨ ب] حجتكم في تقديم أبي بكر على الناس جميعاً حتى وليّتموه أمراً ما كان للنبي (صلع) أن يتقدم فيه ولا يتأخّر إلا ﴿بِإِذْنِ رَبِّهِ﴾[6]. وإذا جعل الله ذلك إليه لم يُجز أن يولي على القوم إلا أفضلهم وأقرأهم للقرآن وأعلمهم بالحلال والحرام وأبصرهم بالتدبير والسياسة. لأن الحكيم لا يفرض على الناس طاعة من هم أطوع

---

[1] في أ: فقد قدمناه   [2] في أ وب: يأمر   [3] ساقطة في أ   [4] في ب: والدين   [5] في ب: مجدودة   [6] سورة سبأ (٣٤):١٢؛ سورة الأعراف (٧):٥٨.

له منه ولا يأمرهم بالانقياد لمن هم أعلم بدين الله منه ولا يحوجهم إلى
من هو محتاج إليهم. وقد يجوز عندكم في التقدمة بالصلاة رجلٌ من
عُرض الناس، فكيف جعلتم ما يجوز عندكم فيه ويجزي به رجل قياساً
على ما لا يجوز فيه إلا من لا مِثل له فيكم ولا نظير. ويقال لهم: [٢٩ أ]
خبّرونا هل كان يجوز للنبي (صلع) أن يقدّم للصلاة بكم من هو دونكم
في الفضل والعلم والسبق إلى الإسلام وقراءة القرآن والمعرفة بالله
وبالحلال(١) والحرام؟ فإن قالوا: لا يجوز له ذلك ولا يكون هذا منه، قلنا
لهم: قولكم هذا يدل على أن عمرو بن العاص وعلي بن أبي طالب
وأسامة بن زيد وعبد الرحمن بن عوف وعتاب بن أسيد وابن أم مكتوم
وأبا مجدودة(٢) خيرٌ من أبي بكر وعمر، لأن رسول الله (صلع) أمّرهم
على أبي بكر وعمر وقدّمهم للصلاة. ويدل قولكم أيضاً على أن صهيباً
عند عمر بن الخطّاب أفضل الأمة، إذ أمره بالصلاة عليه وقدّمه للصلاة
بالناس جميعاً(٣)، ويدل على أن أبا طلحة كان أفضل أهل [٢٩ ب] دهر
عمر بن الخطاب، لأن عمر حكّمه في دمائهم وأشعارهم وأبشارهم،
وفيهم علي بن أبي طالب وعثمان بن عفّان والزبير وطلحة وسعد وعبد
الرحمن وفلان وفلان. وذلك كله بحضرة المهاجرين والأنصار. فإن
قالوا: بلى يجوز للنبي (صلع) أن يقدّم للصلاة بالناس من فيه(٤) خير منه
وأقرأ للقرآن وأعلم بالحلال(٥) والحرام، قلنا: فإذا كان هذا جائزاً من

١ في ب: بالحلال ٢ في ب: مجدورة ٣ ساقطة في ب ٤ في ب: فيهم ٥ في
ب: بالحلال والحلال

رسول الله (صلع)، فما حاجتكم في فضل أبي بكر وعمر؟ إذ كانت دلالتكم على فضله قد بطلت، لأن الدلالة التي استدللتم بها على فضله كانت التقديم للصلاة فقط. والتقدمة للصلاة عندكم الآن لا توجب فضلاً ولا علماً [30 أ] ولا سبقاً إلى الإسلام ولا معرفة بالحلال والحرام. هذا لو سلّم لكم أن النبي (صلع) قدّمه للصلاة مع علمكم أن الناس مختلفون عليكم في صلاة أبي بكر بالناس. ذكرتم أن بلالاً أتاه(¹) عن أمر عائشة، فهذا الخبر في نفسه لا يصلح(²) بلا برهان ولا حجة ولا بيّنة. وقد زعم أكثر الناس أن النبي (صلع) لما بلغه ما صنع القوم في تقدمة أبي بكر غضب غضباً شديداً وقال لعائشة: « أنتنّ! صويحبات يوسف! » ثم خرج على حال لا يخرج على مثلها من العلّة والضعف حتى أزاله عن القبلة وصرفه عن الموضع الذي وضعه القوم فيه. وهذا يدلّ على شدّة إنكاره على أن هذا المقام [30 ب] يصلح(³) للجمهور والعامة والبر والفاجر أيضاً عندكم دون الخاصة. فكيف جعلتم ما يصلح للعامة منكم دون الخاصة قياساً على ما لا يصلح له إلا من لا مثل له ولا نظير فيكم. وأيضاً إنه لو ثبت أن النبي (صلع) قدّمه للصلاة لم توجب له الصلاة فضلاً ولا علماً ولا عملاً، إذ كان (ع م) قد قدّم الصلاة بالناس من هو دون الجماعة في الفضل والعلم وقراءة القرآن والمعرفة بالحلال والحرام. ولا يجوز أن يستخلف الرسول (صلع) على الناس إلا أعلمهم وأفضلهم وأخصّهم بوصيّته وخلافته، وأقومهم بأمر(⁴) الصلاة والدين

---

¹ في ب: أتاهم   ² في ب: لا يصح   ³ في ب: يصح   ⁴ في أ: بأمره

والدنيا، يقوم فيهم مقامه ويحذو مثاله. كذلك يكون وصيه وخليفته.

عدم جواز استخلاف المفضول بوجود الفاضل

[٣١ أ] ويقال لهم: خبّرونا، هل يجوز عندكم للنبي (صلع) أن يستخلف عليكم رجلاً وفي الجماعة مَن هو خير منه وأعلم بالحلال والحرام والفرائض والأحكام؟ فإن قالوا: بلى يجوز أن يستخلف المفضول العاجز على الفاضل الحازم. قلنا لهم: فلا حجة لكم في تفضيل أبي بكر على غيره، إذا كان النبي (صلع) يرى أن يستخلف من هو دون أبي بكر على فضله بمائة درجة ودونكم جميعاً. وما فضله بذلك المقام الذي يصلح لكل الناس عندكم؟ فإن قالوا لا يجوز للنبي (صلع) أن يستخلف رجلاً وفي القوم من هو خير منه ولا أفضل ولا أعلم بالحلال والحرام وما يحتاج الناس إليه من أمر الدين والدنيا [٣١ ب] قلنا لهم فهذا فرق ما بين الصلاة وبين الإمامة والقيام بأمر الأمة والاستخلاف. فلِمَ حجرتم على رسول الله (صلع) وأقمتم مقامه رجلاً ليس بأعلمكم ولا أفضلكم ولا أقرأكم ولا أعملكم[١] بالفرائض والأحكام وفَرقٍ ما بين الحلال والحرام؟ إذ كان كذلك رسول الله (صلع) عندكم ليس بأعلمكم ولا بأفضلكم ولا بأقرأكم[٢] ولا أبصركم بالحلال والحرام؟ فهذا مثله ونظيره ويقوم عندكم مقامه؟ أو كان لا مثل له ولا نظير؟ فلِمَ جعلتم قياس ما لا مثْل له ولا نظير مثل قياس من له 'المثل والنظير'[٣]؟

ويقال لهم: خبّرونا، هل يجوز أن يقوم بكم بعد الرسول (صلع) رجل

---

[١] في أ: أعلمكم   [٢] في أ: أقرأكم   [٣] في ب: مثل ونظير

منافق أو كافر في الباطن؟ فإن قالوا: نعم، [32 أ] قلنا لهم: فما حاجتكم في تفضيل مَن يقوم مقام النبي (صلع)؟ إذ(١) كان يصلح لذلك المقام رجل منافق أو كافر في الباطن، وهذا مقام يصلح لأشر الناس؟ فإن قالوا لا يجوز ذلك، قلنا لهم: فهل يجوز أن تختاروا رجلاً منافقاً في الباطن مؤمناً في الظاهر؟ (أو مؤمناً في الظاهر)(٢) كافراً في الباطن؟ فإن قالوا هذا لا يجوز علينا، قلنا لهم: فأنتم تعلمون من الغيب ما لا(٣) يعلمه رسول الله (صلع)؟ لأن الرسول (ع م) قد مكث حيناً لا يعلم بهم حتى عرّفه الله ذلك منهم، فإن قالوا: بلى(٤)، يجوز ذلك علينا، ويمكن أن نقف باختيارنا على رجل ظاهره الإيمان وباطنه الكفر والنفاق، قلنا لهم: فَمِثْل هذا يجوز [32 ب] عندكم على الله وعلى(٥) رسوله؟ فإن قالوا: نعم، قلنا: فالله ورسوله لا يعلمان مِن ذلك إلا دون ما تعلمون؟ فإن(٦) قالوا: لا يجوز ذلك على الله ورسوله؛ فلا يختار الله ورسوله للمسلمين والقيام بأمر الدين إلا مَن لا مِثْل له ولا نظير، ظاهره كباطنه وسره كعلانيته، لأنه عالِم الغيوب لا يخفى عليه خافية فيختاره على علم على العالمين. قلنا: فمن أمَرَكم بالاختيار؟ مع عجزكم عن درك الصواب فيمن يصلح للدين والقيام بأمر المسلمين ومن يحتج به على العالمين؟ وهو يقول: ﴿لَا تُقَدِّمُوا بَيْنَ يَدَيِ اللَّهِ وَرَسُولِهِ وَاتَّقُوا اللَّهَ إِنَّ اللَّهَ سَمِيعٌ عَلِيمٌ﴾(٧)

ويقال لهم: خبّرونا كيف كانت القصة في نصب [33 أ] الإمام وفرض

---

١ في أ: أن ٢ ساقطة في ب ٣ في أ: لم ٤ في ب: بل
٥ ساقطة في ب ٦ ساقطة في أ ٧ سورة الحجرات (٤٩):١

طاعته عليكم: قبل النصب أو بعده؟ بالنص تنصبونه أو بالاستخراج؟ فإن كان بالنص، فمن هو؟ وإن كان بالاستخراج، فمن فرض عليكم طاعته؟ ومن يتولّى نَصْبَه وإقامته؟ وذلك شيء إلى جماعتكم أم إلى بعضكم دون البعض؟ أم إلى قوم يُعرفون بأسمائهم؟ أم إلى أهل بلده دون بلد؟ أم إلى عدد يُعرف مبلغهم؟ فإن كان إلى جماعتكم، فمن يضبط عددهم مع تبيانهم وتباعد من بينهم؟ وإن كان إلى قومٍ يُعرفون بأسمائهم وأنسابهم، فمن هم؟ وأين هم؟ وإن كان إلى أهل بلدٍ دون بلدٍ، فهل يجوز ذلك لغيرهم ؟ أم لا يجوز ذلك إلّا لهم؟ وإن كانوا بالعدد، فكم ذلك العدد؟ وهل يخلو ذلك العدد أن يكون شفعاً أو وِتْراً؟ فإن كان [٣٣ ب] شفعاً، قلنا: فهل يجوز أن يكون وِتراً؟ وإن قالوا: لا يجوز ذلك، قلنا لهم: فمن جعله وِتراً أو شفعاً؟ وهل[١] يجوز في ذلك العدد الزيادةُ والنقصان؟ فإن قالوا: نعم، يجوز أن ننقص واحداً، قلنا وكذلك يجوز أن ننقص واحداً بعد واحد. لأن حكم الواحد مثل حكم الاثنين وحكم الثلاثة أبداً حتى يبلغ إلى واحد.

ومن جعل الأمر في نصب الإمام إلى ذلك الواحد، وإذا ثبت أن الأمر إلى واحد فقد بطل قولكم[٢]: رأينا كذا، ⟨وقلنا كذا وفعلنا كذا[٣]⟩، ومن جعل ذلك الواحد أحق بنصب الإمام من واحد غيره، وما الفرق بينه وبين غيره؟ وكذلك السؤال عليكم فيمن [٣٤ أ] جعل الأمر منكم إلى

جماعتكم، أو(١) إلى بعضكم دون بعض، أو(٢) إلى أهل بلد دون بلد، أو إلى قوم يُعرفون بأسمائهم وأنسابهم، أو(٣) إلى عدد – وإذا تكامل ذلك العدد نصبوا الإمام – أو إلى واحد دون الناس جميعاً. وذلك واحد بالنص ينصبه أم بالاختيار. ولا بد في كل قول قلتم وإلى مذهب ذهبتم من أن تأتوا على ما تدعون من ذلك بحجة من الله ورسوله. فهل من حجة أو برهان؟ وهل يردعكم ما ترون من فساد مذهبكم إلى الرجوع عن سوء الثناء على الله ورسوله؟ وهل في هذا بيان ﴿لِقَوْمٍ يَعْلَمُونَ﴾(٤)

ويقال لهم: خبرونا: ما كانت العلّة من الله ورسوله(٥) [٣٤ ب] في نصب الإمام وإلزام فرضه؟ فإن قالوا: نظراً منه لخلقه وتعبّداً لهم(٦) بطاعته وطاعة رسوله وطاعة من أمرهم بطاعته، قلنا فما باله الآن لا ينظر لهم ذلك النظر ولا يتعبدهم ذلك التعبد؟ ما(٧) الذي يمنعه من حسن نظره؟ أترونه كان لهم في ذلك العصر والزمان أنظر لهم من 'هذا العصر والزمان؟ أم ترونه الآن(٨) أنظر لهم من حينئذٍ؟ وما الذي أزال عنهم فرض الطاعة للإمام المنصوص عليه؟ فإذا كان الإمام بعد النبي بالنص فقد نرى الآن بطلان ذلك النص، وإن كان بالاختيار من الأمة وجماعة المسلمين فهذا والنص في البطلان سواء. فقد زال [٣٥ أ] التعبد وسقط الفرض وجرت الأمور على عصيان الله ومخالفته وتعدّي أمره وحدوده.

ويقال لهم ألسنا وإياكم مجتمعين على أنه لا يخلوا أمر الإمام من

وجوه ثلاثة: إما أن الله قد نصبه وافترض على الخلق طاعته وأمرهم بالانقياد لحكمه والقبول منه وجعل الحكم في الدم والفرج والمال والقيادات إليه دون غيره ولم يجعل لأحد أن ينظر عليه ولا معه – إذ كان الناظر عليه فوقه والناظر معه مثله. فإذا(١) كان في القوم من هو فوقه والمولّى عليهم(٢) دونه كان ذلك مفسداً لدينهم ودنياهم، لأن الله لا يحتج بالأقل على الأكثر ولا بالجاهل [٣٥ ب] على العالم ولا بالمفضول على الفاضل والا بالكافر على المؤمن.

وإذا(٣) كان في القوم مثله لم يكن لهم حاجة إلى مثلهما لأن الحكم المفتري على الناس غير مسلّم سيّما إذا كانوا لا يرون له فضلا عليهم في دين ولا دنيا. وهذا والأول في سقوط الحجة سواء؛ فإذا(٤) كان فوقهم فلا بد أن يكون أفضلهم وأعلمهم بالدين وأبصرهم بالسياسة والتدبير إذ(٥) كانوا مأمورين بطاعته وترك مخالفته وقبول خبره. وفي نصب الله له قطع الحكم وإلزام التعبد والطاعة له فيطيعه من يطيع الله ورسوله(٦) ويعصيه من يعصي الله ورسوله ﴿لِيَهْلِكَ مَنْ هَلَكَ عَنْ بَيِّنَةٍ وَيَحْيَا [٣٦ أ] مَنْ حَيَّ عَنْ بَيِّنَةٍ﴾(٧). فإن أقروا بهذا أقروا أنهم كلهم قد عصوا الله ورسوله بنظرهم مع الإمام في الدم والفرج والمال وخلافهم عليه في ذلك كله في حياته وبعد وفاته. والخلاف على الإمام العادل المفروض الطاعة كالخلاف على رسول الله (صلع). وسبيل هذه الأمة سبيل أختها(٨) في

---

١ في ب: وإذا   ٢ في أ: عليه   ٣ في أ وب: وإذ   ٤ في أ: وإذا   ٥ في ب: إذا   ٦ ساقطة في أ   ٧ سورة الأنفال (٨):٤٢   ٨ في أ: أخرها

النظر بلا حجة والقول بلا برهان والحكم بالظن والشهادة على الله فيما أحلَّ وحَرَّم بغير الحق، كأن لم يسمعوا قول الله (ع ج)، ﴿وَلَا تَقُولُوا لِمَا تَصِفُ أَلْسِنَتُكُمُ الْكَذِبَ هَذَا حَلَالٌ وَهَذَا حَرَامٌ لِتَفْتَرُوا عَلَى اللَّهِ الْكَذِبَ﴾[١] وقوله ﴿وَقَدْ خَابَ مَنِ افْتَرَى﴾[٢] وقوله ﴿وَلَا تَقْفُ مَا لَيْسَ لَكَ بِهِ عِلْمٌ إِنَّ السَّمْعَ [36 ب] وَالْبَصَرَ وَالْفُؤَادَ كُلُّ أُولَئِكَ كَانَ عَنْهُ مَسْئُولًا﴾[٣]، وقوله ﴿وَلَا تَقُولُوا عَلَى اللَّهِ إِلَّا الْحَقَّ﴾[٤]، وقوله ﴿إِنِ الْحُكْمُ إِلَّا لِلَّهِ﴾[٥]، وقوله ﴿فَالْحُكْمُ لِلَّهِ الْعَلِيِّ الْكَبِيرِ﴾[٦].

أو يكون الإمام منصوباً لنا ومأموراً بسياستنا ونحن غير مأمورين بطاعته ولا محرَّم علينا خلافُه ومعصيتُه ولنا أن ننظر عليه ومعه ونتأمل أحكامه وفتياه وقضاياه. فما كان صواباً عندنا أمضيناه وما كان خطأ رددناه. فهذا حينئذ غير مفروض الطاعة ولا محظور الخلاف[٧] والمعصية ولا مؤمر[٨] على الرعية. وهذا لا يجوز على الله فيمن يختاره للدين ويحتج به على العالمين ويجعله الحَكَم على الناس أجمعين والفاصل [37 أ] بين المحقين والمبطلين. وما الحاجة بالناس إلى إمام غير مفروض الطاعة ولا محظور الخلاف والمعصية ولا مأمون السريرة ولا يقوم بأمر الدين والدنيا إلا كما وصفتم. وما الفرق بين الراعي والرعية؟ فإذا كان الأمر كذلك فليس لقوله

---

[١] سورة النحل (١٦):١١٦ [٢] سورة طه (٢٠):٦١ [٣] سورة الإسراء (١٧):٣٧ [٤] سورة النساء (٤):١٧١؛ في ب: ولا تقولوا على الله ما لا تعلمون [٥] سورة الأنعام (٦):٥٧؛ أنظر أيضاً سورة يوسف (١٢):٤٠ [٦] سورة غافر (٤٠):١٢ [٧] في أ: الخلافة [٨] في أ وب: مامر

(تع): ﴿أَطِيعُوا اللَّهَ وَأَطِيعُوا الرَّسُولَ وَأُولِي الْأَمْرِ مِنكُمْ﴾[١] معنى، ولا لقوله ﴿فَإِن تَنَازَعْتُمْ فِي شَيْءٍ فَرُدُّوهُ إِلَى اللَّهِ﴾[٢] معنى. وكل واحد يقول: سأنزل مثل ما أنزل الله.

ويقال لهم خبرونا، هل تشهدون على رسول الله (صلع) أنه استخلف عليكم رجلاً بعينه تعرفونه باسمه ونسبه يقوم فيكم مقامه؟ أو تشهدون أنه[٣] خلاّكم [٣٧ ب] وترككم – ولا بد من شهادتكم أنه خلاّكم –فلم يستخلف[٤] عليكم رجلاً بعينه تعرفونه[٥] باسمه ونسبه. فإن كان لم ينصب[٦] ولم يستخلف عليكم أحداً فاتركوا عنادكم الإمامَ ونصبَهُ، فإن 'لنا ولكم برسول الله أسوة حسنة'[٧]. فإن كان قد نصب رجلاً فأسقطوا الآن[٨] ذكر الاحتجاج في[٩] نَصْبِكم من نَصَبْتُم من طريق العدالة والتفضيل والتقدمة للصلاة وغير ذلك. ثم أَسقطوا قوله[١٠]: « أما بعد فإن المسلمين قد استخلفوني ورضوا بي ». وقولَهُ: « وُلِّيتُكُم[١١] ولست بخيركم ». وأُلزموا لأنفسكم الخطأَ والعصيان لله ورسوله في ترككم المنصوبَ لكم والرغبة عنه والخلاف عليه والنّظر معه فيما لم يجعله الله ولا رسولُه [٣٨ أ] لأحد سواه.

وفي اصطلاحكم على نصب رجل لم ينصبه الله ولا رسوله دليلٌ[١٢]

---

[١] سورة النساء (٤):٥٩ [٢] سورة النساء (٤):٥٩ [٣] في أ: أن [٤] في أ: ويستخلف [٥] ساقطة في ب [٦] ساقطة في أ [٧] إشارة إلى الآية القرآنية ﴿لَقَدْ كَانَ لَكُمْ فِي رَسُولِ اللَّهِ أُسْوَةٌ حَسَنَةٌ﴾ سورة الأحزاب (٣٣):٢١ [٨] في ب: لإن [٩] في ب: من [١٠] في أ: لقوله [١١] ساقطة في أ [١٢] في أ: دليلاً

على خلافكم على الله ورسوله فيمن نصب لكم إذا كنتم قد أجمعتم على أن الله لم يهملكم وأن الرسول لم يترككُم حتى نصب لكم رجلاً إليه مفزعُكم. وهذا هو العدل من فعل الله ورسوله. وترجعون إلى الطعن على رسول الله (صلع) وسوء الثناء على الله سبحانه في أنه خلّاكم وأهملكم وتركَكم. وبأي الأمرين أقررتم فلا حجة لكم ولا عذر عند الله ولا عند رسوله في نصبكم من نصبتم، لا عن أمر الله وأمر رسوله.

من إمام هذا العصر؟

ويقال لهم: خبرونا، أبحكمٍ من الله ورسوله في نصب الإمام في هذا الدهر؟ [٣٨ ب] وهل يلزم الخلقَ فرضُ الطاعةِ لأحدٍ معروف؟ فإن قالوا: نعم، وسمّوا رجلاً، قلنا: فمن افترض طاعته؟ ومتى أمر الله ورسوله بذلك؟ ثم ما صِفتُه: بَرّاً أو فاجراً؟ فإن قالوا: بَرّاً، وجب أن يكون الإمام خير الخلق وأفضله، وإن قالوا فاجراً، أبطلوا طاعتَه وأسقطوا حجّته، لأن الله لا يَحتَجّ بالفاجر على المؤمن ولا بالجاهل على العالِم ولا بالمفضول على الفاضل.

ويقال لهم: خبّرونا(١)، أيما أولى بنا وبكم؟ أن نقبل قول أبي بكر وحكمَهُ فيما خالف فيه عمر ومَن قال بقول عمر من المهاجرين والأنصار وجلّة أصحاب النبي (صلع) أو قول عمر ومن ذكرنا؟ فإن قالوا: نقبل قول أبي بكر وحده، [٣٩ أ] فإن الحق ما حكم به؛ قلنا: أرأيتم؟ أنْ لو جاءكم أبو بكر ولا أحد معه فشهد على درهم واحد، أكنتم قابلي

---

١ ساقطة في أ

شهادته؟ فإن قالوا: نعم، فقد خرجوا مما عليه الجماعة وخالفوا حكم الكتاب والسنة، وإن قالوا: لا نقبل قول رجلٍ واحد ولا نجيز شهادته، فإن جاء عمر والذين معه من المهاجرين والأنصار شهدوا على ذلك الرجل بذلك الدرهم، أكنتم قابلي شهادتهم؟ فإن قالوا: نعم، قلنا: فهذا عمر والجماعة ومن قال بقولهم جميعاً قد فارقوا أبا بكر في أحكامه وفتياه وفرائضه، وذلك تخطئةً له وشهادةً منهم عليه أنه قد حكم بخلاف الحق، وهو عندكم مُزَكّى. والحكم بغير ما أنزل [٣٩ ب] الله يدعو إلى الكفر والفسوق والظلم، فلو كان الرجل عندكم إماماً ومفروض الطاعة، لاتّبع القوم حكمه وفتياه ولرضوا بقضاياه، إذ كان الله قد نصبه وأوجب على الخلق طاعته والقبول لقوله والانقياد لحكمه، ولا يجعل لأحد أن ينظر عليه ولا معه. وقد حَكَم في الدماء والفروج والأموال والقيادات.

وقد خالفه القوم وحكموا فيه(١) بغير ما حكم وقالوا بخلاف ما قال. ولن يخلو أمر القوم وأمرُهُ أن يكونوا علموا أنه ليس بإمام ولا مستحق لذلك المقام ولا فرض الله طاعته ولا أمر بولايته ولا نهى عن خلافه ومعصيته. وبعد أن علموا [٤٠ أ] أيضاً وشهدوا أنه قد حكم بغير الحق وبغير ما أنزل الله تعالى(٢) فمن ذلك خالفوه وهذا من فعلهم يدل على أن هذا اعتقادهم فيه. وتركهم الإنكار عليه(٣) دليل على ما ذهبوا إليه من ذلك الفعل. أو قد علموا يقيناً أنه الإمام الفاضل المستحق الصادق في خبره العالم القائم(٤) بأمر الدين والدنيا قد حكم بالحق وبما أنزل الله (تع)، ثم

خالفوه فيه إلى الضلال عن اليقين والمعرفة. فهم حينئذٍ ضُلَّال فسّاق بخلافهم على الإمام الفاضل العادل. فإن زعموا أنهم كانوا أولى بالحق فيما فعلوه من أبي بكر، قلنا: فاحكموا على أبي بكر بالخطأ والضلال، إذ تعدى حدود الله [40 ب] وحكم بغير ما أنزل الله. فإن[1] كان أبو بكر أولى بالحق فيما فعل فاحكموا على عمر والذين[2] معه بالعصيان لله والخلاف على الإمام العادل الفاضل. أو تزعموا أنه لا تبعة عليكم جميعاً فيما فعلتم؟ فنحن أيضاً، إن خالفنا الإمام العادل الفاضل[3] المفروض الطاعة فلا تبعة علينا؟ وكذلك إن (خالفنا الجماعة، وكذلك إن حكمنا بغير ما أنزل الله، وكذلك إن)[4] تعدينا حدود الله؟ ثم ليس الخلاف والإجماع إلا سواء على أهل القياس، ولا الطاعة ولا المعصية إلا سواء، ولا الكفر ولا الإيمان إلا سواء على قياسكم هذا، وإلا فالزموا كل فريق ما يلزمه، ثم أعلمونا أي الفريقين أصاب وأيهما أخطأ؟ وماذا عليهم من الله فيما [41 أ] فعلوا، وهل على الناس أن يقتدوا بإحدى الطائفتين أو يخالوهما[5]، ومع هذا فأعلمونا ما على من خالفهما من العقاب وما لمن وافقهما من الثواب. ثم ائتونا بالبرهان على ما تذكرونه[6] من ذلك. و﴿لَا قُوَّةَ إِلَّا بِاللَّهِ﴾[7] ﴿الْعَلِيُّ الْعَظِيمُ﴾[8].

ثم[9] يقال لهم: خبّرونا، هل رأيتم في الحقيقة رجلاً يطعن على أبي

---

[1] في ب: وأن   [2] في ب: ومن كان   [3] ساقطة في ب   [4] ساقطة في أ   [5] في أ: يخالفهما   [6] في ب: تذكرون   [7] سورة الكهف (١٨):٣٩   [8] سورة البقرة (٢):٢٥٥؛ سورة الشورى (٤٢):٤   [9] في ب: و

بكر وعمر؟ فإن قالوا: نعم. قلنا: فهل يخلو ذلك الرجل من أن يكون منكِراً لعقد ولايتهما أو تَقَدُّمَهما بين يدي الله ورسوله بلا حجة من الله ولا برهان، أو يكون قائلاً بإمامتهما ثم قد(١) خالفهما في الدم والفرج والمال والقيادات ورغب عن حكمهما وقال بخلاف ما قالا ودان [٤١ ب] بخلاف ما دانا. وهذا من أعظم الطعن عليهما لأنه ليس بين الحلال والحرام منزلة تصير إليهما، وإنما غاية الناس فيما تعبّدوا به أن يقولوا هذا حلال وهذا حرام؛ لا يجدون قولاً ثالثاً فيصيرون إليه.

ونقول فيما ادُّعي من إجماع الأمة على الرجلين أن الحجة قد قامت بكون ولايتهما بالحد الذي ذكرناه. ولم يُنقل عن رسول الله (صلع) الأمر(٢) بولايتهما ولا 'اجتمعت الأمة اليوم'(٣) إلا أن الأمّة اجتمعت عليهما رأياً لا نصاً عن رسول الله (صلع) كما اجتمعت 'عليهما بأنهما أولى(٤) ولا اجتمعت(٥) الأمة إلا أن الإمامة، بل الأمة في ذلك مختلفة والدعوى في ذلك [٤٢ أ] كاذبة، بوجود الاختلاف على ما ذكرنا في عصرنا.

ثم(٦) يقال لهم: خبّرونا، أليس قد فرض الله تعالى(٧) أموراً أوجبها نصاً وأغنى فيها عن الاستنباط والاستخراج والرأي(٨) والقياس، وأوجدها بأعيانها وصفاتها، ومع هذا لا يقوم ولا يكون ولا يصلح ولا يتم إلا بإمام. فلا بد من نعم. قلنا فلِمَ(٩) كان فرض ما نرى 'أنه لا يقوم(١٠) ولا

─────────────

١ ساقطة في ب   ٢ ساقطة في أ   ٣ في أ: اجتمعت اليوم   ٤ في أ: كما اجتمعت بأنها أولى   ٥ في أ: أجمعت   ٦ في ب: و   ٧ ساقطة في أ   ٨ ساقطة في ب   ٩ ف أ: فلمّا   ١٠ في أ: أنه ما لا يقوم

يتم ولا يكون إلا بإمام أولا من فرض نص الإمامة على الإمام بعينه حتى يغني فيه عن الاستنباط والاستخراج والرأي والقياس إذ كان المقيم[1] بالدين والحاكم على المسلمين وحجة رب العالمين.

وجوب النص بالإمامة كوجوب النص بالدعائم

ويقال لهم: خبرونا، هل كان يجوز عندكم أن يكلفنا الله (ع ج)[2] الصلاة [42 ب] والزكاة وغيرهما من طريق الاستنباط والارتياد من غير أن ينص بهما لنا؟ فمن قولهم لا، فيقال لهم: فلمَ لا كان الأمر الذي لا تقوم[3] هذه الأمور إلا به بأن[4] لا يجوز الأمر فيه إلا به من طريق الاستنباط والقياس والارتياد ولا تكون إلا نصاً، كما لا تكون هذه الأمور إلا نصاً.

ويقال لهم: أليس الرسول مأموراً بنص هذه الأمور من بعده؟ فلا بد من نعم. فيقال لهم: فلم ما[5] قلتم أنه مأمور بنص من لا يقوم هذه الأمور إلا به من حيث كان مأموراً بنصهما من بعده؟ فإن قال قائل إن النبي (صلع) لم ينص على كل الفرائض من ذلك لم ينص على أعيان الدراهم في الزكاة، ولكن أخبر أن في مائتي درهم خمسة دراهم. وكذلك لم ينص على شخص الإمام[6] [43 أ] ولكن دل على أنه إذا[7] كان عالماً فاضلاً، اتّخذ إماماً طُولب بالدليل على أن النبي أوجب إقامة إمام، وإن لم ينص على عينه، كما أوجب دراهم في الزكاة وإن لم يدل على

---

¹ في ب: القيم   ² في أ: ع م   ³ في أ: لا يقوم   ⁴ أولى بان   ⁵ في
ب: لا   ⁶ ساقطة في أ   ⁷ في أ: إذ

أعيانها بإجماع أو بخبر في غير إجماع. ولن يجدوا إلى ذلك سبيلاً. أو
'يقال لهم خبرونا لو'[١] كان واجباً على المسلمين إقامة إمام بأنْ فُرِضَت
عليهم هذه الأمور دون أن يكون واجباً على رسول الله (صلع) نصها
لهم[٢]؟ إذ كان قد أوجب الله عليه نصاً لهم، فإن قالوا: ليس كل
الفرائض نصاً لنا، قلنا: هذه دعوى فاسدة، وسنقول في[٣] ذلك في
موضعه إن شاء الله تعالى. ولا يُنكَر أن الأصول[٤] عندكم من الصلاة
والزكاة والحج [43 ب] والجهاد وصوم شهر رمضان لأمور قد نصّها
الله (ع ج) لرسوله (ع س) ونصّها الرسول لنا وأمرنا بها في عهده ومن
بعده. فلِمَ لا يلزمكم ما قلنا من نص الرسول (صلع) للإمام مِن بعده؟ 'إذ
كان مأموراً بنص ما قد أقررتم من الأصول والأمر بها من بعده'[٥] ولِمَ كان
قولكم في إيجاب فرض الإمامة على المسلمين بفرض هذه الأمور عليهم
أولى من قولنا في إيجاب فرض نص الإمام على الرسول (صلع) بالفرض
عليه في نصها ولا أعلم في ذلك فرقاً مع ما لزمكم من إبطال الإمامة
إذ[٦] كنتم تزعمون أن الرسول (صلع) لم ينص على رجلٍ بعينه، وأنه لم
ينص فرضاً، وكان ادعاؤكم [44 أ] فرض ما ذكرتم من فرض هذه الأمور
فاسداً لِما فيه من تنافيه.

ويقال لهم: خبرونا، هل أمر الرسول من ناءت داره عنه بهذه
الفرائض؟ فلا بد من نعم. فيقال لهم: فإذا كان قد أمر بها وكان في

---

١ ساقطة في أ   ٢ في أ مرددة مرتين   ٣ ساقطة في أ   ٤ في ب: العقول

٥ ساقطة في أ   ٦ في ب: إن

أمرهم بها أمرَ إقامة الإمام. فكان علي من شهد رسول الله (صلع) في مواقفه وهو يأمر بإقامة إمام في بلد بعد رجعته إليه، فإن قالوا نعم، خرجوا من قول الإمامة، وإن زعموا أنه لم يكن واجباً عليهم بفرض هذه الأمور فرضٌ لإقامة(١) الإمام لقضوا قولهم، وإن زعموا أنهم أُمروا بذلك على عهد رسول الله (صلع) لم يكن في فرضها عليهم فرض إقامة الإمام بمقام(٢) رسول الله (صلع) كان في فرض [44 ب] ذلك عليهم إقامة الإمام، قيل لهم: ثم لم تنفصلوا ممن زعم أن فرضها بعد الرسول (صلع) غير دالٍّ على إقامة إمام(٣) كما كان على عهد رسول الله (صلع) غير دال على ذلك إن كان غير جائز فوت الرسول إلا بعد نصٍّ مَن يقوم مقامه في أمته، لأن ذلك واجب عليه بما ذكرنا بدياً؛ وكان غير جائز ترك الواجب، لأن في تركه إهمالهم، وإلا أدى إلى إفسادهم في فرائضهم. فلا يجوز فيهم إلا النص على الإمام كما لم يجز في دين الله إلا النص على الرسول. وفي نص الرسول لمن نأت داره عنه على أميرهم وتركه ان يكلهم(٤) [45 أ] فيه إلى اختيارهم خوفاً من فرقتهم وفساد ذات بينهم وعموم ذلك في جيوشه وبعوثه والحوطة في ذلك على رجلٍ بعينه 'بعد رجلٍ٥، كما فعل في غزوة مؤته وفي توليته أحد أصحابه على الجيشين إذا اجتمعا على الجيش. والنصُّ على ولي كل جيش دليل على فساد ترك النص على خليفته وإمام أمته. ولا الفساد في جميع الأمة أصل والصُّور فيه أهل.

١ في ب: إقامة   ٢ في أ: لمقام   ٣ في ب: الإمام   ٤ في ب: يكلمهم
٥ ساقطة في ب

عدم وجود إجماع على النص لا يعني إبطال النص

فإن قالوا إن الأمر لو كان على ما ذكرت منه[1] وجوه النص على الإمام لكان قد نصه، ولو نصه لنقلته الأمة، وفي أن الأمة لم تنقله ما صح أنه لم ينصه. قيل لهم هذه علّة غير العلل الأولى، وإنما أردنا مطالبتكم [ب 45] بالاستدلال[2] بفرض ما ذكرتم[3]، على فرض الإمامة وعارضناكم بما تقدّم من الكلام، لتتبيّنوا[4] أنه لا حجة[5] لكم في الولاية ولا بيّنة على قولكم فيها. وقولكم لو كان واجباً عليه، لنصه (صلع) – وإنه قد نصّه – ونقلت ذلك طائفة من الأمة؛ ولم ينقل الباقون[6] أنه لم ينص[7]. ولو لم يقل الباقون أنه لم ينص[8]. لم يكن ذلك نقلاً، لأنه نفيٌ مع كثرة الدلائل لمن نقل أنه نصّ على صحةِ قولهم وقرب شبهة النص[9] بأفعاله في حياته من توليته[10] الولاة ونص الكفاه. فإن اعتل بأنهم لم ينقلوه[11]، فإنه لم ينص. قيل لهم ولما[12] كان في ذلك دليل على ما ذكرت، دون أن يكون في نقلٍ مَن نَقَلَ [أ 46] أنه نصٌّ. وصحة القياس لهم في ذلك دليل على فساد عقد من عقد وتكلفهم ما لم يأذن الله به، مع نفينا جماعهم على ما ذكرت، وإن كان أكثر ما وصفت كافياً في أول الكتاب. ولو أن قائلاً[13] قال في إجماع النصارى على أن المسيح

---

١ في أ: من   ٢ في ب: الاستدلال   ٣ في أ: بفرض على ما ذكرتم   ٤ في ب: لتبينوا   ٥ في أ: لا صحة   ٦ ساقطة في ب   ٧ في أ: نص   ٨ في ب: نص   ٩ ساقطة في ب   ١٠ في أ: توليه   ١١ في ب: وإن لم ينقلوه   ١٢ في ب: دليلا   ١٣ في ب: يقول

غير عبد وتسميتهم إياه [إلهاً] دليل على أن المسيح لم ينص لهم أنه
عبد لكان في نقل من نَقَل أنه عبد، مع فساد كونه إلها ووجوب الإقرار
عليه بأنه عبد غيرُ جائز فيه ترك الإقرار[١] بما وجب عليه الإقرار به ما دلّ
على أن إطباقَ من أطبق[٢] منهم فاسد، وإذا أمكن أن يطبقوا على القول
الذي هو ضد ما نص لهم المسيح من أنه عبد وإذا جاز في أمتنا أنه
يطبق [٤٦ب] أكثرها على الفعل[٣] الذي هو خلاف لما نص الرسول
(صلع) ولا يكون ذلك دليلاً أنه لم ينص، كما لم يكن في إجماع أكثر
الأمة التي تبعت المسيح لمّا اجتمعت على القول الذي ينفي عنه أكثر
العبوديّة دليل على أنه لم ينص لها. فإن قال: إن النصارى، وإن قالوا في
المسيح ما قالوا، فلم يمتنعوا من النقل عنه أنه قال: إنني عبد[٤]، ولم
نجد في[٥] أمّتنا مجتمعة على أن الرسول نص على رجل، قلنا له: فهذا
أوكد فيما قلنا، لأنه إذا جاز فيهم مخالفة ما نقلوا عن المسيح (ع م)
من ذلك (بضرب من الضروب[٦] لم[٧] يستنكر في مثلهم ومَن كان في
طبعهم مخالفةُ ما نص لهم ولم يكن في [٤٧أ] فعلهم خلاف في ذلك،
دليل على أنه لم ينص لهم. فإن قالوا إنه لو كان نص لهم على رجل
لنقلوا بأجمعهم أنه نص عليه، وإن خالفوا ذلك بضرب من التأويل، كما
نقلت النصارى أن المسيح نص على أنه عبد وإن تأوّلت. قيل: أوليس قد
صح أن المسيح نصّ على محمد باسمه؟ والنصارى غير ناقلة لذلك بل

---

¹ في ب: الإقرار عليه ² في ب: طبق ³ في ب: الفصل ⁴ في أ: عبده
⁵ ساقطة في ب ⁶ ساقطة في أ ⁷ في أ: ولم

جاحدةٌ له. وهل في جحدها، على كثرتها وتركها. أن تنقل ما نُص؟ فإنه إن ﴿لم يكن﴾[١] ترك مَن ترك أن ينقل النص عن النبي (صلع) في ذلك الرجل وفعلهم في ذلك دليل على أنه لم ينص. فإن قالوا إن النصارى، وإن لم ينقلوا[٢] أنه سماه باسمه فقد نقلوا ما يدل على نبوّته، [٤٧ب] قيل له: لأنّا[٣] إنما[٤] أردنا أن يزول احتجاجكم بأن تركّكم أن تنقلوا[٥] دليل على أنه لم ينص؛ فأوجدناكم نصاً لا شك فيه ومن[٦] نقله ونص له. والأمة، وإن لم تنقل كلها أن النبي (صلع) نص على رجل بعينه، فقد نقلت فيه ما يدل على إمامة ذلك الرجل، كما أن النصارى، وإن لم تنقل أن المسيح نص على محمد (صلع). فقد نقلت ما يدل على نبوّته. وإما قول من قال إن في كتاب الله (ع ج) والمجتمع عليه من سنّة نبي الله (صلع) مخرجاً لما ابتُلي به الناس، أو ينقلون ما جاء عن الله، فإنا نقول: إن الأمر على ما قال الله (ع ج)، وإن ذلك في الكتاب والسنة من عَلِمُهما أو جَهِلَهما وجميع الغناء [٤٨أ] عن غيرها.

ولو كانت السنة ليست إلا ما اجتمعوا عليه لخسَّت ونقصت. ولسنا نلتفت إلى إجماع أهل فرقة. إذ قد يجوز التفرّق عن الحق والجهلُ به كيف ما كان ولا يكون ذلك من كتاب الله وسنّة نبيّه. والله (تع) يقول في كتابه: ﴿مَا فَرَّطْنَا فِي الْكِتَابِ مِنْ شَيْءٍ﴾[٧] وقوله (تع): ﴿الْيَوْمَ أَكْمَلْتُ لَكُمْ دِينَكُمْ وَأَتْمَمْتُ عَلَيْكُمْ نِعْمَتِي وَرَضِيتُ لَكُمُ الْإِسْلَامَ

---

[١] في ب: يكون ترك   [٢] في أ: ينقلوه   [٣] في ب: انا   [٤] في ب: إذا
[٥] في أ: ينقلوا   [٦] في أ: من   [٧] سورة الأنعام (٦):٣٨

دِيناً‏(١). فإن‏(٢) فيما قال الله (تع) من ذلك لقطعاً‏(٣) للحجة وحظْراً على التقوّل‏(٤) على الله بغير علم، والارتياب في كتاب الله (تع) ما لم يأذن الله به والقياس في حكمه بما لم يوجد إليه سبيلاً ولم يجعل به سلطاناً مع قوله: ﴿وَمَنْ لَمْ يَحْكُمْ بِمَا أَنْزَلَ [48 ب] اللَّهُ فَأُولَئِكَ هُمُ الظَّالِمُونَ﴾‏(٥) والكافرون والفاسقون أمراً لنا بالحكم بما حكم الله واختار ما لم يحكم به مع منعِهِ نبيّه (صلع) من القول بغير ما نص في فرائضه وأحكامه، لقوله: ﴿وَلَوْ تَقَوَّلَ عَلَيْنَا بَعْضَ الأَقَاوِيلِ لَأَخَذْنَا مِنْهُ بِالْيَمِينِ ثُمَّ لَقَطَعْنَا مِنْهُ‏(٦) الْوَتِينَ﴾‏(٧) وعيداً له في فضل‏(٨) ذلك وقد جرى له عنده وإذا كان هذا محظوراً عليهم (صلع)، وهو أكمل الناس عدلاً وافتق الناس رأياً وأقرب الناس من صواب وأبعدهم من إغفال. كان حظره ذلك على غيره أحرى والله فيه أولى ممّن الخطأ عليه أغلب والإغفال منه أقرب والزلل [49 أ] والصواب منه أبعد. ولعمري إن معنى قولهم إنه ليس في كتاب الله (ع ج) ولا في سنته (صلع) كفاية للناس 'ولا سد‏(٩) لحاجتهم، وزعموا أن الله ينص لهم جميع ما يحتاجون إليه حتى وكلهم في أكثر ذلك إلى الآراء المتخبطة‏(١٠) والأهواء المردية.

---

¹ سورة المائدة (٥):٣   ² في ب: وإنما   ³ في أ: قطعاً   ⁴ في ب: القول   ⁵ سورة المائدة (٥):٤٤؛ تقول الآية ﴿فَأُولَئِكَ هُمُ الْكَافِرُونَ﴾ وليس الظالمون ⁶ في ب: عنه   ⁷ سورة الحاقة (٦٩):٤٤-٤٦   ⁸ ساقطة في ب   ⁹ في أ: والأشد ¹⁰ في أ: المختبطة

السنة أصل آخر بعد الكتاب

وأما قولهم: فما وجدنا فيهما[١]، فلا نغيّر حكم الله جل جلاله. وما لم
يوجد فيهما. فعلى ولاية العلماءِ به النظرُ فيه والتشاور واجتهاد الرأي. فإنا
نقول: قد ثبتنا أن في الكتاب والسنة بيان كل شيء، ثم نقضتَ ذلك
بقولك: « وما لم يوجد فيهما »، فتناقضتَ بنفي ما ثبت، ثم رجعت
فثبَّت مما نفيت من كون البيان في الكتاب والسنة في قولك: [ب ٤٩]
« فعلى ولاية العلماء به[٢] والنظر والتشاور واجتهاد الرأي » فإنا نقول: لو
ثبت عليكم بما نفيت كونه، إذ في كونهم علماء به تثبيت لكونه. إلا أن
يكون ذهب إلى أنهم علماؤهم من غير الكتاب والسنة فضلال وبدعة.
فإن قال لهم: لم يخرجه من الكتاب والسنة إن لم يكن منصوصاً إذا
كان معاني نسبته بهما، قيل له: لِمَ لا أخرجه[٣] من الكتاب والسنة[٤] إن
لم يكن منصوصاً؟ إذ لم يجد في كتاب الله أباح للرسول[٥](صلع)
الحكم بما لم ينص فيما وافق وخالف وهو أعلم الناس بالتمثيل والتشبيه
بل قد حظّره عليه ومنعه من الحكم إلا بما أنزل[٦]. ثم نسأله فنقول: من
أين أوجب[٧] [أ ٥٠] عليهم بالنظر والارتياد، وأبحتم التشاور في جميع
الأحكام، وقد حظر الله ذلك على رسوله (صلع) بما قدّمنا وبما حُكي
عن الأمم الماضية من ضلالهم بالرأي، فقال حاكياً عنهم[٨] وذاماً لهم

---

¹ في ب: فيها   ² ساقطة في ب   ³ في ب: أخرجته   ⁴ ناقصة في ب   ⁵ في
ب: لرسوله   ⁶ في ب: أنزل الله تعالى   ⁷ في ب: أوجبت   ⁸ في أ: أنهم

(وقالياً) لهم)، ﴿وَقَالُوا مَا فِي بُطُونِ هَذِهِ الْأَنْعَامِ﴾(٣) إلى قوله ﴿قُلْ آللَّهُ أَذِنَ لَكُمْ أَمْ عَلَى اللَّهِ تَفْتَرُونَ﴾(٤) وهل عدا أولئك أن يكونوا ارتأوا أو قاسوا وهل لتقوّله(٥) على الله إلا القول بما ليس في الكتاب والسنّة، ومَن الدافع لقول الله سبحانه ﴿الْيَوْمَ أَكْمَلْتُ لَكُمْ دِينَكُمْ وَأَتْمَمْتُ عَلَيْكُمْ نِعْمَتِي وَرَضِيتُ لَكُمُ الْإِسْلَامَ دِينًا﴾(٦) وقوله (تع) ﴿مَا فَرَّطْنَا فِي الْكِتَابِ مِنْ شَيْءٍ﴾(٧) وقوله ﴿لِيَهْلِكَ مَنْ [ب ٥٠] هَلَكَ عَنْ بَيِّنَةٍ وَيَحْيَا مَنْ حَيَّ(٨) عَنْ بَيِّنَةٍ﴾(٩) ومَن(١٠) زعم أن الله قد أخرج في عامة فروضه وأحكامه إلى الأذهان الضعيفة والعقول السخيفة وعرض بذلك خلعه(١١) لمّا نهاهم من الاختلاف وترك ما أمرهم به من الائتلاف. فإن اعتَلَّ بقوله(١٢) (ع ج): ﴿وَشَاوِرْهُمْ فِي الْأَمْرِ﴾(١٣)، قيل له: إنما ذلك في طريق يُسلك أو منزل يُنزل أو ما أشبه ذلك ليس من الحكم والشرائع في شيء يدل على ذلك. إن النبي (صلع) لم يشاور أحداً في فريضة ولا ناظره في سنّة فإن اعتَلَّ بحديث معاذ بن جبل عن النبي (صلع) أنه قال: « بِمَ تَحكم؟ » قال: « بكتاب الله ». قال: « فإن لم [أ ٥١] تجده في كتابه؟ » قال:« فبسنّة(١٤) رسول الله (صلع) ». قال: « فإن لم تجده

---

١ في الأصل: قال ٢ ساقطة في أ ٣ سورة الأنعام (٦):٣٩ ٤ سورة يونس (١٠):٥٩ ٥ في أ: التقوى ٦ سورة المائدة (٥):٣٨ ٧ سورة الأنعام (٦):٣٨ ٨ في ب: يحيى ٩ سورة الأنفال (٨):٤٢ ١٠ في ب: من ١١ في ب: خلقه ١٢ في ب: بقول الله ١٣ سورة آل عمران (٣):١٥٩ ١٤ في أ: فسنّة

فيها[١]؟ » قال: « أجتهد برأيي ». فقال: « الحمد لله الذي وُفق بقول
النبي (صلع) ». قلنا: قد[٢] قدّمنا لك[٣] حديث الأخبار. وهذا خبر لم
نقم بصحته الحجة إذ قد وجدنا من الأمة من يدفعه، مع ما فيه من
خلاف الكتاب لما فيه على تأويلك من إلزام الكتاب والسنّة بالنقض[٤].
وذلك خلاف ما أخبر الله في كتابه من الكمال والتمام، ثم ما فيه من
إباحة ما حظره الله ونهى عنه من القول بما لم ينزل الله به سلطاناً.
والحديث الذي لا تدفعه الأمّة قول النبي (صلعم): « ما أتاكم عني
موافقاً لقول الله (ع ج) فأنا [٥١ ب] قلته وما أتاكم عني مخالفاً لكتاب
الله فلم أقله ». وفي ذلك دليل على باطل هذا الحديث، ﴿إن فيه خلافاً[٥]﴾
للقرآن وإباحة ما منع الله منه وزجر عنه. ولو كان الحديث صحيحاً
والبرهان بمجيئه عن الرسول (صلع) قائماً، كان المعنى غير ما ذهبتَ
إليه، وكان معناه عندنا[٦] في قوله: « إن لم تجد[٧] » في قول الله تعالى
ولا سنّة رسوله اجتهدت برأيي » يعني أن علمه فيها، كما يعلم بعض
الناس من كتاب الله (تع) ما لم يجد من جهل فأعلم هو منه ولا يوجب
ذلك ما جهل من الكتاب والسنة أن ليس فيهما. فيكون[٨] معنى
قوله: اجتهد برأي بعلم[٩] ما جهله والحكم [٥٢ أ] بما علمه من المسائل
والتحرز[١٠] من النسيان. ولذلك قال تبارك وتعالى لنبيّه (صلع): ﴿وَأَنِ

---

[١] ساقطة في ب   [٢] ساقطة في ب   [٣] في أ: لكم   [٤] في ب: والنقض   [٥] في
ب: إنه فيه خلاف   [٦] ساقطة في ب   [٧] في ب: يجد   [٨] في ب: ويكون   [٩] في
ب: تعليم   [١٠] في ب: التحرز

احْكُمْ بَيْنَهُمْ بِمَا أَنْزَلَ اللَّهُ﴾[١]، وقال ﴿لِتَحْكُمَ بَيْنَ النَّاسِ بِمَا أَرَاكَ اللَّهُ﴾[٢]. وليس ذلك القياس والارتياء، ولكن[٣] احكم بينهم بما علّمك الله. يدلّ على ذلك أمرُه إياه بالحكم بما أنزل. فإن اعتلّ في فِدَى الصيد مثل ما قتل من النَّعَم يحكم به ذوا عدل منكم فذهب إلى أن قوله « مثل » إباحةُ الرأي والتمثيل. قلنا: إن الله (ع ج) قد نص أن جزاء الصيد مثله، ولم يقل: اجتهدوا في المثل ولا الارتياء فيه ولا القياس. فمِن أين ثبت قولك إنه أباح القياس في المثل والارتياء؟ بل الثابت أن يكون الواجب قد [٥٢ ب] عرّفه بَيّنَةَ المثل كما عرفه أن عليه المثل. ولن يجد في الآية[٤] دليلاً على إباحة القياس والرأي في المثل. فإن قال إن الناس لما كانوا لا غناء بهم عن معرفة المثل من الصيد وعن معرفة النوازل، ولم يكن في الكتاب والسنة من النص على ذلك ما يجمع لهم حاجتهم وجب بذلك القياس والرأي، قلنا له: من أين زعمت أن ليس في الكتاب والسنّة نص جميع ما يحتاج إليه؟ وإن اعتلّ بجهله وجهل أكثر الأمة حاجتهم إليه من ذلك، قلنا: وإن كان في جهلك وإياهم به ما أوجب أن يكون غير منصوص دون أن يكون [٥٣ أ] في جهلك وإياهم به وامتناع ذلك من أن يترك قياساً أو رأياً مع الحاجة[٥] إليه دليل على أنه منصوص لمن يقوم بعلمه لمن علينا الحجة ويقوم مقام الرسول في الأمة. فإن قال قائل: ومن أين امتنع أن يدرك[٦] قياساً أو رأياً؟ قلنا له: الدليل

---

[١] سورة المائدة (٥):٤٩   [٢] سورة النساء (٤):١٠٥   [٣] في ب: لكن   [٤] في أ: إيمانه   [٥] في أ: الحجة   [٦] في أ: يترك

على ذلك إجماعنا وإياك وسائر الأمة على امتناع درك ما علمنا نصاً من الصلاة والزكاة والحج والصوم والجهاد وغير ذلك مما سميت أصلاً من غير(١) أن يدرَك قياساً(٢) ورأياً، قلنا: إن كان ذلك كذلك وكانت النوازل داخلةً في معانيها في أنها أحكامٌ لله(٣) وفرض له كانت لا يجوز أن تُدرَك قياساً ولا رأيا [٥٣ب] ولا يكون إلا نصاً، كما لم يجز غير ذلك فيما دخلت في معناه مما سمّيته أصلاً. فإن قال: لِمَ أحكمت لنا أشبه هذه الأصول لحكمها في أنها لا تُدرَك إلا نصاً دون أن يُحكَم لها بحكمه في أن ما أشبه الحلال منها فحلال وما أشبه الحرام فحرام؟ قلنا له: تركُنا من ذلك من جهات: منها أن الله لم 'يبح لنا' التحليل والتحريم. بل حظرها علينا بما ذكره منها، بل رأيناه(٥) قد حكم في المتشابهات بأحكام مختلفات. مثل ما حكم في قضاء الحائض الصوم وما وضع عنها من قضاء الصلاة وما أوجب من قضاياهما جميعاً إذا تركهما عامداً، وما أباح من الإفطار [٥٤أ] في السفر، فأوجب به القضاء، ولم يبح ترك الصلاة، ثم لم يكلف قضاء ما أباح تركه منها. وما وضع عن(٦) الذمية من الجزية وأمر به في الدماء وما أمر به من قتال مشركي العرب حتى يؤمنوا وما أمر به من قبول الجزية من مشركي أهل الكتابين(٧) وما حكم به في الحُر والعبد من الأحكام المختلفة مع اتفاقهما في الأعيان والوجود الحرِية مع الذي يحكم له به بحكم ما أشبه، لا يخلو من أن

---

¹ ساقطة في أ ² في أ: قياسة ³ في ب: الله ⁴ في ب: يبحنا ⁵ في ب: رأينا ⁶ في أ: من ⁷ في ب: الكتابيين

يكون شبه من كل وجوهه أو من بعض وجوهه. فإن ادّعى اشتباهه من كل وجوهه، قلنا له: فهو هو، فما هو حاجتك إلى قياس الشيء على نفسه، وإن رجعت على أنه موافقة من جهات [٥٤ ب] مخالفة من جهات، قلنا له: فَلِمَ حكمت له بحكمه من الجهة التي أشبهه فيها دون أن تحكم له بخلاف حكمه من الجهة التي خالفه(١) منها؟ فإن رجع إلى أنه كان(٢) أكثر وجوهه شبهةً له وإن خالفه من جهات هي أقل من الجهات التي يشابهه منها، قلنا له: هل تكون الموافقة بين شيئين أكثر منها بين ما ذكرنا من الحر والعبد والذمّية؟ فإن ادّعى ذلك أكذبه، وإن لم يدّعه كان في حكم الله سبحانه في هذه المتشابهات(٣) بالأحكام المختلفات دليلٌ على أن الأحكام لا تقع بقلّة الاشتباه ولا بقلّة الاختلاف. وإن رجع إلى أن يقول: لو كانت الأحكام في النوازل منصوصات لكان رسول الله [٥٥ أ] (صلع) قد ألقاها إلى أصحابه. ﴿ولو كان ألقاها إلى أصحابه٤ لَنُقِلت إلينا وفي ألّا يكون ﴿نقل ذلك دليل على أنه لم يُلقِهِ، وفي ألّا يكون٥ ألقى دليل على أنه لم يُنَصّ له. لأنه لو نُصّ له لكان لا يعدو واحداً من أمرين: إما أن يكون كتمه الجميعَ، وذلك نفيُ صفته لكثرة تعليم من بُعث لتعليمه، أو يكون ألقاها إلى بعضٍ دون بعض. ففي ذلك ما أدّى إلى المحاباة(٦) في الدين والأثرة. وهذه خروج من صفة النبوّة.

---

١ في أ: خالفته   ٢ ساقطة في ب   ٣ في ب: المتشابهات   ٤ ساقطة في أ
٥ في أ: أصل ذلك دليل على أنه لم يقلد وفي ألا يكون   ٦ في ب: المحابات

عدم نشر النص على جميع الأمة لا يبطله

قلنا له: إن علم النوازل ليس على كافة الناس علمُها، ولا كلَّهم محتمِل لذلك مضطلع به، لما بُني [١] عليه الناس من السهو [٢] ولما [٣] في تكليف الجزء منه فضلاً عن الكل من التشاغل عما لا يجوز لهم التشاغل عنه من معاشهم وما [55 ب] في ذلك، لو كُلِّفوه من تكليف أكثر من الطاقة إذ هم عاجزون من حمله. وإذا كان كلهم كذلك، ليس له محمل [٤] ولا في طاقته ذلك، ولم يكن كلهم يعلم ما ليس في طبعه احتماله، وكان غير جائز أن يكون كلَّهم، لجهلهم [٥] بقلّة حاجتهم إلى من يعلمه تبيان فيهم [٦] من يعلمه ولا يكون على رسول الله (صلع) إلقاء ذلك إلى الناس عامةً، لأنه لا يسعهم تركُهُ. فليس، كما لا يسعهم ترك تعليمه [٧] مما لا يجوز، إلا أنْ [٨] يلقيه إليهم. ونقول: إن رسول الله (صلع) قد أبان الحكم فيما ورد عليه من النوازل، وليس كلها ترد في عهده. وليس في إعلام النبي (صلع) ذلك بعض الأمة دون بعض ما أدّى إلى المحاباة [٩] من حيث [56 أ] كان يزكّي [١٠] بعض الأحكام في النوازل بحضرة نفرٍ من أصحابه، وقد غاب أكثرهم، يعلمه من حضر وجهله من لم يحضر. ولا تكون في ذلك محاباة وقد قلنا إن في حاجة الناس إلى علم الأحكام والنوازل ما أوجب أن ليس كل الناس يحتمله. وفيما ذكرنا من صفتهم

---

١ في ب: بين   ٢ في أ: الشهود   ٣ في أ: لما   ٤ في أ: محملاً   ٥ في

ب: بجهلهم   ٦ في ب: منهم   ٧ في أ: تعليم   ٨ في ب: إلى   ٩ في

ب: المحابات   ١٠ في أ: يذكر

وضعفهم وعجزهم دليل على أن ليس كل الناس يعلمه مع ما وجدنا من جهل أكثر الناس به. وإذا كان ذلك كذلك كان لا بد من عالِمٍ لِما جهلوه من ذلك محتملٍ لما لم يحتملوه خارج من صفتهم، غير جائزٍ ما يجوز عليهم من الجهل والخطأ وارتكاب الكبائر فيرجع ويرجعوا به من الجهل إلى ما منعوا به. فإن [56 ب] قال: لا تزول المحاباة(١) فيما(٢) يخبر به بحضرته بعض أصحابه وفي حال غيبة الأكثر منهم وجهلهم به؛ لأن الحاضر مؤدي علم ذلك إلى الغائب. قلنا له: وكيف يزيل ما عنه المحاباة(٣) في إعلامه واحداً دون الجميع أن جعله معلماً ومؤدياً علمٌ(٤) نازلتهم في وقت حاجتهم. وأما قول من قال: إنه لا يجوز أن يحكموا حتى يعلموا أن الأمر على ما قالوا، ولا يجيئون بما لا يعلمون، فإنه لن يعدو غاية العلم عنده ⟨بذلك إصابة التشبيه في القياس أو الحكم للشيء عنده° بنظره⟩(٦) أو الاجتهاد(٧) في الرأي. وقد بيّنا من فساد ذلك ما فيه كفاية. وإذا كان ذلك فاسداً(٨) لم يعدْ(٩) أن يكون حاكما بما لا يعلم. إذ كان مأموراً بالحكم(١٠) بما يعلم منهيّاً عن الحكم [57 أ] بما لا يعلم. إذْ(١١) كان مأموراً بترك الحكم ⟨بالرأي والقياس⟩(١٢) إذ كان على ما بيّنا وشرحنا والحمد لله رب العالمين.

---

¹ في ب: المحابات ² في أ: فيها ³ في ب: المحابات ⁴ في ب: على ⁵ ساقطة في أ ⁶ في ب: ينظره ⁷ في ب: لاجتهاد ⁸ في أ: فاسد ⁹ في ب: ينفذ ¹⁰ ساقطة في ب ¹¹ ساقطة في أ ¹² في أ: بالقياس والرأي

كما أن الرسول منصوص عليه كذلك أولو الأمر

(ثم قالوا¹) وقد قال الله (ج): ﴿لَوْ رَدُّوهُ إِلَى الرَّسُولِ وَإِلَى أُولِي الأَمْرِ مِنْهُمْ لَعَلِمَهُ الَّذِينَ يَسْتَنبِطُونَهُ مِنْهُمْ﴾(²). ولاة أمورنا علماؤنا. وقد قال تبارك وتعالى: ﴿أَطِيعُوا اللَّهَ وَأَطِيعُوا الرَّسُولَ وَأُولِي الأَمْرِ مِنكُمْ﴾(³). وأعظم أمور ديننا وإن الذي فرض الله على المسلمين من توليه إمام عليهم من الأمور التي لم تُسَمَّ بأعيانها، (وإن كان⁴) قد سميت من الخصال التي قد ذكرناها، فإنا نقول: إن الأمر في مَن أمر الله بالرد إليه والطاعة له، ووعد العلم بالرد إليه فيما ينبغي استنباطه منهم ما قال الله تعالى على تأويلكم [٥٧ ب] والدليل على ذلك أن الله جل ثناؤه أمر بطاعة نفسه بعد أن عرّفنا نفسه، وبطاعة رسوله بعد أن عرفنا رسوله بالنصّ عليه، وكذلك أمر بطاعة ولاة الأمر بعد أن عرّفهم بالنص عليهم(⁵) بأعيانهم كما نص على رسول الله (صلع) بعينه. لأنه لما جعل طاعته لا تتم إلّا بطاعة رسول الله (صلع) لم يجز إلّا بنص عليه. وكذلك لما جعل طاعة رسوله لا تتم إلا بطاعة ولاة الأمر⁶ ثبت أن لا تتم طاعة رسوله إلا بطاعة ولاة الأمر⁶ منصوصاً كما نص على الرسول (صلع). ولو جاز أن يأمر بطاعة ولاة الأمر وولايتهم ولا ينص عليهم لجاز أن يأمر بطاعة الرسول ولا ينص عليه. وكذلك لو جاز أن يكل إلينا [٥٨ أ] اختيار ولاة الأمر، وقد قرنهم برسوله، لجاز أن يكون إلينا⁷ اختيار رسوله (صلع). وكذلك لما كان في أمره

إيانا بطاعة النبي (صلع) دليل على خروج النبي من حدّ مَن يجوز عليه
المعاصي والجهل والخطأ وكان أمرنا بطاعته بمثل ما أمرنا به من طاعة
نبيّه غير جائز عليه ما لم يجز على النبي (صلع)، إلا ما اجتمعنا عليه من
القرآن والخبر أنه لا يشركه فيه أحد من النبوّة واتصّال الوحي والرسالة، إذ
كان الأمر على ما وَصَفْنا وكان لا يجوز عليه ما ذكرنا وكان لا يدرَك من
طريق الرأي[١] والاختيار إلا من[٢] لا يجوز عليه ذلك أو غير مدرك من
تلك الطريق وكذلك قوله: ﴿وَلَوْ رَدُّوهُ إِلَى الرَّسُولِ [58 ب] وَإِلَى أُولِي الأَمْرِ
مِنْهُمْ لَعَلِمَهُ الَّذِينَ يَسْتَنْبِطُونَهُ مِنْهُمْ[٣]﴾[٤] وعداً منه لنا أنّا متى رددنا ما
جهلنا إلى الرسول علمناه من قِبَلِهِ[٥]، وكذلك إذا رددناه إلى أولي الأمر
علمناه. وكما أنّا نعلمه من رسول الله (صلع) نصاً بلا رأي منه ولا قياس
'ولكن نصاً'[٦]، وكذلك نعلمه من ولاة الأمر بلا رأي منهم ولا قياس
ولكن نصاً، ولو كان أولي[٧] الأمر علماؤكم وكان ردّنا إليهم إنما هو ليروا
وليقيسوا لم يعدُ أن يمكن فيهم الاختلاف. فإذا كان الممكن من ذلك
فإنّا نعلم الحقّ منه. أوليس في ذلك تكليف الجاهل التمييزَ من العلماء؟
وذلك ما علم الله عجزهم عنه وأشفق عليهم منه، والقبول من الجميع.
[59 أ] ففي ذلك قول التضادّ والذي ذمه الله.

وإذا جاز ذلك ثم اختلف خصمان، فبأيّ الحُكْمين يُحكم عليهما؟
فأيهما أوجب به الحُكم: لمن يكون عليك في إيجابه إلا ان يقول: قال

---

¹ في أ: الوحي   ² في أ و ب: مر   ³ ساقطة في أ   ⁴ سورة النساء (٤):٨٤

⁵ ساقطة في أ   ⁶ ساقطة في ب   ⁷ في أ: أولو

بعض العلماء[1]، قيل لك: بل أحكمُ بالآخر، فقد قال به البعض الآخر، وإن أوجب عليه الحكمَ[2] بالقولين جميعاً رجعتَ إلى ما بيّنّا من إثبات المحال. وإن أثبتَ[3] الحكمَ الآخر عليه بأحد القولين طولبتَ بالدليل على ما ادّعيت من ذلك، وقيل لك: مَن زعم أن ليس عليه ان يحكم بهما؟ بل عليه ان لا يحكم بواحد منهما واعتلّ بما بيننا مما فسد له الرأي في الأحكام والقياس وأنهما ليسا[4] من أحكام الله (ع ج)، [ب 59] لقول الله سبحانه: ﴿وَلَوْ كَانَ مِنْ عِنْدِ غَيْرِ اللَّهِ لَوَجَدُوا فِيهِ اخْتِلَافًا كَثِيرًا﴾[5] ونقول: إن أولي الأمر منّا هم علماؤنا وأئمتنا وخلفاؤه فينا، وهم الذين «كسفينة نوح من ركبها نجا»[6][7]، الذين أمرنا باتّباعهم والتعليم منهم، ونهى عن تقدمهم، وأخبرنا نبيُّنا محمد (صلع) أنهم غير مفارقي كتابه حتى ﴿يرد معهم حوضَهُ، وأنّا لا نضلّ ما تمسكنا بهم﴾[8].

---

¹ في ب: الحكماء   ² ساقطة في أ   ³ في أ ابيت   ⁴ في أ: ليستا

⁵ سورة النساء (٤):٨٢   ⁶ في أ مرددة مرتين   ⁷ إشارة إلى الحديث: « مثلُ أهل بيتي فيكم كسفينة نوح من ركبها نجا ومن تخلّف عنها غرق وهوى ». يذكر القاضي النعمان هذا الحديث مرتين في كتابه دعائم الإسلام، (ج ١، ص ٣٥ و٩٩) غير أنه في كل مرة يذكره مع شيء من الاختلاف قليل. أما من علماء الحديث السنة فإن الخطيب التبريزي يذكره في كتابه مشكاة المصابيح (ج ٣، ص ٢٦٥) عن أحمد بن حنبل ولكننا لا نراه في مسند ابن حنبل. غير أن جميع المحدثين السنة يعدون سلسلة إسناده ضعيفة (انظر الخطيب التبريزي، مشكاة المصابيح (ج ٣، ص ٢٦٥) ونور الدين الهيثمي، مجمع الزوائد ومنبع الفوائد (ج ٩، ص ١٦٨). راجع أيضاً كتابنا *The Political Doctrine of the Ismāʿīlīs (The Imamate)*، ص ٣٠ و٤٢ والحاشية ١٢٢، ص ٨٤   ⁸ راجع ٤٣٤

الفرق بين النبي والإمام

فإن قال: قد أوجبتهم لهم المساواة بالنبي (صلع) إذ زعمتم أنهم لا
يُدرَكون إلا نصاً كما لا يدرَك النبي إلا نصّاً وأنه لا يجوز على النبي، قيل
له: لا يجب علينا بذلك مساواتهم بالرسول لأمور قد خالفت بينهم وبين
الرسول (صلع) منها: عدم الوحي، وتفضيل النبي (صلع) عليهم[1] [60 أ]
وجواز النسخ في عهد النبي (صلع) وامتناعه في عصرهم، ولو كان ذلك
لنا لازماً للزمكم مساواة الإمام عندكم بالرسول، لإيجابكم من طاعته إذا
عدل مثل ما أوجبتم من طاعة الرسول (صلع) حين استحللتم دم من
خالفه وغزوتم من نابذه 'لنا. فإن قال قائل'[2] قد[3] صح لما ذكرتم أنه لا
بد من مستخلفٍ يُنَصُّ عليه، وأنه ليس ينفي استخلافه إلا بأن تكون
الأمة لِما ذكرتم من العلل في ذلك وإنه لا يكون إلا عالِماً بما تحتاج
إليه الأمة معصوماً من المعصية، فما الدليل لنا بأنه علي بن أبي طالب
دون غيره من المسلمين؟

---

[1] إشارة إلى الحديث: « خلقت فيكم الثقلين كتاب الله وعترتي أهل بيتي ما إن
تمسكتم بها لن تضلوا بعدي، وقد سألت ربي حتى يردا عليّ الحوض غداً كهاتين »،
وأشار بالمسبّحتين من يديه جميعاً وقرنهما وقال: « ولا أقول كهاتين، وأشار بالمسبّحة
والوسطى، لأن لا يسبق أحدهما الآخر، ناصرهما لي ناصر وخاذلهما لي خاذل ووليهما
لي ولي وعدوهما لي عدو ». (القاضي النعمان، دعائم الإسلام (ج ١، ص ٣٥)، راجع
أيضاً أبا جعفر الكليني، الكافي (ج ١، ص ٢٩٤): مسلم بن الحجاج، صحيح مسلم
(ج ٧، ص ١٢٢)؛ أبا عيسى محمد الترمزي، الجامع الصحيح (ج ٥، ص ٦٦٢-
٦٦٣)؛ أحمد بن حنبل، المسند (ج ٣ وص ١٤)   [2] ساقطة في أ   [3] في أ: وقد

وجوب إمامة علي بن أبي طالب

قيل له إذا كان ذلك كذلك، وكان لا بد أن يكون المنصوص[1] [ب 60]
عليه موجوداً، وكان كل من يقصد إليه من قريش وغيرها خلا علي بن
أبي طالب فقد زال[2] عنه بإجماع الأمة أن يكون المنصوص[3] بهذه
الصفة، ولم يزُل ذلك عن عليّ بإجماع الأمة بل قد بينه فيه ونقله له
بعض الأئمة. فلما كان ذلك كما وصفناه، كان لا بدّ من أن يكون علي
(ع م) هو المستخلف، لأنه لو كان 'ليس هو هو'[4] لم يكن فيهم
مستخلفاً[5]. وقد بيّنا فساد عدم المستخلَف خلا واحداً[6] بيّنه [7] أنه هو
ذلك المستخلف. وكذلك قد صح[8] في كل واحد منهم أنه ليس
معصوماً من ذلك ولا عالماً بجميع حاجة الأمة خلا[9] علي بن أبي
طالب (صلع). فلم تجمع الأمة أن ليس هو كذلك. وقد بيّنا أن من لم
يكن كذلك فليس بإمام.

[أ 61] قال: فلمّا أوجب الله تبارك اسمه مَن فرضه في ذلك نفى إقامة
الإمام في الدين أشباهُه[10]. من ذلك قوله: ﴿وَأَشْهِدُوا ذَوَيْ عَدْلٍ
مِنْكُمْ﴾[11]. ولم يُسَمِّ العدول بأسمائهم وأعيانهم. ولكنه إنما أعلمنا
بالعدل. فإذا علمناه في أحدٍ شهدنا له بذلك وقبلنا شهادته. قال

_____

[1] في أ مردده مرتين [2] في أ: أزال [3] ساقطة في أ [4] في ب: ليس هو [5] في
ب مستخلف [6] في أ وب: واحد [7] في أ وب: بينت [8] في ب: صح
[9] ساقطة في ب [10] في أ: وأشباهه [11] سورة الطلاق (٦٥):٢٠

فكذلك⁽¹⁾ أولو الأمر علماؤنا وحَمَلةُ ديننا ورعاة سياستنا. فنقول: قد
ألّفتَ بين مفترقات⁽²⁾ وشبّهت بين مختلفات: زعمتَ أن فرض الإمامة
غيرُ منصوص، وأنها من جهة الاستنباط، واستدللتَ في ذلك بما
ذكرتَ، ثم زعمت أن لها أشباهاً في الدين، منها قول الله
(تع): ﴿وَأَشْهِدُوا ذَوَيْ عَدْلٍ مِنْكُمْ﴾⁽³⁾ [61 ب] نص عند
جميع عند الأمة بإشهاد العدل فيما يدّعي فيه التأويل. فَلَعَلَّكَ أن تستطيع أن
تدّعي أن الله أمَرَ باختيار إمام، فلن تجد ذلك إلا بأن تطاوِل وتقول
له: إذا تم باسم الله عدلاً فيقول⁽⁴⁾: فلان عدل فاشهِدوه. أوجب بذلك
أن يكون الأمرُ بإشهاد العدول مأموراً⁽⁵⁾ به من جهة النظر. فإن قالوا نعم،
أكبَرتْه الأمة بجحد النص، وإن رجع إلى أنه نص تبيّن خطأه. وأيضاً⁽⁶⁾
فيما شبّه⁽⁷⁾ بغير النص. ويقال له فيما ذهب إليه من أن الله (ع ج) لم
ينص عدلاً بالعلم ضرورةً، وإنما يُظهر من حاله في نفسه وبما يبدو من
أفعاله⁽⁸⁾ لا يحتاج فيه بعينه، أن العدالة أمرٌ ظاهرٌ يُدرك⁽⁹⁾ [62 أ] بالمشاهدة
في من⁽¹⁰⁾ هي أو بالخبر. فيجب بذلك التمييز بينه وبين غيره بأكثر من
الظاهر المشاهَد⁽¹¹⁾ كما مُيّز بين الليل والنهار والحرّ والبرد والحسن
والقبيح والطيب والمنتِن. فهذه الأمور علومُها ضروريات عندك لا تحتاج
فيها إلى رأي ولا إلى قياس⁽¹²⁾ ولا ما يُستدلُّ به على استحقاقٍ⁽¹³⁾ في

---

¹ في ب: وكذلك ² في أ: متفرقات ³ سورة الطلاق (٦٥):٢٠ ⁴ في ب:
ويقول ⁵ في أ وب: مأمور ⁶ في ب: أيضاً ⁷ في ب: شبهه ⁸ في ب: أفعال
⁹ في ب: تدرك ¹⁰ في أ وب: فيمن ¹¹ في ب: الشاهد ¹² في أ: إلى قياس

الإمامة عندك مخالف لما ذكرناه، لأن الإمامة(١) عندك تدرَكُ بالنظر والمقايسة(٢) بين الفقهاء والامتحانِ والسير حتى يتخيَّروا(٣) أعلمَهُم وأفضلهم وأكثرهم عندك احتمالاً لها؛ مع تقليد الأمة من العدالة فيما يتبيَّن لك الخطأ من(٤) غلطِ ما ذهب إليه من العدالة [٦٢ ب] مع قول الرسول (صلع): « لا تجوز شهادة ظنين ولا متَّهم ولا كذَّاب »(٥) زيادةً في نصّها وتبياناً لنا مما يدل بالنظر إلا أن يذهب ذاهبٌ في النظر إلى جهة التعليم والمسألة فيها نظر(٦)، فلا يمنعه ذلك إلَّا اختيار(٧) الاسم.

ويقال له: قست الإمامة بعدالة الشهود لأنها فرع لها أم لا؟ فإن زعم أن الإمامة فرع لعدالة الشهود بَان خطأه وقيل له: أنت ممن زعم أن الإمامة أصل العدالة؟ فإن ذهب أن الإمامة أصل في نفسها وعدالة(٨) الشهود أصل(٩) في نفسها بان خطأه في قياسه أصلاً بأصل. ويقال لهم: أليس الواجب أن(١٠) يقاس الشيء بما أشبهه من أقل وجوهه؟ [٦٣ أ] فلا بد من نعم. يقال له: فإنما أشبه مقام الإمام بمقام الرسول فينا منه مقام الشاهد العدل أشبه بمقام رسول الله (صلع) فينا بَان(١١) أيضاً خطأه لأن ما قام به الإمام مثل ما قام به الرسول من جهاد العدو وقسم الفيء وإنصاف المظلوم وحج البيت وجمع الكلمات وإقامة الحدود وما أشبه ذلك. وما

---

١٣ في ب: استحقاقه   ١ في أ: الامة   ٢ في ب: للقائسة   ٣ في أ: يختبروا
٤ في ب: ومن   ٥ في أ: كذا ولا كذا   ٦ في أ وب: نظراً   ٧ ساقطة في
ب؛ في أ: الأخ   ٨ في أ: عدالة   ٩ في أ: واصل   ١٠ في أ: أنه
١١ في أ: بأن

أوجب الله من طاعة ولاة الأمر به من الرد إليهم. وإن رجع إلى أن مقام

أوجب الله من طاعة ولاة الأمر به من الرد إليهم. وإن رجع إلى أن مقام الإمام فينا أشبه بمقام الرسول منه من مقام الشاهد العدل قلنا بهما مِن أنه لا يدرك بالتشاور كما(١) كان النبي لا يدرك بالتشاور وبطل تشبيهم(٢) إياه بشاهد عدل. قال: وكذلك فرض الله الصلاة. فمن ابتلي فيها [٦٣ب] بالسفر الذي تقصر(٣) فيها الصلاة(٤)، ووقت الصلاة في الغيوم. وقال ﴿إِنَّمَا الصَّدَقَاتُ لِلْفُقَرَاءِ وَالْمَسَاكِينِ﴾(٥). وإنما يعرف الفقير والمسكين والغني بالنظر. وقال: ﴿لَيْسَ... عَلَى الْمَرِيضِ حَرَجٌ﴾(٦). وإنما يدرك المريض الذي لا حرج عليه بالنظر فيما يجب من الجهاد وقام في السنّة، ومن بلغ من الصبيان لإقامة الحدود وإقامة السنة في رمي الجمار وقدر الحجارة بالنظر. وفرض(٧) القصاص في قتل العمد، وإنما يدرك ذلك بالنظر. وكذلك ما وجب من إقامة المسلمين فريضةً، ولم يسمّها الله (تع ذكره) بعينها لأنها لا تُدرك من طريق النظر. فنقول(٨): هل خرجت الصلاة في الحضر [٦٤أ] والتقصير في السفر والوقت في يوم الغيم(٩) وفرض الصدقات لمن فرضت له من أن يكون منصوصات في الكتاب على(١٠) غير ما ذهبتم إليه من فرض الإمامة بالتأويل؟ فإن قال نعم، أكذبته الأمة ولم يجد سبباً إلى إيجاد النص، إذ لم يكن هذا نصاً. فإن أقرّ بأنها نص – فلا بد من ذلك – بَان خطأه في تشبيهه ما هو نص

بما ليس هو بنص. والسفر أمر لا يحتاج فيه المسافر إلى نظر ⟨في أنه مسافر ولا يحتاج إلى⟩[١] النظر فيما يجب فيه التقصير، إذ كان ذلك منصوصاً بالخبر وكان اختلاف الناس فيما اختلفوا فيه مما[٢] يقصر فيه المسافر إنما هو الخبر لا أنهم أدركوا أن المسافر [٦٤ ب] يقصر في كذا بالنظر. وهذا لا يجهله مفطور على إسلامه. وكذلك الأمر بالصوم برؤية الهلال والإفطار، وكذلك الزكاة في كذا[٣] إبنة مخاض وفي كذا وكذا، وكذلك الفقراء والمساكين، فلزم في العلم بظاهر أحوالهم وبما[٤] لزم في علم ظاهر[٥] العدول يعلم ذلك ممن شوهد بظاهره ويوجب له به الحكم ويعلم ممن غاب بالخبر أن لا حاجة في شيء مما ذكرنا إلى النظر، وبما يدرك بالسمع، وكذلك مما أسقطَ الله من الحرج عن المريض أمر قد نصه وأبان المريض في عينه بما أقام من الحجة بالمشاهدة[٦]. وقد يكون من الأمراض [٦٥ أ] ما يشهد ظاهرها على عجز صاحبها عن المرض فيشهد له بزوال الفرض عنه عند الله سبحانه. ويكون منها ما يشكل، فيجوز فيه العجز. فحُكم الله في ذلك برد الأمر فيه إلى المريض. وهو عالم بحقيقة ذلك ضرورة، وهو على نفسه فيما[٧] علم [ذو عين] بصيرة. ولم يكلف الله (ع ج) علم الباطن في ذلك، ولو كان يحتاج في علم ما أمر به المريض إلى نظرٍ جاز أن يحتاج في علم ظاهر الصحة إلى نظر. وكذلك لم يجز أن يحتاج المريض في نفسه إلى نظر يدرك به

---

[١] ساقطة في ب   [٢] في أ: فلا   [٣] ساقطة في أ   [٤] في أ: وما   [٥] في أ: الظاهر   [٦] في ب: بالمشاهد   [٧] في ب: مما

أنه مريض؛ ولو كان ذلك مما أُدرِك بالنظر جاز الخطأ فيه حتى يجهل فيكون المريض لا يعلم أنه مريض وهو صحيح العقل. ولو جاز [٦٥ب] ذلك جاز في الشبع مثله وفي الجوع مثله، وكذلك الذي في النطق والسكوت، وكذلك في النكاح وترك النكاح، وكذلك في الري والظمأ، حتى يجهل ولا يدري لعله ينكح في حال تَرك أو لعله تارك في حال نكاحه. وفي ذلك خروج(١) من المتعارف(٢). وكذلك ما ذُهب إليه من بلوغ الصبيان أمراً(٣) إذا قامت به الحجة بمشاهدته. وكذلك القول في رمي الجمار أمر قد فرضه(٤) الله وعرّف نبيّه قدر الجمار. وكذلك مثل حصى الحذف(٥). وذلك يُدركُ بالعيان. لم يكلّف الله فيه إلا أن يكون أقل من جزء لا يتجزّأ(٦) ولا أكثر بمثله، إنما هو على التوسّع(٧). والذي ذُكِر أيضاً من القصاص [٦٦أ] أمر قد نصه الله وعرّفنا ما قتل العمْدِ وما قتل الخطأ، وما الموضحة وما المأمونة، وما الجائفة وما السمحاق، وما الحكم فيهم؛ لا يحتاج(٨) في معرفته إلى نظر أو قياس. فإن اختلف المختلفون في معنى من معاني القتل، عمَداً هو أم خطأ، أو شجّة هو من أي صنف هي، كان اختلافهم غير مُوجِب أن الحقيقة ما اختلفوا فيه يدرَك بطريق النظر، وكان الواجب فيه ردَّه إلى أولي الأمر حتى يعلم أنه قتل كذا وشجّ كذا نصاً كما علم فيه نصّاً. وكلّ هذه الأمور قد بان فساد

---

١ في أ: الخروج   ٢ في أ: التعارف   ٣ في ب: أمر   ٤ في ب: فرض   ٥ في ب: القذف وكُتب فوقها الحذف   ٦ في أ وب: يتجزى   ٧ في ب: التوسعة   ٨ في أ: تحتاج

قول مَن ذهب إليها بحمد الله. ولئن خرجت هذه الأشياء من أن تكون نصاً ليُخرجنّ صاحب [٦٦ ب] هذا القول من أن يكون في الوجود، وليخرجنّ الليل من معنى الظلام والنهار من معنى الضياء، وأوضح قياسَه، ثم قاس الإمام على هذه الأمور، لأوجب أن الإمام لا يكون إلا منصوصاً، كما كانت هذه الفرائض لا تكون إلا نصاً.

وجوب استخلاف الرسول أماماً بعده

فإن قال قائل: هل استخلف رسول الله (صلع)؟ قيل له: نعم كما أجاز شهادة العدل. وقد اجتمعت الأمة على[١] أنه خليفة رسول الله (صلع). ومعنى الاستخلاف لا على ما ذكرنا، لا على أنه نص[٢] بعينه، كما أوجب شهادة العدل، ولم ينصه بعينه، ولكنه أعلمنا ما العدل فيما وجدناه في الشاهد أجزنا شهادته بأمر الله وامر رسوله (صلع) وقد أعلمنا بالصلاح [٦٧ أ] والفضل. فإذا ابتلينا بإقامة إمامنا نظرنا في من[٣] ذلك، فاتخذناه إماماً. فنقول: إنا فيما مضى من جوابنا أغنى عن الكلام فيما ذكرت، ولن[٤] ندع أن نقول إن رسول الله (صلع) قد نص لنا ما العدالة[٥] وأجاز[٦] شهادة العدل. فمن وجدناها فيه شهدنا له[٧] بالعدالة. فكذلك[٨] نص لنا الفضل والصلاح. فمتى وجدنا فيه شهدنا له به. وقوله: اتخذناه إماماً أمرٌ يلزمه الدليل على أن رسول الله (صلع) أمر به وأن الكتاب نصه. فقال: مَن وجدتموه فاضلاً فاتخذوه إماماً، كما قال:

من وجدتموه عدلاً فاتخذوه شاهداً، ولن نجد ذلك. وأمّا ادعاؤه بأنه خليفة [٦٧ ب] رسول الله (صلع) وأن الأمة اجتمعت على ذلك، فقد أبطل في دعواه إجماعها على ذلك. وقد قدّمنا من الكلام في فساد ما أُجمع عليه بالرأي ما يدل على فساد إجماع من أجمع منها عليه، ولأنه لا تقوم الحجة به، وبيّنّا منه ما يُغني عن ذكره، والحمد لله كثيراً.

مَن يعقد الإمامة

ويقال له: من الذي يعقد الإمامة؟ أجماعة الناس أم طائفة من أهل بلد معروفون؟ فإن قال: إن الذي يعقدها علماء المسلمين، قلنا له[١]: جميعهم حتى لا يبقى منهم أحد أو عدة معلومة؟ فإن قال: بل جماعة منهم لا يجوز أن يُجمعوا في اختيارهم على باطل. وليس ذلك بعدة محدودة. ونظير ذلك ما علمناه من أخيار [٦٨ أ] البلدان الغائبة عنا من غير تحديد. وقد يحتاج إلى الخبر من هو كذلك فيستغنى في ذلك بأخبار البعض عن أخبار الجميع. وإن كان الخبر كذلك قائماً[٢] عندنا وعند غيرنا مقام العيان، فهذا وجه قولنا وغيرنا. فإذا اجتمعت جماعة من العلماء على أنه أفضل مَن يعلمون من الفقهاء عقدوا عليه الخلافة وحرّم عليهم الإنباء. فنقول له في ذلك: خبرونا عن الجماعة التي أجزتَ خبرها وجعلتَهُ حجّة، ثم جعلت إجماعهم على ما استخرجوه حجّةً قياساً على كون اختيارهم حجة، أم جماعة مؤتلفين مجتمعين نقلوا الخبر جملة واحدة؟ فإن قال: نعم خرج من قوله في الخبر، وذلك أن هذه [٦٨ ب]

---

[١] في ب: لهم   [٢] في ب: قائم

الجماعة، وإن كثرت، فليست خارجة(١) من حد من يجوز عليه التواطي (والخبر الذي لا تقوم به عندنا وعنده الحجة(٢) (ما لم يكن في ناقليه التواطي(٣) وإذا خرجت هذه الجماعة من أن يكون خبرها حجة، بما وصفناه، فسد عليه أن يكون إجماعها على رأي واحد حجةً. لأنه إنما قاس في ذلك على قيام الحجة بخبرها. فإن قال قائل: إن هذه الجماعة، وإن كانت لا تقوم بخبرها مجتمعة حجةً، فإنها، ممن تقوم بخبرها الحجة، إذا جاءت مجيئاً يفوق التواطي. فلذلك(٤) جعلت(٥) [إجماعها على أدائه حجة. قلنا: أخطأت القياس من وجوه نحن نبيّنها، وذلك أن فعلهم إنما كان حجة لأنه محال منهم(٦) تقليد بعضهم بعضاً. فلما نقل كل واحد منهم من حيث عَلِمَ مواطاتَه صاحبَهُ ثم تواتر بذلك الخبر وجاءت الحجة، فكان على ذلك الوزن يجب أن لا يقبل رأي جماعة ولو كان الارتياء جائزاً لا ما رآه رجل ثم رآه بعينه قد علم فيهم المواطاة، ثم آخر حتى يجتمع عليه من حيث لا يكون أحد منهم واطأ عليه أحد ولا جاهل فيه قلّد(٧) عالماً ولا وضيع اتّبع فيه رفيعا فهذا لا يجوز في الرأي. إذ الرأي لا يسلم مرتابه فيه من تقليد أعمهم وأخصهم وأكثرهم وأقلهم. ولا بد من الاجتماع والتناظر. وكل ذلك موجبٌ إنكار(٨)

التواطي، بل لم يكن فيهم عند التواطي. وفي ذلك دليل على فساد قياسه وبطلان مذهبه. ويقال له: أرأيت الخبر هل يقوم بعامة النصارى أو غيرهم من الملحدين؟ أخبرونا أن فلاناً كان أسقفاً[١] معظّماً أم مترهّباً[٢] متخشّعاً أو فيلسوفاً عارفاً إذ فات خبرهم التواطي. فلا بد من نعم. يقال لهم: فهل تقوم[٣] الحجة بمدى تلك العدة؟ لو استنبطوا مذهباً أو استخرجوا. أوليس قد قامت الحجة بإبطالهم فيما اجتمعوا عليه أيضاً من المسيح عليه السلام، وأن ذلك من أعظم الضلال والكفر؟ ولم تنفذ تلك الحجة بخبرهم عن كون يونس ولوط ومرقس ويحيى، فإن ذهب إلى أن النصارى كفار والأمة ليس كذلك قلنا: وهل أخرجهم كفرهم من أن يقوم بخبرهم الحجة، إذ كان فائتاً للتواطي، وإذا قال لنا قلنا له: فإن اجتمعتْ فيمن ادّعيت الحجة بإجماعهم بأن الحجة تقوم بخبرهم فأوجدناك مَن تقوم بخبرهم الحجة... ولا برأيهم وقد قامت الحجة بأن خطأه في رأيه بيّن وضلاله في ذلك بيّن وفي فساد ما ادعى من قيام الحجة بأن إجماعهم على ما ارتأوه واستخرجوه باطل، ويقال لهم: أليس قد يجوز أن يخبر قوم أن مدينة فلانة أعظم مدينة رأوها ولا يدفع ذلك أن يكون في غير ما شاهدوا مدينة أعظم منها؟ فلا بد من نعم. يقال له: وكذلك لا يدفع أن تجتمع هذه الأمة على أن رجلاً أفضل مَن علمته ولا يدفع أن يكون فيمن لم يشاهدوا مَن هو أعلم منه وأفضل؟ فإذا أن

يولوهما أفضل مَن تعلمون وأن يكون جائزاً[١] أن يكون غيره أفضل منه.
قلنا له: فإذا [٦٩ أ] أجزت في اختياره من لا يدري أن غيره أصلح منه
اختار الأخسّ وترك الأفضل في الدين. قيل له وكذلك اختيارك من لا
تدري، لعلّ غيره أصلح منه وأفضل إيثاراً منك للتفريط واستقامةً للتقصير
واختيار ما لا تدري لعله الأخسّ. فلا بد من الإقرار أنه المفضول أو ترك
قوله بفقد الجماعة تقوم بخبرهم[٢] الحجة حتى لا يرجع الآن إلى أن
الحجة لن تقوم باختيار رجل حتى يتخيّر له منابر البلدان وتجمع عليه
علماء الأمة كلها. وهذا ما لا سبيل إلى كونه؛ ففساد واتّباع المفضول
واضح وبطلان إمامة المساوئ قائم بما ذكرنا. ووجبت للفاضل الذي
علم استحقاقه بنص المستحق [٦٩ ب] لما قبله عليه، إذ هو لا يجوز عليه
الخطأ ولا المحاباة[٣] ولا سوء الظن للأمة.

ويقال لهم: أخبرونا عن الجماعة التي اجتمعت على رأي قامت
بإجماعها الحجة ما يجوز أن يختلف فيفضل بعضها رجلاً وبعضها
رجلاً. فإن قال: ذلك جائز إلا أنه لا بد من أن يكون أحد الفريقين
مُصيباً والآخر مخطئاً. قيل له: والدليل على إصابة المصيب منها ما هو؟
فإن قال: إجماعهم عليه[٤]، قيل له: فإجماع الآخرين أيضاً حجة ولزمه
أن النصف الآخر مصيب لأنهم[٥] أجمعوا، فإن قال: ليس إجماعهم
حجة، ولكن أن يعدموا قيام حجةِ ما أجمعوا عليه حق[٦]، قيل له: فما

اعتلالك(١) بالإجماع؟ وقولك الواحد قد تقوم عليه الحجة [٧٠أ] بأنه حقٌّ. فيجب قبولك. ثم يقال له: أي شبهة(٢) إجماع مَن قد يجوز أن يضاده إجماعٌ على باطل ممن يوازي عدة أهله ويجودهم(٣) بخَبَر جماعةٍ لا يجوز أن يضادّ خيرَها مساويها في العدة ثم حملت ما لا غِناء لمن أجمع عليه على الدلالة على أن ما أجمعوا عليه حق، والخبر الذي هو نفسه(٤) الحجة. ثم يقال له: هل يجوز في بعض الجماعة التي اجتمعت على أنه أفضل وأنه مستحق، وقامت الحجة بإجماعها ترك التقصير في النظر والإغفال حتى يؤدي ذلك طائفةً منها إلى الجهل بالفاضل وينابذ طائفةٌ منهم الفاضلَ بعد علمٍ بفضله، إما لنفاسته أو لمحبته، ويقوم بعضُها للفاضل [٧٠ب] بفضله يختارونه على غيره. فإن زُعم أن ذلك يجوز ولا يكون إلّا علم الجميع بفضله، فأحال الجهل من كلهم ومن بعضهم بفضل الفاضل، وجعل ʼإدراكهم ذلكْ(٥) إدراكاً طبيعياً. وذلك خروج من قوله. ثم أبطل ذلك حاجتهم إلى التشاور والنظر والاستخراج، لأن ما عملوا طبيعياً لا يُحتاج إلى التشاور والنظر والرأي(٦) والاستخراج(٧) وذلك بمنزلة ما يُعلم من ضياء النهار وظلمة الليل. وإن رجع إلى ʼما يجيزْ(٨) ذلك قيل له يجوز(٩) في الدين، ويقوم(١٠) بخبرهم حجة الجهل(١١) بما عنه أخبروا، حتى يكونوا قد رأوا مسجد دمشق بعلم مَن فعل أنه

---

¹ في ب: اختلالك ² في أ: شبهت ³ في أ: وبوجودهم ⁴ في ب: نفيه
⁵ ساقطة في أ ⁶ ساقطة في أ ⁷ ساقطة في ب ⁸ في ب: أن يخبر ⁹ في
أ: تجوز ¹⁰ في ب: يقوم ¹¹ ساقطة في ب

وجهل ذلك بعضهم. ثم أتوا في ذلك مختلفين، فمن مقرٍّ [71 أ] بزخرفته(١) 'عالم بذلك ومن مصرٍّ لها جاهل بذلك ومن جاحد بزخرفته(٢) جاهل بها'(٣). وكلهم قد 'عاين ورأى'(٤) في صحةٍ من عقولهم. فإن أجاز ذلك خرج من الوهم، وإن منعه خرج تشبيهه الرأيَ بالخبر. فقد(٥) وجب في الرأي ما امتنع في الخبر ممّا ذكرناه. ثم يُقال له: أخبرنا عن هذه الجماعة، هل يجوز أن تتنافى آراؤها وتختلف أخبارها ويكون كل طائفةٍ عند أمتها مصيبة فلا يكون منهم إجماع، ثم يجتمعون فيعلم المخطئ أنه أخطأ. فتقوم بإجماعهم الحجة؟ فإن قال: نعم، قيل له: فهل يجوز(٦) بأن تقوم بخبرهم(٧) الحجة أن يُتَبَايَن(٨) في أخبارها، فتخبر طائفة أن الخليفة صام يوم الأحد، [71 ب] ويخبر آخرون أنه أفطر يوم الأحد، ويعلم الكاذبون أنهم 'كانوا كاذبين'(٩) بعد أن لم يكونوا يعلمون ذلك. فإن قال قائل: إن ذلك جائز لنسيانٍ وَقَعَ إلى عدة ألفٍ من الناس وأكثر منها، جاز أن يشك نصف الناس في يوم الفطر والأضحى، خرج من المعقول، وإن لم يُجزْ ذلك فرّق بين الخبر والرأي وبطل قياسه في ذلك. ثم يقال له: ما دليلك على أن على جماعةٍ أن تعتقد الإمامة، وعلى الأمة كلها أن تفعل(١٠) ذلك، وأن على بعضها قبول ذلك إذا عقدته له وأن ذلك واسع لها أو لئن(١١) عقدوا له الحكم(١٢) في كتاب الله أو يقوم من سنّة رسول

الله (صلع) أو بإجماع[1] من رأي المسلمين، أو سوغنا [٧٢ أ] لك الرأي ولم نجده من كتاب الله لأنه إنّما فرع من الكتاب إلى التأويل، وقد بيّنا فساد تأويله ولم نجده[2] خبراً عن رسول الله (صلع)، بل أفعال رسول الله (صلع) شاهدة على خلافه لأنه لم يكل ذلك إلى أحد قط[3] في الجمع[4] اليسير ولا في البلد الصغير فضلاً عن جهات الأرض وجميع الأمة، ولم[5] يصل في الدعوى إلى أن[6] رسول الله (صلع) أمر بذلك. وإن ادّعى إجماع المسلمين بانت فضيحته باختلاف الأمّة في ذلك وإكفار بعضهم من أجاز ما قال، وتضليلهم. فإن رجع إلى القلّة والكثرة أحد بما تقدم في ذلك وعورض بما لم يجمع عليه حرمة الأمة، من ذلك خلقُ القرآن [٧٢ ب] ونفي[7] الجسم مع إيجابه الخطأ على من خالفه. وإن ذكر أن الفقهاء ينصبونه سألناه: هل للفقهاء حد يعرفون به من الفقه مَن بلغه منهم كان فقيهاً ومن قصّر عنه لم يكن فقيهاً؟ فأجاب أن قال: إن ذلك غير محدود عندنا وعند جميع الأمة وسائر الأمم. ولو كان الفقيه لا يكون فقيهاً[8] إلّا بعلم جميع الدين – وذلك عندهم ليس إلى من ادّعوا له الإمامة ما كان من المسلمين في زمن النبي (صلعم) ولا بعده إلّا فقيه واحد – وكيف يكون[9] ذلك كذلك وقد قال الله (تع): ﴿أَوَلَمْ يَكُنْ لَهُمْ آيَةً أَنْ يَعْلَمَهُ عُلَمَاءُ بَنِي إِسْرَائِيلَ﴾[10]، والآية

---

[1] في ب: إجماع [2] في ب: يجد [3] في أ وب: فقط [4] في ب: الجميع [5] في ب: ولن يصل [6] زائدة في ب [7] في ب: وهي [8] في أ: الفقيه [9] ساقطة في أ [10] سورة الشعراء (٢٦):١٩٧

حجة. ففي ذلك دليل [٧٣ أ] على أن علماء المسلمين، إذا علموا فضل الفاضل، قامت الحجة بولايته. ومن كان عالماً بالأصول التي نزلت في الكتاب والسنّة فهو فقيه، وإن زلّ عنه بعض علم ذلك ما لم يبلغ أن يسمّى جاهلاً. إذاً كان علمه ذلك في علمه. وليس أحد يجمع علم جميع الدين فيكون مساوياً للنبي (صلع) في علمه، وكان إذا طلب إلى الله سبحانه أن يزيده(١) علماً كان يطلب(٢) مثل علم النبي (صلعم) ولكن قد ترك الخصلة عن العالم ويكون موجودةً في الآخر. فنقول في ذلك: إنا لم ندّع(٣) أن في الأمة(٤) فقيهاً، وإن لم يعلموا جميع العلم، إذ علموا من ذلك ما يُخرجهم من الجهل. ونقول فلان [٧٣ ب] فقه من فلان يدعي أن في الأمّة(٥). وليس عن هذا سألناه، وإنما سألناه عن الفقهاء الذين يختارون الإمام: هل لهم حدٌّ معروف مثل أصحاب مالك وأصحاب أبي حنيفة وابن أبي ليلى وغيرهم. فلا بد من أن يكونوا من أصحاب مَن ذكرنا أو لا يكونوا. فإن زعم أنهم من إحدى(٦) هذه الفِرَق، قلنا له: ومَن جعل فقهاء هذه الفرقة أولى من فقهاء غيرها؟ وإذا لم يكن معنى يستحق به أحد(٧) الفرق اختياراً لإمام دون صاحبها لم يبق إلا مناظرة أهل الفِرق بعضها بعضاً مَن المحقّ في قوله والمصيب في مذهبه. فيجب له في أقواله اختيار الإمام أو أن يجتمع من (قول الفقهاء)(٨) كل عصبة فيختارون

_____

¹ في ب: يزيد   ² في ب: يطلبه   ³ في ب: ندعي   ⁴ في ب: الإمامة   ⁵ في ب: الإمامة   ⁶ في أ وب: أحد   ⁷ في أ وب: أحد   ⁸ قوله فقهاء

[٧٤ أ] جميعاً. وفي ذلك رجوع إلى الاجتماع وعدم الإمكان(١) أو(٢) لكثرة المقالات واتساع البلدان وسائر الأقوال وتعادي أهلها والموجود من إكفار الأمة بعضها لبعض. ولن يسلم أيضاً المجيب(٣) بأحد القولين من أن يسأل الدليل في الكتاب والسنة كما سأل(٤) قبل ذلك عن قوله أيَّ هذه الفِرق يختارون دون هذه، وأيُّهما جائز لها(٥) جميعاً ذلك، ولن(٦) يجده بأكثر من الدعوى. ونقول: إن(٧) في علم علماء بني إسرائيل دلائل النبي وجوب الحجّة عليهم بنبوّته وأن في ذلك أن يعلم أمتنا الدلائل على إمامة إمامنا لوجوب الحجة عليهم بإمامته وأن في ذلك لما كان من [٧٤ ب] النبي (صلعم) ومنه إنما هو بأن نص الله عليه ولم يحوج الناس فيه إلى اختيارهم ولا المقايسة(٨) بين الناس فيه كان علم علماء أمتنا باستحقاق، إنما هو بالنص عليه من رسوله (صلع) ومَن يقوم مقام رسوله، وفي ذلك فساد ما ذهب إليه. وليس في أن خليفة رسول الله (صلع) يعلم ما تحتاج(٩) إليه الأمة ما أوجب له لحوق النبي (صلع) ولا مساواته عليه وآله الصلاة(١٠) كما قد قرأ القرآن أقوام(١١) وحفظوه ولم يجب لهم بذلك مساواة النبي في حفظ القرآن، وقد كان ينزل عليه الوحي فيعلمه أصحابه ولا يكون في ذلك ما أوجب لهم مساواته (صلع). ولن يدفع أن يكون علوم غير علوم [٧٥ أ] النوازل من لطائف

---

١ في ب: المكان ٢ ساقطة في ب ٣ في ب: والمجيء ٤ في ب: سئل ٥ في أ وب: كلّيهما ٦ في ب: وأن ٧ ساقطة في أ ٨ في ب: القائسة ٩ في أ: يحتاج ١٠ في ب: السلام ١١ في ب: أقواه

خلق الله وعجيب[١] صنعه قد علمها رسول الله (صلعم) لم يعلمها غيره ويكون العالِم بجميع النوازل، لدعاء أن يزاد علماً، يعني حفظاً لِما علِمَ وفهماً لِما حفظَ، وقد يحفظ القرآن رجلان ويكون أحدهما أحفظ من الآخر، وهما لا يحيطان فيه، ولكن ذكره على أحدهما أسهل منه على الآخر. وقد نزَّل جبرئيل على النبي (صلع) ولم ينبغ[٢] لنا أن نقول حُذَيْفَة في ذلك الوقت ساوى النبي في العلم وقد اختار بعض أصحابنا أن دعاء القائم بعيد، كما كان النبي (صلع) يدعو: ﴿اهْدِنَا الصِّرَاطَ الْمُسْتَقِيمَ﴾[٣] وقد هُدي. ويقول اغفر لنا، وقد غُفِر له.

ونقول أيضاً: إذا كان الفقيه [75 ب] (عند أهل كل[٤] فرقة من المعتزلة والخارجة والحشوية والشيعة وغيرهم إنما هو من قال[٥] بقولها ودان بمذهبها، وكذلك أصحاب مالك وأبي حنيفة وغيرهما. ولن تجمع هذه الفِرَقُ الفقهاء فرقةً أنهم مستحقون لاختيار الإمام دونهم، وكان التنازع في ذلك قائماً والأمر فيه عندهم مشكلاً لم يكن لذلك[٦] حدٌّ أجمعوا عليه وعرفوه، إذْ[٧] كان الأمر على ما وصفنا من اختلاف أهل كل فرقة ليكونوا المستحقين لاختيار الإمام غير معلومين ولا معروفين ولا مستحقين لاسم الفقه، إذ ليس كل فرقة عند مخالفيها بمقبول قولُها ولا صواب مذهبها. وإذا [76 أ] كانوا لم يجمعوا لأهل فرقة بالصواب في مذهبها لم يستحق مَن لم يصح صوابه أن يكون فقيهاً. وكل فريق منه

---

[١] في ب: وعجب   [٢] في أ: يبلغ   [٣] سورة الفاتحة (١):٦   [٤] في ب: عند كل أهل   [٥] في أ: قاله   [٦] في ب: ذلك   [٧] في ب: إذا

بالبدعة والضلالة(١) وليس المختار على أهله للأمة إلا من أُجْمِعَ على(٢) عدله وفقهه؛ ولم تجمع الأمة لأحد على ذلك. لأنه ليس في اجتماع أهل كل فرقة على رجل منهم أو على جماعة منهم ما أوجب لهم الحجة. لأن كل فرقة ساوتهم في الاجتماع على من ادعوا أفقه منهم وأنبأ علماً(٣) 'ما ادعوه'(٤) مخالفوهم. وإذا كان الأمر كذلك فقد صحّ أنه ليس أحد يعلم بإجماع أنه فقيه.

ونقول: أنه(٥) إذا بان علامة الإمام وجب على الأمة اختياره 'على من سواه'(٦) كما وجب عليهم اختيار النبي (ص) [٧٦ ب] على(٧) مسلمة وكما وجب اختياره الصلاة على تركها والزكاة والفرائض بالنص عليهم.

ونقول: أن عليهم الإقرار بأن غيبَهُ كظاهره إذا صح أنه الإمام ونص عليه الإمام قبله له، كما كان عليهم الإقرار بذلك في النبي (صلع) وإذا كان عليهم أن لا يقولوا بالظن والرأي كان عليهم تركُ إقامة إمام لم ينص لهم الكتاب أنه إمام ولم يخبر الرسول(٨) بذلك في ترك تعاطي من لم يفترض عليهم. لأن ما لم ينصه(٩) الكتاب عليهم ولا(١٠) الرسول غير(١١) خارج من الظن والرأي.

ويقال لهم: خبّرونا، هل أمر الفقهاء بنصبِ رجلٍ له صفة(١٢) ليس لأحد مثلها، عليهم إصابته دون سواه [٧٧ أ] فمن قولهم في ذلك إنهم

مأمورون برجلٍ له صفة وهو أظنُّ يكون أفضل الفضلاء والعلماء، معلوم في كتاب الله (ع ج) وسنة النبي (صلعم). وليست بصفة محدودة من نسب معلوم، ولكنه الفضل في العلم والعمل والقول. وذلك إذا ابتلوا به فقد جعل الله مخرجاً لأنه[١] لا يكلفهم إلا ما إليه لهم السبيل.

ونقول لهم: أرأيتم إذا زعمتم أنهم مأمورون بالرجل الذي ذكرتم، وليس من عشير ولا نسب معلوم ولا بلد معروف، هل لهم بدّ من امتحان البلدان والأمصار على بلده[٢]؟ فإن[٣] أجازوا الاقتصار على فاضل في بلدهم، قلنا: ولمَ قد فرض عليهم الأفضل، وجاز أن يكون الأفضل [٧٧ ب] في غير هذا البلد. ولم يقل الأفضل من غير بلد (كذا وكذا[٤] ولا قبيلة فلانة وإن أفسد ذلك لم يكن على أصلكم بد من استبراء غير ذلك البلد، ثم غيره حتى سمرقند والأندلس وغيرهما. فإن وقفتم عند غايةٍ قلنا لكم: ومَن جعل لكم الوقوف عند هذه[٥] الغاية وترك بعض[٦] نقص[٧] ما بعدها، ومن جعل هذه أولى من التي قبلها، حتى يلزمكم امتحان جميع البلدان، هذا بعد أن يَجمع فقهاءَ الأمة ويختار من جميعهم من جميع الآفاق من يختار الإمام والامتناع في الفقهاء المجتمَع على فقههم على ما ذكرنا بدياً[٨]. وأتى بالإجماع على الفقهاء[٨]، ثم أنّى لهم ذلك ببعض الأرض[٧٨ ا]! وامتحان علماء أهلها وتخيّر[٩] الأفضل في العلم والورع. وفي امتناع ذلك دليل على أن الله لم يكلّف

خلقه ولم يبتلهم به لأنه لا يكلف إلا ما يوجد إليه السبيل. وهذا ما قد
بيّن الله أنه لا سبيل إليه(١). كما لم يكلّف الله الصلاة إلا 'بعد أن'(٢)
حدّها، والزكاة إلا بعد أن سمّاها، والرسول إلا بعد أن نصّ عليه بعينه.
ولكنه تبارك وتعالى لا يبتلي بفقد الرسول إلا بعد أن يبيّن خليفته ووَصيّه،
ثم يبتليهم بالإقرار به، بعد العلم به والنص عليه وفي امتناع إمكان ما
لزمه من(٣) تفتيش الأرض وعجزهم عن الدلالة على الأمر بذلك غير
ممتنع من كتاب الله نصاً أو من سنّة رسوله المجتمع عليها [78 ب] ما دلّ
على ما ذكرناه من النص على الإمام كما قدّمنا بدياً. فإن قال قائل: إنهم
قد يعلمون الفاضل من أهل كل مدينة ومبلغ فضله بالخبر حتى يميّزوا
بين فضله وفضل من شاهده فلا يحتاجون في ذلك إلى النظر ولا دوران
البلدان. بذلك حاجةُ من حضر من أهل الشورى إلى النظر في أفضلهم
وجب أن الخبر لا يقع إلا بعد المعرفة بأفضل الناس دون المشاهدة.
كما لم يقع بالمشاهدة في أصحاب الشورى دون النظر. فإن كان قد
يقع الخبر أن فلاناً فاضل(٤) ولكن حتى يُعلم أنه أفضل الناس، فهذه لا
تكون إلا من هذه الجهة. قال: فإن اختلف رأيهم [79 أ] فقال قوم رجل
وقال آخرون رجل آخر. قال: فجوابنا في ذلك أنهم إذا اختلفوا، فأحد
الفريقين مخطئ والآخر مصيب، وعلى أهل الخطأ الرجوع إلى
المصيبين. وقد جعل الله (تع) لأهل الصواب حجةً ودليلاً ليست لأهل

الخطأ. فإن كانا جميعاً ولا حجة لهما[١] في فضل من ادّعيا فكلاهما مخطئ[٢] وعليهما أن[٣] لا يدعوَا إلا لمن قامت له الحجة بتفضيله. فنقول لهم عند ذلك: أخبرونا، إذا اختلفوا على تحقيق ما يقولون[٤] – والأمر من رسول الله (صلع) وبإجماع الأمة، فإن ادّعوا النص لم يجدوا، وإن فزعوا إلى التأويل لم يكونوا أولى به من خصومهم، وإن ادّعوا أمر الرسول لهم [٧٩ ب] كانوا منه أبعد. واختلاف الأمة دليل على يديهم إن ادعوا الإجماع فإن[٥] كان ذلك[٦] كذلك تبيين أن تناظرهم في الإمامة وعقد الجميع إن اتفقوا، وعقد كل فرقة إن تفرقوا[٧] خطأ، وجب عليهم ترك الخطأ. وفيما قدمنا من صفة الإمام والأمر الذي يجب فيه إمامته وساد غيره ما أوجب ما أوجب إلا الحجة[٨] مع جميعهم أو كلِّ فرقة منهم وأن عليهم تكليف ذلك إذا قامت الحجة بابتداعهم وفعل ما لم يُؤذن لهم في تكليفه.

ويقال لهم: هل يجوز أن يجهل الإمام بعض ما تحتاجون إليه؟ فإن جاز في بعض[٩] جاز في الكل. فإن قالوا: ليس ذلك لأنه إذا كان الغالب عليه الجهل خرج من اسم الفضل، كما أنه إذا كان الغالب عليه [٨٠ أ] السوء سمّي رجلَ سوء وقد ذمّه الأنبياء صلوات الله عليهم وإن لم يسمّوهم[١٠] بذنوبهم أنهم قوم سوء. وقد أنبأناكم أنه لا يجوز أن يولّوا إلا

---

١ في ب: لها   ٢ ساقطة في ب   ٣ ساقطة في ب   ٤ في ب: تقولون   ٥ في ب: إذا   ٦ ساقطة في ب   ٧ في أ: يتفرقوا   ٨ في ب: حجة   ٩ في أ: البعض   ١٠ في أ وب: يسمونهم

أفضل الفضلاء. فنقول له: أرأيت إذا أجزت فيه الجهل ببعض الفقه، أيمتنع أن يُعلم 'منه إلا ما جهل'(١)؟ فإن منع ذلك أُخذ بما لا يدفع من جهل غيره ما يعلمه غيره، فإذا تنبّه له رجع عن ذلك ما ردّه على غيه من رجم المرأة وغيره مما يطول ذكره، وإن لم يدفع(٢) ذلك قليل فليس ممتنع أن يكون غيره أفقه منه، وإن لم يخرج ذلك من اسم الفقه. فإن قال نعم – وهو قوله – قيل له: [٨٠ ب] وكذلك ليس بممتنع أن يكون الذي هو أفقهُ منه أعبَدُ منه. فإن لم يخرجه ذلك إلى الاستخفاف(٣). وكذلك ليس بممتنع أن يكون ذلك العابد أزهد منه ما لم يخرجه ذلك إلى الكلَب 'على الدنيا'(٤)، وكذلك أورَع(٥) منه ما لم يخرجه ذلك إلى انتهاك الحرم(٦)، وكذلك أزكى في الجهاد منه ما لم يخرجه ذلك إلى التفريط في الجهاد والفرار من الزحف، وكذلك أقرأ للقرآن(٧) إذا لم يخرجه ذلك إلى الجهل به. وإذا أجاز ذلك لم يمتنع أن يكون أفضل منه. فإذا(٨) قال: قد يجوز أن يفضل 'في خصلة من هذه الخصال ولا يجوز أن يفضل(٩) في كلها لأنه إذا فضله غيرُه في هذه الخصال كلها كان [٨١ أ] مفضولاً لا يصلح(١٠) للإمامة(١١)، وإذا فضل 'في خصلة وكانت فيه الفضائل(١٢) في هذه الخصال ما يوازي(١٣) به في تلك الخصلة ويزيد

---

١ في ب: من الأمة ما جهل   ٢ في ب: يرفع   ٣ في أ: الاستخفاف ٤ ساقطة في أ
٥ في أ وب: أروع   ٦ في ب: الحرام   ٧ في ب: القرآن   ٨ في ب: فإن
٩ ساقطة في ب   ١٠ في ب: يصح   ١١ في ب: للأمة   ١٢ ساقطة في أ
١٣ في ب: يوارى

عليه، فلم يكن مفضولاً قيل له: وكذلك قال خصمك: لما كان في أن
تفضل[١] هذه الخصال أوجب بعضه، فإذا كان إمامه في كلها كانت كل
خصلة منها لا غناء[٢] بالإمامة على أن يستكملها إمامها، لم يَجُز أن
يفضل في بعضها، لأنه لو جاز أن يَفضَل في الفقه كان ناقصاً عمَّن هو
أفقهُ منه. وإمامة الناقص غير جائزة. ولئن[٣] جازت إمامة المفضول في
الفقه جازت إمامة المفضول في غير الفقه وقول ذلك جائز في الفقه
[٨١ ب] وليس ذلك جائزاً[٤] في غير هذه الخصال بحكمٍ لأن العلة التي لها
أثبتُ أن الفضل في كل هذه الخصال إنما هو التقصير. وليس المفضول
في الفقه سالماً[٥] من التقصير[٦] في الفقه. فإذا كان إمامة المفضول في
كلها غير جائزة لهذه العلة، كان إمامة المفضول في بعضها غير جائزة
لهذه العلة.

ثم يقال لهم: ما تقولون لِمَن عارض؟ فقال: لا يكون إلا أفقه الناس
وقد يجوز أن يكون ليس بأفضل الناس. واعتلّ بأن الحاجة في الفقه أشد
لأنه به تقوم الفرائض وتقسم فيهم. وإنما حاجتهم في الفضل والورع إلى
أن لا يخرج إلى الفسق، فيكون غير مأمون [٨٢ أ] وليس حاجة الأمة إلا
أن يكون مأموناً. ولا غناء بهم عن أن يكون أفقه الناس لأنّ جهلهُ ببعض
الفقه ضارٌّ[٧] بهم 'فيما ينزل'[٨] بهم مما جهله، وكان لا بد للأمة مما ينفي

الضرر عنها في إمامتها.

أما قوله: قد أنبأناكم أنه لا يجوز أن يولوا إلّا أفضل الفضلاء، يقال له: وكذلك لا يكون إلا أفقه الفقهاء. قلنا: واعلموا(١) أنه ليس أحد من ضَعَفَةِ المؤمنين ولا أقويائهم إلا وقد فُرِض عليه علم صلاته وفسادها، وذلك أن لا يَرَى في شيء حتى يتبيّن له أنه حرام عليه. وإذا لم تقم عليه الحجة بتحريمه فإنه له حلال، وإن من الأمور التي حرّمها الله في كتابه وسنّة نبيّه (صلع) [82 ب] على من بلغه ذلك وقامت الحجة ‹به عليه›، فمن يعلم فهو آثم ومن لم تقم عليه الحجة(٢) بما في الكتاب والسنة فليس عليه فيه وزر. فنقول: إن الله تعالى(٣) لا يفترض على كل أحد أن يعلم، لأن العلم صنعةٌ لا يجوز للعباد القدرة عليه. ولو قد فَرَض على المؤمنين أن يتعلموا شيئاً من مصالحهم وأشياء أخرى يعلمها من مصلحتهم لم يفرض الله(٤) عليهم تعليمها(٥) بما كان من صوم شهر رمضان وصلاة الخمس والحج والزكاة. فهذا ما لم يسع جهله ولا يجوز أن [لا] يعلمه. وما كان من علم النوازل فأمرٌ لم يفرضه الله على كل المسلمين. والله(٦) قد جعل لهم إذا علم حاجتهم إليه وقلة احتماله لهم يعلم جميعَهُ(٧) من خلفاء نبيه [83 أ] وأوصيائه(٨) من عند(٩) شدة حاجتهم. ونقول: الحجة لن تقوم على من لم يعلم، ولكن أن يعلم هو قيام الحجة ‹وأن تقوم(١٠)

---

١ في أ وب: وعلموا ٢ ساقطة في أ ٣ في ب: تبارك وتعالى ٤ ساقطة في أ
٥ في ب: يعلمها ٦ في ب: ولكنه ٧ في ب: جميعهم ٨ في ب: وأوصياء ٩ في
ب: عنده ١٠ في ب: يقوم

الحجة هو أن يعلم، وكل من لم يقم عليه الحجة في صغير من الدين أو جليل فلم يعلم. وإذا لم يعلم لم يجُز تكليفُه ولا يصلح أمرهُ[١] ونهيه. قالوا: وقد يزلّ[٢] عن والي[٣] المسلمين علم شيء من النوازل، فإذا شاء[٤] تشاور[٥] وبصر انتبه لموضع ذلك من الكتاب والسنة[٦] يعلمه[٧]، فإن لم يعلمه بعد قيام الحجة عليه من الكتاب والسنّة فهو عاصٍ. فنقول: إنه لن يجوز أن يزلّ[٨] عن والي المسلمين علم شيء من النوازل، ولا يكون إماماً والحجة قائمة [٨٣ ب] عليه يعلم[٩] ذلك من غير التشاور والقياس لأنهما ممّا[١٠] لم يبحه الرسول (صلع)[١١] ولم يوسعه الكتاب. ولو جاز أن يجهل ذلك لجاز أن لا يعلمه، ولو جاز أن لا يعلمه لكان الدين ناقصاً، وقد أخبرنا الله سبحانه بكماله، وإذا كان قد أكمله، معما[١٢] تبين من فساد القياس والأحكام والارتيا كان كماله وتمامه أن يعلم خليفة نبيّه جميع[١٣] نوازل خلقه في دينهم، ولا يُبتَلى بشيء إلا عنده مخرج منه. فالحجة ما مضى الحكمُ فيه. ولو جاز عليه الجهل بشيء من ذلك لم يجز أن يكون والياً، أحق بأن يكون مُولّى عليه، ولا مؤدِّباً دون أن يكون مؤدَّباً[١٤]، ولا يجوز أن [٨٤ أ] فيما تحتاج[١٥] الأمة إلى طاعتهم فيه ولا فيما يجب عليه فيه الحدود، كما لم يجز ذلك على من

---

[١] في ب: أموره   [٢] في ب: نزل   [٣] في أ: وال   [٤] في ب: تشاء

[٥] ساقطة في أ   [٦] ساقطة في أ   [٧] في ب: يعلمه   [٨] في ب: يزل   [٩] في

أ: بعلم   [١٠] ساقطة في أ   [١١] ساقطة في أ   [١٢] في ب: فيما   [١٣] في أ:

وجميع   [١٤] في ب: مؤدياً   [١٥] في ب: يحتاج

استحق مقعد رجل في(١) أمته بمنزلته(٢) (صلع). قالوا: وهل هو في ذلك إلا بمنزلة من كان النبي يوليه بعض البلدان النائية عنه يعمل بالحكم فيوفقه(٣) فيفقّهه حتى يأتيه علم ذلك يتلي به الناس. فإذا ابتلى الوالي عَمِل على(٤) استنباط ذلك واستعان بأهل العلم، فإذا أرادوا الإصلاح وفّقهم الله سبحانه وسدّدهم لأنه لا يكلّف عباده إلا ما يطيقون. ونقول في ذلك لِما جعلتم الإمام فيما يتلى(٥) به بمنزلة ولاةٍ. فهل يقولون إن النبيّ (صلع) وسع لأحد منهم [٨٤ ب] أن يستنبط في النازلة حكماً أو يشاور(٦) فيها أحداً. وإذا كان ذلك لم يوسع فيه لأحد لولاة البلدان وكنتم قد أنزلتم الإمام بمنزلةٍ(٧) لم يكن ذلك موسعاً مع حاجته إلى علمه عند(٨) رسول الله (صلع) كان لا يجوز مضى الرسول حتى يعلّمه ذلك، فيكون مفزعه إلى ما نص من سنّته ⟨قياساً على فرع الوالي ما يرد عليه من سنّته⟩(٩) ويكون ممتنعا في الإمام المشاورة والاستنباط كما امتنع ذلك في والي البلد علم قياس قولكم: «ولعمري إن في كتاب الله (ع ج) وسنّة رسوله(١٠) (صلعم) لكمال الدين ونص ما فيه حاجة المسلمين». ولو كان الله (ع ج) وَكِلَنا إلى المقايسة(١١) والمشاورة [٨٥ أ] في الأحكام لَلَحِقَ(١٢) ذلك بالكتاب والسنّة النقصان وأوجب فيهما عدم الكمال.

---

¹ في ب: منه   ² في ب: في منزلته ³ في أ: فيوقفه   ⁴ في ب: في   ⁵ في أ: يتلا وفي ب يتلى   ⁶ في ب: شاور   ⁷ في ب: بمنزلة   ⁸ في أ: غيبة   ⁹ ساقطة في أ   ¹⁰ في ب: نبيه   ¹¹ في ب: القائسة   ¹² في ب: لا لحق

ومن أراد الحق وفقه الله وفقه له ومن 'لم يُرد' الحق فيمن أعمل في دين الله رأيَهُ وابتدع في أحكامه ما لم يجعل الله به سلطاناً، ولعمري ما كلف الله الإمام من الحكم في النوازل إلا ما يطيق، إذا أعلمه[٢] ذلك ونص له علمه[٣] فالحمد لله على نِعَمه وإحسانه. ويقال لهم: يجوز أن يخطئ في قياسه؟ فقالوا: إن أخطأ فعاصٍ، وقد كلِّف[٤] الصواب، وهو يطيقه لأنه إنما أخطأ في ترك ما قامت به حجته، ويقال لهم: أخبرونا[٥]، فما وجه العلم فيما أخطأ وعصى فيه؟ فإن قالوا بيّنه[٦] العلماء، قلنا لهم [85 ب] قد اختلفوا في ذلك. فقال بعضهم بقوله وخالفه البعض[٧] الآخر. وكلٌّ عند تقدّمه مصيب. وقد نزلت بالمسلمين نازلة لا بد من إمضاء الحكم فيها. فإن قالوا: ينظرون، قيل لهم: قد نظروا، فثبت لكل قوم على ما قالوا به[٨] وإن كان بعضهم مخطئاً، كما قد رأينا بعض القياسيين مختلفين في نازلةٍ من[٩] مائة عام وأكثر، لم يزد[١٠] كل يوم كثرة النظر إلا تمسكاً بقولهم. فإن قالوا: يمضي الحكم رأي[١١]، قيل لهم: ولِمَ وهو عاصٍ[١٢] وكيف [لا] يسع المسلمين تركُهُ وإمضاء الحكم بما هو معصية؟ فإن قالوا: بمضي الحكم بقول من خالفه من العلماء، قيل: وكيف الصواب عند غيره؟ [86 أ] وكيف ترك رأيه والذين[١٣] وافقوه[١٤] وأمضى القول بخلافه؟

---

١ في ب: يرد   ٢ في ب: عليه   ٣ في أ: عليه   ٤ في أ: كان   ٥ في ب: خبرونا   ٦ في ب: أبينه   ٧ ساقطة في أ   ٨ في أ: فيه   ٩ في أ: مذ   ١٠ في ب: يرد   ١١ في أ: رائ   ١٢ في ب: عاصي   ١٣ في أ: والدين   ١٤ وافقوه

فإن قالوا: إنه متى قصد للحق فقد جعل النظر سبباً لإدراك النازلة. قلنا
لهم: وما الدليل على أن الله (ع ج) جعل النظر سبباً لذلك، فإن كان
القياس في الأحكام لا دليل عليه وكان الأمر فيه داعياً إلى تعطيل الحكم
وإنفاذه بغير الحق، كما ذكرنا، كان لا يكون إلا مستغنياً عن القياس بما
علمه ونصّ، وبطل ما قال المبطلون في ذلك. والقوة لله. وقالوا: قلتم لا
بد من إمام عادل يعرف كل ما بُلينا به. فقالوا: إن الإمام هو رسول الله
(صلع) وقد ورثنا كتاباً وسنّة فيهما[١] بيان كل شيء، وهو [٨٦ ب] بين
أظهرنا، وهو ما اجتمعت عليه (عوام الناس والفرق المنتحلة[٢] لدينه[٣].
فكما جاز أن على والي[٤] من غاب عنه ما لا يعلم جميع علمه، كان
مفزعة إلى رسول الله (صلع) هل كان إلا كتاب الله وسنّة رسوله(صلع)
نصاً لا قياساً ولا رأياً ولا مشورة، وكذلك يجب على قياسك أن يكون
مفزع من ولي إمامة كتاب الله وما نصه رسول الله (صلع) من سنّته.
ويكون امتناع القياس والمشورة في والي من غاب[٥] من رسول
الله (صلع). وقد بيّنه لمن يقوم بعده مقامه. ولو جاز أن يلينا من لا يعلم
جميع نوازل ديننا، لأنه لو جاز ذلك في والي بلدٍ لجار أن يلينا من ليس
[٨٧ أ] بأفضلنا، لأنه جاز ذلك في والي بلد، وهذا خروج من قولهم بإمامة
الفاضل.

ونقول: إن رسول الله (صلع) إمام الأئمة وإن ما نقلت عوام الفرق

---

١ في أ: فيها   ٢ في ب: عوام الفرق والمنحلة   ٣ ساقطة ففي أ   ٤ في
ب: ولى   ٥ في أ: ما

وفات نقلها فيه التوطى، فمن سنته، وإن كان في كتاب الله وسنَّة
نبيّه(صلعم) غنى عن غيرها، وأنهما مفزع الإمام كما قلنا قبل هذا. وقد
بيَّنّا من استحالة إدراكه بالقياس مع مَنْع الله (تع) ذلك في كتابه وحظره
بما قد اتينا على ذكره.

قالوا: وقلتم: لا يكون معصوماً من جميع الذنوب. فهل تزعمون أن
ولاة النبي(صلعم) كانوا كلهم على ما تصفونه[١]؟ فقدّ ولَّى من ليس عنده
جميع العلم، ولا معلوم أنه لم يزل[٢] ويتبع [٨٧ ب] شهوة. وقد فرض الله
على الناس ألا يتّبعوه إلا بما يعلمون صوابه، وأنه قبلةٌ عن رسول الله
(صلع)، ولا يساعدونه على الخطأ. فنقول: إنه إذا[٣] كان الدليل عندكم
على أن الإمام يكون غير معصوم. ولأن ولاة الأمصار غير معصومين، فَلِمَ
لا كان الدليل على جواز كون الإمام غير الفاضل، لأنه[٤] جاز في ولاة
الأمصار غير الفاضل. وكذلك يقال لهم: إذا جعلتم الإمام قياساً على
والي المصر، لم يكن إلا بنصّ الرسول (صلعم) وإن لم يكلّفهم إلى
اختيار إمامهم، كما لم يكل أهل المصر إلى اختيار أميرهم. فإن قال: إذا
ألزمتني هذا ألزِمك مثلَهُ[٥]. ولم يكن كون والي المصر منصوصاً عليه
[٨٨ أ] لوجب[٦] كون الإمام منصوصاً كما لم يكن والي المصر غير
منصوص موجباً أن الإمام غير منصوص. قيل له: إذا[٧] ألزمنا ذلك على
قياسك وارتيائك[٨] أنه بك لاحق، وإنما معنى أن يكون الإمام معصوماً

---

١ في أ: تصف   ٢ في ب: يزول   ٣ في أ: إذ   ٤ في أ: لأن

٥ ساقطة في ب   ٦ في ب: لوجوب   ٧ في أ: أنا   ٨ في أ: إرتيابك

للعلة التي وجب لها ذلك في الرسول (صلع)، لأن موقف الإمام بمواقف الرسول أشبه من موقفه[١] بموقف والي مصر. وإذا كان الله لم يكلنا[٢] في رسولنا إلى أن نستخرجه أو نقيمه حتى نصبه[٣] باسمه وعينه، وكذلك من يقوم مقام الرسول. وإذا كان الله عزّ وجل فكرامتنا من رسولنا أن[٤] يركب بنا خطيئة أو يوبقنا بمعصية أو يبتلينا بتغييرٍ أو تبديل كان ذلك كذلك في خليفته [٨٨ ب] وولي عهده. لأن حاجتنا إلى ذلك في وصيه كحاجتنا فيه إليه (صلعم).

ونقول: إن الله تبارك وتعالى قد افترض على الناس طاعة إمامهم وأخبرهم أن حُكمه فيهم حق وأنه عن الرسول قبله، وأنقذهم من أن يحملهم على خطأ، إذ نصه لهم رسوله وأمرهم بالانقياد له وأوجب[٥] له عليهما ما وجب له (صلعم). قال: فإن قلتم لا يجوز أن يستخرج رجل يصلح للإمامة باختيار وكان رسول الله (صلع) يولي الرجل على عمل، فيختار الرجل عاملاً له فيوليه على بعض أعماله الغائبة عنه، وجاز الخيار في عدل الرجل وصلاحه، فحكم الشهادة والدعاء[٦] بالصفة التي وصف [٨٩ أ] النبي صلى الله عليه وآله من الصلاح والعدل. ﴿وكذلك يجوز أن تختار[٧] الأمة بالصفة التي وصفت من الصلاح﴾[٨]، وليس على الناس علم ما غاب من عصمة الإمام كما لم يكن عليهم علم ذلك من المشهور،

---

١ في ب: موقف   ٢ في ب: يكلفنا   ٣ في أ: نصه   ٤ في ب: أنه   ٥ في ب: وجب   ٦ في أ: والدماء   ٧ في ب: يختار   ٨ مرددة مرتين في ب

وأمر بإثبات الإيمان للمؤمنين، وقد علم أن في بعض[١] الناس من يضيع بعض أعماله الغائبة. فهل رأيته سوّغ الموالي أن يكل ذلك للمسلمين دون أن ينص عليهم رجلاً يتخيره لهم. وكذلك يجب عليك أن يكون النبي (صلع) أو من قام مقامه لا يكل اختيار الإمام إلى المسلمين دون أن ينصبه لهم ويختاره منهم. ولم ننكر[٢] الاختيار من هذه الجهة وإنما أنكرنا إهمال الناس وتوكيلهم [٨٩ ب] إلى الاختيار لأنفسهم إذ لم تقم بذلك حجة مع ما قد بان فيه من الفساد. وقد كررتم تشبيه اختيار الإمام الشاهد العدل[٣]. وقولكم[٤]: وكذلك يجوز أن نختار[٥] بالصفة التي وصف من الصلاح. يقال له: هل تجد الرسول (صلعم) أمرك أن تقيم والياً إذا كان صالحاً كما أمرك أن تشهد عدلاً صالحاً؟ فإن ادّعى ذلك بَانَ كذِبُه. وإن قال: قست[٦] الإمام على ذلك في الشاهد. قيل له: فأجِز في الإمام أن يكون[٧] غير قارِئٍ للقرآن وغير فقيه، لأنه جاز ذلك في الشاهد[٨]. ويعارض ذلك[٩] فيما شُبِّه من عصمة الإمام بالشاهد وبظاهر المؤمنين. وقد قلنا في غير موضع من كتابنا [٩٠ أ] هذا إن الإمام لا يكون إلا معصوماً، باطنه كظاهره[١٠]. وثبت أن مقام الإمام بمقام الرسول أشبه من مقام الإمام بمقام[١١] الشاهد[١٢] العدل. وأن يحكم على الشيء بحكم ما أشبه أكثر وجوهه[١٣].

---

١ ساقطة في أ   ٢ في ب: ينكر   ٣ إشارة إلى الآية القرآنية: ﴿وَأَشْهِدُوا ذَوَيْ عَدْلٍ مِنْكُمْ﴾ (٦٥:٢)   ٤ في ب: وقولهم   ٥ في ب: يختار   ٦ في أ: قست   ٧ في ب: يكون إلى   ٨ ساقطة في ب   ٩ في ب: بذلك   ١٠ في ب: كظاهر   ١١ ساقطة في ب   ١٢ في ب: بالشاهد   ١٣ في ب: من وجوهه

قرابة النسب بين الرسول والإمام

ولا يجوز أن تقوم الحجة بقوله، ولا يكون إماماً إلا وله قرابة من رسول الله (صلعم) وقد يكون أقرب منه فلا يكون له من الفضل ما له، فيكون الأقرب لا يصلح لها. فقالوا لنا: إذا لم يصلح ذلك أن يكون في العم، فكان في ابن العم، فهل يجوز أن يكون لابن ابن العم أو الآخر أبعد منه حتى يكون ذلك قرشياً[1] ولا يكون هاشمياً[2]، ثم يرجع[3] إلى مضري ونزاري إذا جوّزتم أن يكون [90 ب] لم يوجد أقرب منه. وسألوا عن الحد الذي يصلح أن يكون لأمته فإنه يجوز أن يكون الإمام أخاه[4] فيختلط عليهم أمره كما اختلط إذ كان من غير فخذه، فنقول: إن خروجها من أقرب القرابة لأنه يكون غير موجبة خروجها من جميع القرابة كما أجزتم كونها فيمن زلّ عنه جميع الأبواب. وكذلك جائز[5] كونها[6] فيمن زل عنه جميع «أبواب الفقه[7]» وكذلك جائز كونها فيمن زلّ عنه معاني القرابة. والحد الذي لا يكون الإمام إلا منه القرابة بحد محدود حتى يكون ابن ابن العم وأسفل من ذلك أو ارفع. ولكن هي التي يتعارف الناس ويوقعون[8] على أهلها اسم القريب والقرابة، وإن كان معنى من [91 أ] المعاني التي يستحق بها الإمام الإمامة فإنه لن يستحق بها ذلك دون أن يراد بها غيرها من الفضل والعصمة. وإذا كان للإمام[9] أخوة أو

---

[1] في أ: قرشي؛ في ب: قريش   [2] في أ وب: هاشمي   [3] في أ: نرجع   [4] في أ وب: أخوه   [5] في ب: جاز   [6] ساقطة في ب   [7] في أ: لأبواب   [8] في أ: يوقعوا   [9] في أ وب: الإمام

قرابة قد تساووا من ولد[1] أو غيره، لم يجز إلا أن يبيّن الإمام منهم بالوصية أو بفضل ورع يظهر منه[2] ومعنى من معاني الخير لا يلحق به من ساواه[3] في القرابة أو تقدمه فيها. هذا ما كان في نعته[4]. وأما إذا كانت الدار داره فالنصُّ عليه وعقدُ ولايته. فإن قال قائل: فإذا كانت القرابة لا يستحق به وحدها الإمامة دون الفضل، فقد خرجت[5] مما يستحق به الإمامة، وثبت أن ذلك بالفضل الذي [ب 91] لا يستحق القوم الإمامة إلا منه. وإذا كان الفضل هو المعنى الذي يُستحق به كان مَن وُجد فيه ذلك المعنى هو فضل من قريب أو بعيد ﴿فهو مستحق﴾[6].

ويقال له: أخبرنا عن الفقه، هل هو من المعاني الذي يستحق بها عدل الإمامة؟ فإذا قال: نعم، يقال له: هل يجوز أو يولّى فقيه ليس بِوَرِع؟ فإذا قال: لا، قيل ذلك: فإذا كان الفقه مما يستحق به الإمامة وجب تولية الفقيه الذي ليس بورع. ﴿فإذا كان الورَع هو الذي يستحق به الإمامة[7]﴾ لأنه قد يوجد فقيه ليس بورع فلن[8] يستحق الإمامة. ثبت أن الورِع هو المستحق كان [أ 92] فقيهاً أو غير فقيه. فإن اعتلّ بأن الفقه على حالةٍ لا يُستحقّ بها حتى يكون معه الورع ولكن بهما جميعاً: فإذا كان ورِعاً فقيهاً استحق بهما. ولم يوجب أن الفقيه خارج من المعاني التي[9] يستحق بها الإمامة. فإن لم يستحق به على حالة فأوجب عليه بمثل ذلك في الكتاب. وأن خروجها من أن يجب بها حدّها الإمامة غير

مُخرِجٍ لها من أن يكون وغيرها أنّ[1] يجب الإمامة.

وسألوا أيضاً: من كان الإمام في زمن دعوة النبي (صلعم) القابل من عيسى (ع م)؟ وقالوا: كيف يجوز أن يُعلم بين[2] الأخبار[3] عن[4] الإمام وإن لم يُكن[5] قلنا: كما[6] نعلم عن النبي (صلع) وإن لم يكن[7]. [٩٢ ب] وكيف جاز ٬أن يُعلم من الأخبار[8] عن الإمام في حياته ولا يُعلم بعد موته؟ ونقول: ٬إنا نعلم[9] أن لعيسى (ع م) وصياً وخليفةً تناهت وصيته إلى حجةٍ في زمن النبي (صلع) وإن لم نعلم اسمه ولا من هو بعينه من حيث قلنا إنه لا يجوز في إمامٍ نَصبّه حتى يُنصَّ على من يقوم مقامه. وليس جهلُنا لمن هو موجبٌ علينا الجهل بأنه قد علم أن مِنّا[10] كثيراً لم يعلم أيهما هو[11] فلم يوجب جهلنا ٬مَن هُم[12] جهلاً بأنهم[13]. ونقول إن خليفة عيسى عليه السلام لم يخلُ أن يكون قريباً ٬أو أن يكون بعيداً[14][15] من أنه غير موجب أن يكون في قرب الأم أم من أمه لأن الذي أجاز [٩٣ أ] ذلك في عيسى (ع م) عدم الأب. كما أنه[16] جازت[17] في ابن العم لأنه فيمن هو أقرب منه[18] لم يكن ذلك مجوّزاً أقربهما في ابن العم إذا زالت[19] الأمة عن أقرب منه. ولو أن مجيزاً أجازها فيمن ليس

---

[1] ساقطة في أ   [2] ساقطة في أ   [3] في أ: الأخبار   [4] في ب: من   [5] في أ: يكنى   [6] في أ: لم   [7] في أ: يكنى   [8] في أ: أن يعلم الأحبار   [9] ساقطة في أ   [10] في أ: إماما   [11] في أ: هم   [12] في ب: منهم   [13] في أ: أنا   [14] في أ: قريباً   [15] ساقطة في ب   [16] في أ: أن   [17] في أ: أجازت   [18] ساقطة في أ   [19] في ب: زلت

بقريب(١) من المسيح وغيره من الأنبياء أو(٢) عمل بإرسال الأنبياء واتصال الوحي ونسخ الشرائع لكان ذلك(٣) سائغاً جائزاً وكان ذلك غير جائز خروجُها من قرابة النبي (ع م) لانقطاع الوحي وعدم الرسل. ٬ولعمري لو خرجت من قرابة النبي (صلعم)٬ مع انقطاع الرُّسُل وغلبة الجبابرة وتقية الأئمة من على خلفائها بعقد الولاية، لكان ذلك موجباً لإشكال الأمر [٩٣ب] ولكن(٥) لما حصر(٦) ذلك النسب وكانت الدلالة على موته(٧) القريب كل القرابة مما ذكرنا من الوصية إليه بالأهل وبفضل علم وورع أو طالبة من الاتكال وعدم [الأخذ] فيمن نصح نفسه في [من] الاخلاط. والحمد لله.

وقالوا: إنما يُعرَف ما غاب من الأشياء بالأخبار المُجْمَع عليها على غيره، مواطأة كجماع الناس على البلدان والملوك. على ذلك حمل الناس الذي بخبرِهِم عُرِفت دعوة النبي(٨) وعُرِف ما جاء به أن النبي(صلعم) لمّا قبضه الله ولَّى الناس أبا بكر. وكل الذين حملوا ولايته مُجمعون على أن النبي(صلع) لم يُولِّه، إنما ولَّاه الناس بآرائهم [٩٤أ] وأن المسلمين ٬ولّوه بعلم٬ منهم، بأنه أفضلهم، وأن من دين النبي(صلعم) بفضل الأفضل لم يفعلوا ذلك إلا بعلم وفريضة من الله عليهم. ولو تُركوا كانوا قد جاروا(١٠) عن قصد السبيل. وقد ولَّى الله ورسوله على هذا

---

١ في أ: بقرب   ٢ في ب: و   ٣ ساقطة في ب   ٤ في ب مرددة مرتين
٥ في أ: ولكنه   ٦ في ب: حضر   ٧ في ب: نبوّته   ٨ في ب: الرسول   ٩ في ب: ولو يعلم   ١٠ في أ: جاوزوا

المعنى. كما ذُكرتم بسنة النبي(١)، المؤمنين في كل زمان. فمن كان مؤمنا بالله ورسوله(٢) سماه مؤمنا، وكذلك [من اختاره المؤمنون] سمّاه الله إماما واليا عن الله ورسوله (صلعم). قبلوا ذلك كما قبلوا أشباهه مما سميناه. فنقول لهم: ما الدليل على ‹أن كل٣› المسلمين ولّوه؟ وما الدليل على أن من ولّاه منهم ولأنه أفضل؟ وما الدليل‹على أنهم فعلوا ذلك فلم يفضله [أحد] وأنهم لم يخطئوا في ذلك ولم يضلّوا؟ وما الدليل٤ على أن ذلك فرض عليهم أو أبيح لهم. فإن [٩٤ب] علموا(٥) بما قدّمنا، ولن يَعْدُوها(٦)، حكموا ما مضى من كلامنا. ونقول: إن تولية من ولّاه بدعةٌ جاروا بها عن قصد السبيل. وإن الله ورسوله لم يوليّاه على معنى من المعاني، وإنما تشبيههم(٧) تولية مَن ذكرنا بتسمية من ينتمي إلى المؤمنين مؤمنا فإنّا نقول لهم: أليس الله قد أمر بتسمية من أقر وعمل مؤمنا، وإن لم يسمِّ(٨) رجلاً بعينه؟ فإذا قالوا: نعم، قلنا: فهل سمّى(٩) من اختاره الناس إماماً؟ وان كان لم ينص على عينه، وهل يجد الرسول (صلعم)؟ قال: فمن وجد فاضلاً عالماً فهو إمام. كما قال عز وجل: ﴿أُوْلَئِكَ هُمُ الْمُؤْمِنُونَ حَقًّا﴾(١٠). فإن ادّعوا ذلك بان كذبُهم في أن لم يجدوا عن رسول الله (صلعم) [٩٥أ] أنه(١١) قال: «من كانت صفته كذا وكذا فاتخذوه إماماً وسمّوه واليا»، فإن ذلك موجود(١٢) في المؤمنين ما

أوجب التفرقة(١) بينهم. وقد يجوز هذا المعنى في غير موضع. ودعانا إلى
تكرار الجواب أنّ من وُلّوا لِما كان لم يولّه الرسول (صلع) وأجمعوا أن
من ولّاه إنّما مع ما قد بان من فساد الرأي وحكم قيام الحجة بإجماع،
كانت ولايته ضلالة، ومن ولّاه بتوليته لهم هم يقبلوها ضلالاً
لمخالفتهم(٢) الرسول (صلعم)، وتكليف ما لم يأذن الله به. قالوا: وقد
أجمعوا على تجويز(٣) الرأي والقياس لأصحاب محمد (صلعم). قالوا:
وقد(٤) يجوز ذلك أن يجتهدوا برأيهم ثم لا يقولون [٩٥ ب] حتى يعلموا أن
الحق فيما قالوا. وليس من دين المسلمين أن يقولوا ما لا يعلمون. فنقول
لهم: ما الحجة في الإذن ﴿في الارتياء﴾(٥) في دين الله؟ أبحكمٍ من كتاب
الله عز اسمه؟ أو بظاهر من سنة رسول الله (صلع)؟ فإن عملوا بنقض ما
ذكرناه في أول الكتاب كلفوا بما قدمنا، وإن عملوا باجتماع أصحاب
محمد (ع م) على تجويز اجتهاد الرأي طولبوا الدليل على إجماعهم،
وإن ذهبوا إلى أن أكثرهم أجازه(٦) كلموا الكثير والقلة بما قدمنا. وقيل:
ما الدليل على صواب الأكثر أجازوا الاجتهاد لو ثبت الأكثر إجازة.
وإن(٧) كان من دين المسلمين ترك القول بما لا يعلمون وكان اجتهاد
الرأي بما لا [٩٦ أ] يعلمون أنه حق.(٨) لأنه(٩) لم تقم به حجة وجب أن
من أجازه منهم مخطئ قائل ما لا يعلم ضال بذلك عن قصد السبيل.

---

١ في ب: الفرقة   ٢ في أ: فخالفهم   ٣ في أ: تجوز   ٤ ساقطة في ب
٥ ساقطة في أ   ٦ في أ: أجازهم   ٧ في أ: وإذا   ٨ في ب: الحق   ٩ في
ب: لأنهم

وزعم أن فيما وصفه دلالة على أن إمامة أبي بكر كانت على وجه الخطأ، بعد إقراره أنه مستدل على الفائت(١) من الأمور التي وصف. وقد ذكر أن الناس قد أجمعوا على تفضيله واختياره. وفي اختيارهم إياه وتفضيلهم له وإيثارهم أنه خيرهم عندهم مع علمهم وجوه الخير وهم السابقون الأولون من المهاجرين والأنصار الذين وصفهم الله عز وجل في كتابه وأوجب لهم أنهم صائرون إلى جنته بقوله في سورة براءة: ﴿السَّابِقُونَ الأَوَّلُونَ مِنَ الْمُهَاجِرِينَ وَالأَنصَارِ وَالَّذِينَ اتَّبَعُوهُم بِإِحْسَانٍ﴾(٢) إلى آخر(٣) الآية(٤)، [٩٦ ب] وكيف لا يوقيهم الله الخطأ وقد وصفهم الله ونعتهم بما ذكر. والخبر المرسل في قوم إنما يكون في عامتهم ولا يجوز في خاصتهم. وقد قال الله (ع ج): ﴿إِنْ يُرِيدَا إِصْلاَحًا يُوَفِّقِ اللَّهُ بَيْنَهُمَا﴾(٥). فمن أولى بإرادة الصلاح ممّن(٦) وصفه الله بما وصفه؟ فنقول في ذلك إن الأخبار العامة للتواطي دلالة على الأمر الغائب. من ذلك دلالتها على ولاية أبي بكر، وأنها عن(٧) غير أمر رسول الله (صلع) ولإجماع الأمة. وأن أكثرهم [ادّعوا أنه] قد نص بولايته(٨) وقد كذبوا فيما حكموا من إجماع الأمة على تفضيله، ولم يثبت أن من ولاه لأنه أفضل، بل قد اختُلف في ذلك: من أجاز ولاية أبي بكر من أصحاب إمامة [٩٧ أ] المفضول مع خلاف مَن أبى(٩) إمامته وإلزامه من

____

١ في أ: القاءه ٢ ساقطة في أ، ما في ب فورد « بإحسانهم » بدلاً من « بإحسان » ٣ في ب: آخره ٤ سورة براءة (٩):١٠٠ ٥ سورة النساء (٤):٣٥ ٦ في ب: من ٧ في ب: من ٨ في ب: به ولايته ٩ في ب: أبي

ولاّه فيها الخطأ. وقد فرّقنا بين الإجماع على الرأي والإجماع على الخبر. وأخبرنا أنه لو جاز قبول ما اجتمع عليه رأي سمّوه(١) عالماً. لأن لو قد(٢) قامت بخبره الحجة لجاز قبول رأي جماعة غير عدول. ﴿وقد قامت الحجة بذلك(٣) ملبين(٤) أو ذميين، وهذا ما قد بان فساده. وأما(٥) قوله(٦) ﴿السَّابِقُونَ الأَوَّلُونَ مِنَ الْمُهَاجِرِينَ وَالأَنْصَارِ﴾(٧) وما مدحهم الله به، ولعمري إن ذلك لفضيلة لمن لم يبطلها، كما قال الله عز وجل: ﴿وَلا تُبْطِلُوا أَعْمَالَكُمْ﴾(٨) وقال: ﴿فَمَن(٩) نَكَثَ فَإِنَّمَا يَنْكُثُ عَلَى نَفْسِهِ﴾(١٠). وقد عاتب من ذكرهم(١١) بالجملة فقال(١٢):

[97 ب] ﴿وَتَظُنُّونَ(١٣) بِاللَّهِ الظُّنُونَا﴾(١٤) فإن قلتم إنما كانت خواصاً، قيل: وكذلك مدح خواصاً، وصح هزيمة أكثرهم في غير موطن عن الرسول (صلع) وثبت أن فيهم النفي ولا يعرفون، لا شك(١٥) في انقطاع ولايتهم عند الله. وقد كانت لعمري لهم أفعال جميلة لو أعفوها مما كدّروها، ولو كان من أسبق له المدح (لا يجوز(١٦)) عليه الذم ومن سبق عليه الذم لا يجوز عليه الصواب. وقد ذم الله المشركين ثم آمن منهم خلق كثير فزال

١ في ب: من سموه ٢ ساقطة في أ ٣ في أ: وقامت بذلك الحجة ٤ في ب: ملبيين
٥ ساقطة في أ ٦ في كل من أ وب: قولها ٧ سورة براءة (٩):١٠٠
٨ سورة محمد (٤٧):٣٣ ٩ في كل من أ وب: ومن ١٠ سورة الفتح (٤٨):١٠
١١ في ب: نكرهم ١٢ في أ مرددة مرتين ١٣ في كل من أ وب: يظنون ١٤ سورة
الأحزاب (٣٣):١٠ ١٥ في أ: لا شره ١٦ في أ: ولا يجوز

عنهم الذم ولزمهم المدح. كذا من لم يثبت من الممدوحين زال عنه(١) المدح ولزمه(٢) الذم فإن قال قائل: لم يذم الله إلا من علم أنه لم يؤمن [٩٨أ] وإن كان قد أطلق الذم في الجملة. ولو كان(٣) مدح جملة القوم بنص(٤) كون الخطأ منهم لا ينفي 'الخطأ عنهم'(٥) في ذم بعضهم بعضاً، حتى يكون عثمان وقاتلوه وعلي ومحازبوه مصيبين في ذلك غير مخطئين. ولن يدفعوا أحد(٦) الفريقين وفسق أحد(٧) الخائنين وبان الوعيد على إحدى(٨) الناحيتين. وفيما ذكرنا من كون المنافقين المرتابين المرائين المنهزمين ما دل أن المدح لم يقع على الجملة فيما ذكرنا من أحداث(٩) ما قد زالت به عدالته وانقطعت ولايته ووجبت(١٠) عداوتهما دل على أن ليس ما فعل الممدوحون صواباً(١١) [٩٨ب] ولا حجة وأن(١٢) الحق أن ينظر فيه، فإن كان الكتاب موافقا والسنة مشاكلاً قُبل الأُرقَضُ وشهد على أهله بمبلغ الخطأ فيه من كفر أو(١٣) ضلال أو(١٤) فسق. ونقول إن الحكمين إن يريدا إصلاحاً يوفق الله بينهما وإن يكونا مريدين إلا الصلاح إلا باتباع ما أمر الله به وترك ما لم يأمر به ولم يبح فعله. وكذلك غير الحكمين. وكذلك من أراد الصلاح واتبع ما أمر الله به ووفقه الله. ونقول: أن من ذكرتم لم يريدوا إصلاحاً إذا ابتدعوا في ذلك

١ في أ: عنهم، في ب: عند   ٢ في أ: لزمهم   ٣ في أ: كان لأن   ٤ في أ: ينفي
٥ في أ: الخطايا منهم   ٦ في أ: إحدى   ٧ في أ: إحدى   ٨ في كل من أ
وب: أحد٩ في ب: أحذار   ١٠ في ب: ووجبت به   ١١ في كل من أ وب:
صواب   ١٢ ساقطة في أ   ١٣ في ب: و   ١٤ في ب: و

وفعلوا ما لم يأمر الله به وقدّموا من أخّر الله؛ وكان ذلك من فعلهم ناسخاً فضل من سبق له منهم فضلٌ[١]، [٩٩ أ] ودليلا على نفاق من أسرّ منهم نفاقا وزايداً في كفره وضلالاً. إذ لا سبيل لكم إلى الدلالة على أن ما فعلوا مأمور به من الكتاب نصاً أو من سنة الرسول (صلعم). وليس يدفع دافع وجود مؤسٍّ[٢] عند إجابتهم وطاعتهم ولا زوال المدح ولزوم الذم تغييرهم واتفاقهم على ضلالهم[٣] خلا من عصم الله منهم. ولم يباينهم[٤] هذه الأمة في الخُلُق[٥] ولا في وجوب المعصية ولا في رؤية الأولى وفي أقل ما قلناه كفاية.

ونقول: إنه لمّا كان شأن الإمامة على ما وصفنا وأمرُها على ما ذكرنا وفساد التشاور فيها على ما بيّنا، وكان لا بد من إمام على ما حددنا[٦] وكانت [٩٩ ب] التي أثبتناها قد زالت عن كل من كان بعد النبي من قريب أو بعيد، واجتمعت[٧] الأمة أنه لم ينصّه خليفة ما[٨] لم يكن معصوماً ولا تجتمع المنصوص في أمر النوازل عالماً خلا رجل واحد لم تُجمع الأمة أنه ليس كذلك لوجود بعض الأمة يدّعي كونه كذلك ويأثر فيه الإخبار، فلو جاز أن يكون هذا المدّعي له هذا هو الإمام ليثبت[٩] الإمام وقد بيّنّا أنه لا بد من إمام. فإذا كان قد فسد أن يكون كل من ليست له هذه الصفة إماماً وفسد أن لا يكون إماماً وفسد أن يكون كل أحد غيره إماماً،

---

[١] في أ: فضلاً   [٢] في كل من أ وب: موسى، مزيداً عليها في ب بـ« عليه السلام »
[٣] في ب: ضلالتهم   [٤] في ب: يبائنهم   [٥] في ب: الخلقة   [٦] في ب: عددنا   [٧] في ب: اجتمعت   [٨] في ب: وأنه   [٩] في ب: ليس

لزوال الصفة التي لا يخلو الإمام منها [١٠٠ أ] عن كل واحد منهم(١) بإجماع، لم يبق أحد منهم غير الواحد الذي ذكرنا، فثبت ما قلنا أنه هو. فأما المدعي بلا بيّنة فغير ثابت له الحق ولا مزيل باطل.

ونقول فيما ادّعى من وصية العباس رحمة الله عليه، فإنّا لا نعلم أحداً ادّعى للعباس وصية، وإن ذهبت طائفة إلى أنه كان أولى من طريق التشاور وألزموا من اختار غيره الخطأ في الاختيار واعتلوا له بالوراثة. وكان النقص عليهم شبيه ما(٢) ذكرنا من زوال الإمام عنه كان فاضلا خيراً. وقيل لهم في الوراثة لو وجب إن كان وارثاً يكون إماماً لوجب(٣) للورثة الإمامة بالوراثة مع هذا(٤) [١٠٠ ب] الخلاف في إرث(٥) العم مع الإبنة(٦)، وقولنا إنه لا يرث مع الولد ﴿بين فيه بنوه﴾(٧) غيره فأما من ادعى ذلك عندنا كاذب مبطل على من ادعى(٨) ذلك ما رأينا ذلك ولا سمعناه(٩) إلا من ناصبٍ يشيع(١٠) على شيعة آل محمد (صلع). وإن يكن أحد قاله وادعاه فقد قلنا إنه لا يجب بها حق ولا يزول بها باطل دون البينة عليها والشهادة بها. وقلنا إن من الدلالة على إمامة علي كرّم الله وجهه حديث غدير خم إذ كان مجمعاً عليه. فعارضنا قوم وزعموا أن الاجماع على الخبر لا يكون إلّا أن يكون مجيئه كعدد الصلاة وعدد الزكاة [١٠١ أ] وعدد رمي الجمار والطواف، فأما إذا نظر الناظر في أصله

لوجد[١] إلا على ما روي عن[٢] خاص. فليس بمثله تقوم الحجة. قالوا
وأشهر منه عشرة من أهل الجنة: الصدّيق والفاروق وكذا وكذا، فلم
يُلتَفَت ومثله أو أشهر منه كقول[٣] أهل الجنة. وأشهر منه أو مثله قول
علي (ع م)[٤]: خير هذه الأمة بعد نبيّها أبو بكر وعمر[٤] وما لا يحصى من
الحديث الذي منه أشهر منه ما لم يُلتَفَت إليه. ونقول: إن قائل ذلك فقد
أبطل في تشبيه هذه الأخبار بخبر غدير خم، وذلك ان خبر غدير خم إن
كان في علم الصغير والكبير به ليس بعدد الصلاة، فإنه لا تنازع بين
الأمة [١٠١ ب] فيه، لتواتر الخبر به من من النواحي التي لا يحدث مثلها،
بدليل دافع من الأمة. ولا نقل أحد من الأمة من جميع الأصناف لا
ينفيه[٥] ولا ينقصه ولو لم تقم به الحجة، لأنه ليس في الناس نقلهم بعدد
الصلاة، وكذلك فروض الله في الزكاة[٦] والحج وغيرهما مما لم
يستفض[٧] في الناس كاستفاضة عدد الصلاة، ولو لم يكن مفاخر فيها
بعدد الصلاة فيما ذكرنا مخرج لها[٨] من أن يكون الحجة قد قامت بها
عن رسول الله (صلع) من حيث نقلها حملةٌ[٩] الروايات ولم يدفعها
دافع، ومثل ذلك أشباه من دلائل الرسول (صلعم) مثل تكليم الذئب له
ومخاطبة الذراع[١٠] [١٠٢ أ] وأشباه ذلك وإشباع عالَم من سخلة[١١]. كل
ذلك ليس استفاضة في أيدي الناس مثل استفاضة عدد الصلاة حتى

---

١ في أ: أوبرجد   ٢ في أ: من   ٣ في ب: كقولك   ٤ في ب: كقوله   ٥ في
أ: لا يغيه   ٦ في أ: الديات   ٧ في ب: يستفيض   ٨ ساقطة في ب   ٩ في ب:
جملة   ١٠ في أ: الرزاع   ١١ في ب: سنجلة

يعلمه الجاهل والعالم، وإنما ذهاب من ذهب إلى غدير خم حيلة منهم. وأبطال هذه الأخبار التي يستدل بها المسلمون، يُقيمون^(١) بها الحجة. من دلائل النبي (صلعم) دلائله في غدير خم وما كان مثله أَمُّ الصلاة^(٢) لتواتر الفرائض^(٣) بالصلاة في أوقات من النهار والليل^(٤) فكثر^(٥) ذلك في الليل والنهار. والدليل على ذلك علم الناس بعدد الصلاة أشيع من علمهم عدد الزكاة لأنه ليس من علم من جهة عوام الناس أن الظهر أربع ركعات، يعلم أن في^(٦) مائتي درهم خمسة دراهم وكذلك [١٠٢ ب] العلم أن في مائتي درهم خمسة دراهم في أيدي جهّال العوام أكثر من علمهم بأنه يقام في مِنى أيام التشريق يذبح^(٧) بها، وأنه يقيم لعرفات وأن ذلك بعد زوال الشمس وأنه يزور البيت في وقت كذا وأن عليه صوم عشرة أيام إن لم يجد ما يضحّى به. وقد نطق الكتاب بذلك وجاء بجميع ما ذكرنا بالخبر الذي تقوم به الحجة، وأنّ^(٨) من استقامته الصلاة عدد الصلاة. فكان الذي أوجب في هذه الأخبار مساواة مجيء عدد الصلاة، وإن لم ينقل أحد من فِرق الأئمة ضدها ولا من الأخبار ما ينفيها. كذلك خبر غدير خم لم يردّه أحد من الأمة ولم يُنقل عن [١٠٣ أ] رسول الله صلى الله عليه وآله ولا من فعل القول ذلك فيه ما ينفيه^(٩). وإنما فزع المعاندون فيه إذ لم يستطيعوا ردّه^(١٠) إلى التأويل الفاسد، فإن الأخبار

---

١ في أ: تقيمون ٢ في ب: أم للصلوة ٣ في أ: الفرض ٤ في ب: أو الليل ٥ في ب: يكثر ٦ ساقطة في أ ٧ في ب: بذبح ٨ في أ: بأن ٩ في أ: ما ينفعه ١٠ في ب: ردها

التي ذكروها فمنها لا يعلم أنه جاز إلا من[١] رجل واحد وهو حديث
العشيرة[٢]، وجاء عن سعيد بن زيد وقد نقل بعض فرق الأمة ما ينفيه مثل
أن بعض العشيرة كان في أصحاب الفقه، ونقل عن علي أنه كذّبه في
حديثه، وقال: أشهد بالله أنّك كذبت على رسول الله (صلعم)، وروي
عنه أنه قال: أما أنت شهدت لي وأنا أشهد لك. وكذلك سيد كهول
أهل[٣] الجنة قد نقل بعض الفرق من الأمة أنهما كانا في أصحاب
[١٠٣ ب] الفقه، وأبوا الحديث ورموا ناقله بالكذب. وكذلك ما ذكرنا عن
علي كرم الله وجهه وصلوات[٤] الله عليه[٥] من قوله[٦]: « خير هذه الأمة
بعد نبيها... » وروي عن علي (ع م) ضده مثل ما رماه به من ظلمها[٧]
له واختاره بفضله عليهما الذي نُقل من أفعاله الدالة على فضله عليهما[٨]
وأنه لم يكن كاذبا. أكُلُّ[٩] ذلك ينفي أن تكون هذه الأخبار ضاهت خبر
غدير خم الذي فيه نقله إلى علماء الأمة[١٠] ولم يأبه[١١] أحد من فرّقها ولا
رده. فكيف يشكل[١٢] هذا على ذي علم وفهم؟ وزعموا أن الأمة جاءت
مجمعة[١٣] بولاية أبي بكر وتأخير عليّ ودخوله معهم في ذلك، ثم في
زمن الغار، ومثل ذلك مجتمعون على ذلك. ثم وجه الشورى مع خمسة
فوجّهاهم[١٤] [١٠٤ أ] إلى غيره[١٥] وأخرج نفسه وأخرجوه منها، ثم في

الرابعة ادعاها(١) وحالفه(٢) ثلاثة من أهل الشورى. أما اثنان فحارباه وأما واحد فأبى بيعته، ثم لم يزالوا في حَرْبِهِ حتى ردَّها إلى الشورى بحكم الحكمين(٣)، فأخرجه(٤) منها صاحبه الذي اختاره لنفسه. فكيف يجوز أن يُفضّل هذا بعد هذا على الصدّيق والفاروق لولا جهل الجاهلين؟ فنقول في الخبر المجتمع(٥) عليه حجة وبحجته بيّنا(٦) إن أبا بكر وُلّي (وكذلك عمر(٧) وكذلك(٨) أمر الشورى وبحجة(٩) الخبر علمنا أن القوم ضلوا بما فعلوا وخالفوا الرسول (فيما أرموا. وقد ثبت بالخبر أن ذلك كان من غير أمر الله ولا رسوله (صلعم). ثم أفعالهم(١٠) [104 ب] التي ينقض بعضها بعضاً لأنّ(١١) كان أصلهم أن رسول الله (صلع) وكلّهم فاختاروا لأنفسهم أصلحهم ولن(١٢) نشك أن رسول الله (صلعم) قد كان علم الأصلح. فلئن كان ترك رسول الله (صلعم) تولية الأصلح أصلح لقد ثبت أن الذي فعل أبو بكر من تولية عمر ليس بأصلح ولا كان الذي فعل أبو بكر أصلح ما يخلو ذلك من وجهين: إما أن يكون رسول الله (صلعم) جهل الأصلح بعده وعلم أبو بكر الأصلح من بعده، أو يكون رسول الله (صلع) علم(١٣) أصلحهم وترك توليتهم، وقد عُلم أن تولية(١٤) الأصلح أصلح. وهذان المعنيان كفر بالله، ممّن(١٥) قالهما أو ذهب

---

١ في ب: إدعاءها ٢ في كل من أ وب: خالفه ٣ في ب: الحاكمين ٤ في ب: فأحكمه ٥ في ب: الجميع ٦ في أ: بيننا ٧ في ب: لذلك ٨ في ب: لذلك ٩ في ب: وحجته ١٠ في ب مرددة على الصفحة التالية ١١ في أ: لأنه ١٢ في أ: وأن ١٣ ساقطة في ب ١٤ في ب: توليتنا ١٥ في أ: فمن

إليهما. ثم فعل عمر ما فعل في الشورى [105 أ] ما(١) قد بان فيه خطأه. إذ
لا دليل له عليه من كتاب الله ولا شاهد له به من سنّة رسوله فعله. وإن
أبا بكر أمر به ولم يدفع أن الخبر قد ثبت ﴿بأن أكثر القوم قد دفعوا عليّاً
(صلعم)، ولمّا ثبت٢﴾ من ذلك عندهم(٣) ثبت خطأهم. وقدّمنا في أوّل
كتابنا الدلالة على فساد الإمامة من طريق التشاور والرأي. وأمّا دعواهم
دخول علي كرّم الله وجهه وصلى عليه فيما دخل فيه القوم فأمر تعدّى
فيه الحق وتجاوز فيه الصدق. ولو ثبت أنه دخل معهم بيّنا من فساد
عقدهم واستحقاقه الأمر دونهم لأن لا يكون ذلك إلا تقية وسع الله له
فيها. وأما ادعاؤهم [105 ب] بأنه وجهها مع أصحاب الشورى إلى غيره
فادعوا باطلاً عليه. بل قد بيّن لهم خطأهم وأوضح لهم سبيل نجاتهم
ودلّهم على رشدهم وأعلمهم فساد مذهبهم. فلما أبوا ضعِف عن
جهادهم ووسعه(٤) تركهم، فإن قال: بايعهم قاصرٌ من الفقه فسبيلهم فيها
كسبيله(٥) فيما قبلها. ونقول: إن من خالفه من أهل الشورى غير مزيل
عنه استحقاقها. وكذلك موافقتهم غير مثبتة أشياء لم يكن بغير الموافقة
ثابتاً. وليس مخالفته أهل الباطل يفسد الحق بل يزداد به أهل الباطل
باطلا ويدخل أهل الولاية في منزلة الإغراء. وإنما الأمر الذي ثبّت به
إمامته (صلعم) ما قدمنا [106 أ] من فساد عقد القوم واستحالة خروج
الرسول من غير استخلاف ووجود صفات الإمام التي تزول الامامة عن(٦)

---

١ في ب: مما   ٢ ساقطة في ب   ٣ في ب: عنهم   ٤ في ب: وسعة   ٥ في
أ مردّدة   ٦ في أ: عمن

فقدها لعلي (صلعم)، [إذ](١) كان لا بد أن يكون فيهم مستخلف لتلك الصفة، وكان ذلك زائلا عن جميعهم بإجماع الأمة خلا علي (صلع)(٢) [وأصول مذهبهم يدعوهم إلى الاحتجاج لخلاف من خالفه](٣) وكذلك أبطل فيما ادعوا(٤) من ردّ الأمر إلى الشورى ولها أمر بعض عبيده ورعيته أن يحتج على من ادعى الشك في أمره، وأظهر حربه(٥) ونهض في جهاد عدوه ما أمكنه. ولعمري ما ترك جهاد من كان من أئمة الجور قبله ولا العجز قامت به معذرته ووسعته(٦) نفسه من ذلك ظلمهم له وحملهم النار إلى بيت فاطمة حليلته [106 ب] وابنة نبيّه (صلعم)، ثم إجماع الصلاة منهم على قهره وغصبه الحق من شيعته. وأما قولهم: فكيف يجوز أن يفضل بعد ذلك على الصدّيق والفاروق، فإن هذا جهل من قائله وعمى عن التفضيل. وهذه أمور تجب(٧) بها عندنا ضلالة فاعليها ومبتدعها.

وإنما وجه التفضيل التي تجب حجته علينا وعليهم الأمور التي أجمعنا أنها مرضية لله: فيها جهاد العدو والسبق إلى الإسلام والقراءة للقرآن والعلم بالحلال والحرام والقرابة بالرسول فيما أشبه ذلك. والذي(٨) أوفر حظاً من هذه الأمور هو الأفضل، والذي هو أوفر من الهزيمة نصيبا أخس في العلم [107 أ] حظاً(٩) وأكثر في أمر الرسول شكّاً، مثل ما كان في يوم الحديبية مع الرسول لحذيفة على نفاقه. فواجب أن يكون هو الأنقص

---

١ في ب: إذا   ٢ في ب: مرددة مرتين   ٣ ساقطة في أ   ٤ في أ: ادعى
٥ في ب: حرمه   ٦ في ب: وسعة   ٧ في أ: يجب   ٨ في ب: أو الذي   ٩ في أ: خطأ

وغيره الأفضل. ⟨ونقول⟩[1] إن في افتتان من افتتن بعلي (صلع) دليل على
أنه قد باين من يحصره[2] من الضروب، كإغلاظهم[3] من أجله، وذلك
أنه لا يتصرف[4] ⟨إلا وهم⟩[5] الأغلط في مثل ما غلطوا فيه ⟨لا لمعنى⟩[6] فيه
غلطوا إلا فيمن دار من الناس مثله، ⟨وعندما شاهدوا شبهه⟩[7]، وكذلك
نقول في الأوثان والمسيح (ع م) إن الناس إنما افتتنوا فيه لعلةٍ لا يقوم
في الوهم إلا ذلك. وقد تكون العلة حقيقة ومخوفة ومن ذلك ما كان
من المسيح (ع م) من أفعاله التي [١٠٧ ب] دلّ بها على نبوته (صلعم)
فاستعظمها القوم فأفرطوا فيها، ومن ذلك ما روي من تخوّفه أهل الأوثان
واحتيالهم لصنم مجوّف يُدخلون فيه رجلا يكلّم الناس فيه، وما ذُكِر عن
بعض الأصنام من احتيال أهلٍ فيه حتى أقاموه في بيت بين سقفه وأرضه.
وكان سبب وقوفه من قبل أن سقفوا[8] البيت بأحجار مغناطيس،
وفرشوه بمثله ثم أقاموه بين السقف والأرض وجذبه كل واحد ولم يكن
أحدهما أكثر فيكون أقوى بيت الصنم بين سقفه وأرضه. ثم ما رواه
الأمة من سبب اتخاذ المشركين في ودّ وسواع أنهما كانا رجلين
صالحين يسميان بهذين [١٠٨ أ] الاسمين، فلما ماتا خرج عليهما
أهلوهما، فأتاهم إبليس بهذين الصنمين فقال لهما: هذان مثالهما،
ورضوهما[9] على الأنس[10] بمثل العابدين، ونشأ جيل آخر فأعطوهما أكثر

---

[1] ساقطة في أ   [2] ساقطة في ب   [3] في ب: كاغلاظهم   [4] في ب:
ينصرف   [5] في أ: الوهم   [6] في ب: المعنى   [7] في ب: وعند من شاهد وأشبهه
[8] في ب: يسقفوا   [9] في أ: ووصفوهما   [10] في أ: الأيس

من ذلك الإعظام حتى ترقّى بهم الأمر إلى العبادة لهما. وكان السبب في ذلك فضل الرجلين والإعظام لمثالهما. قلنا: كان غلط الناس لا يخلو من ذلك: إما بمعنى فضل الله بعض خلقه فغلط فيه من جهة مباينة[١] من بحضرته، وإما بحيله يحتال بعض الخداعين[٢] لعوام الناس. وثبتت أن طائفةً قد غلطت في هذا الرجل علمنا ان غلطهم لم يكن إلا لمعنى، إما فضيلة[٣] [١٠٨ ب] قد[٤] أبانها الله بها وعلمٌ ألقاها[٥] إليه رسول الله (صلعم) أو غيره أو لضرب[٦] من ضروب المخوفة[٧]. وإذ كان قد نفي عندنا وعند جميع الأمة عند معاني المخرقين وأمور الخدّاعين لما ثبت من عدالته واتباع أمر نبيه (صلع) وفضله وسابقته كان غلط من غلط فيه من الناس. لم يكن إلا ما ذكرنا من الفضل قد بان به مثل ما روي عنه أنه خبر يوم الجمل الوقت الذي يهزمهم فيه وكم يقتل منهم[٨]، ثم ما خبّر به يوم النهروان وأنه لا ينجو منهم عشرة ولا يقتل من أصحابه عشرة، ثم ما خبّر به من أمر ذي الثدية[٩] وشأنه. كل ذلك بان فيه صدقه. ثم ما روي عنه [١٠٩ أ] من اقتلاعه الصخرة عن البئر في طريقه إلى العراق ونزول الراهب إليه واختباره أنه يجد في كتبه أنه لا يفتحها إلا نبيّ أو وصيّ نبي، ومثل ذلك[١٠] ما روي من رجوع الشمس له حتى صلى العصر مرتين في[١١] حياة الرسول وبعد وفاته. كل ذلك بعلم علمه من

---

١ في ب: مبائنة   ٢ في أ: الخدامين   ٣ في ب: فضيلته   ٤ ساقطة في أ   ٥ في ب: الفا   ٦ في ب: وغيره ولضرب   ٧ في ب: المجوفة   ٨ في ب: فيهم   ٩ في أ: الثدي   ١٠ ساقطة في أ   ١١ في أ: من بين

رسول الله (صله) واسما من أسمائه. تمّت عزيمة الله[١] في إجابة من دعاه بها.

فمن ههنا غلط القوم. وفي غلطهم لعمري دليل على فضله، إذ زال عنهم أمر الخدّاعين كما قلنا.

ولعلّ قائلاً يقول: فقد يجوز أن يكون قوم عادوا الإسلام[٢] فقالوا فيه ذلك القول يريدون بذلك إضلال[٣] الضَّعَفَة من الناس عداوة للدين [١٠٩ ب] إذ قهرهم الإسلام. فيقال لهم: قد يجوز أن يكون هذا كذلك، ولكن لمّا وجدنا فيه معنى باين[٤] به الناس، أمكنه ذلك المعنى التمويه والخديعة. ⟨فإن قال قائل[٥]: فما بال الرسول (صلع) لم يتعدَّ[٦] له[٧] منزلة، وقد كان من أفعاله ما لا يجوز لغير نبي، قلنا له: إنا إذا قلنا إن القوم إنما غلطوا في هذه العجيبة رأوها[٨] فليس يجب علينا أن كل من كانت منه عجيبة فواجب أن يُغلط فيه، كما ⟨قال قائل[٩]⟩ إن عيسى (ع م) إنما غلط من غلط لقلة عجائبه. وقد رأى الناس من موسى وحزقيل عجائب كثيرة لم يغلطوا لها. وبذلك يُحتج على من غلط في المسيح. [١١٠ أ] وكذلك يُحتج على من غلط في أمير المؤمنين بمباينته[١٠] ذلك. على أنّا نبرأ إلى الله فيمن أفرط فيه أو ألحقه بمنزلة الرسول (صلع)، بل كان أخاه ووصيه وخليفته في أمته ووارث علمه. هذه منزلته عندنا، وإليه

---

¹ في ب: بالله   ² في ب: والإسلام   ³ في ب: ضلال   ⁴ في ب: بائن

⁵ ساقطة في أ   ⁶ في أ: يتعدا وفي ب: يتعدى   ⁷ ساقطة في ب   ⁸ في أ: رادها

⁹ في أ: قد ثبت   ¹⁰ في أ: بمناسبة وفي ب: بمباينته

ندعو مَن خالفنا. قالوا: وقد رأينا من يدّعي أنه وصيّ(١)، ما وجدنا الكبير منهم أثراً في علم ولا مخرجاً من لَبَس، ولا ظهر منه فيه بحكم ولا بيان في شيء من لطيف الدين. ونقول في ذلك: ما من أحد تناهت إليه وصية رسول الله (صلعم) إلا وعنده الأثر في العلم والمخرج من اللّبَس والفهم للحكم(٢) والبيان في جليل الدين ولطيفه. وليس بأن نَقْصَ [١١٠ب] علم عالمكم عن ذلك ينفي من كان مستحقه ولا بالمحبة تثبت عندنا إمامة الإمام. (وذلك(٣) أنّا قد أفسدنا إدراك الأحكام بالقياس والارتياء(٤) وأبطلنا علم غير(٥) الإمام بما يعلم الإمام من ذلك، وأن علمه مما يحتاج إليه لا يكون إلا بنص من قبله عليه.

(وأما(٦) الدلالة على الإمام المثبتة(٧) لإمامته إشارة الإمام قبله إليه وإحالة الرعية عليه. وقد قدّمنا الكلام أنه لا(٨) ينصب إلا أفضل الناس علما وورعا، وثبتنا(٩) أنه ذلك الإمام بعد الرسول على ما قدّمنا في أول كتابنا فيمن ثبت له وصية علي (ع م) فهو القائم بما قام به علي (ع م) مقامه وكذلك كل من تناهت إليه الوصية [١١١أ] من عروضٍ لم(١٠) ينقصه ولم(١١) يفسده جهل من جهله وجَحدُ من جحده، كما لم ينقص من كان قبله واحتجوا على الإمام. قد أجمعت(١٢) على من ليس بنبي ولا يعدل بنبي في قول أو علم، ورموا هذا الحديث بالشذوذ(١٣) غير منزل

---

¹ في ب: وصيا ² في أ: للحلم ³ في ب: فذلك ⁴ في ب: بالارتياي ⁵ في ب: عين ⁶ في ب: فأن ⁷ في ب: البتة ⁸ في أ: لم ⁹ في أ: ثبت ¹⁰ في ب: لا ¹¹ في ب: لا ¹² في أ: اجتمعت ¹³ في ب: بالسدود

بحجته. والإمامة في هذا 'الحديث صنفان'': ناقل وغير دافع'''. وليس

بمستنكر جهل من جهل منهم في رد خبر أو في قبوله، وطلب الحجة

في إزالة ما لزمه عند الإقرار به وعند جحده إيّاه وردّه أو رميه بالشذوذ'''،

فإنا نقول: إنه لا يعدل النبي (صلع) من ليس بنبي في قول أو فعل.

وليس في ذلك خلاف الحديث إذ قد استثنى الرسول في الحديث

[١١١ب] النبوّة، وإذا كانت النبوة زائلة أن يكون نزل من الشيء بها منزلة

هرون من موسى. وكذلك الأخوة من الأب والأم. وكانت منزلة هرون'''

من موسى بعد كل المؤازرة''' دون قومه وشد العضد دون أهله، وكان

الحق به الشهادة وأكثرهم بعده علما وفضلا 'وأشدهم لمقعده''' بعده

استحقاقاً. ولو كان رسول الله (صلع) قد أنزل علياً بمنزلة هرون من

موسى على ما استثنى من النبوة وخلا ما زال بالإجماع من أخوة الأب

والأم لم يبق إلا أنه وزيره دون أهله وعضده دون قومه وأقربهم شبها به

وأفضلهم بعده وألحقهم بعلمه وأحقهم [١١٢أ] بمقعده، وإذا كان الامام لا

يكون إلا كما وصفنا ولا ينص الرسول إلا على 'مثل ما ذكرنا كان في

قول الرسول هذا دليل على''' أنه هو المنصوص عليه والمشار إليه بالأمر.

ونقول إنه غير جائز إطلاق رسول الله (صلع) هذا 'الأمر الخاص'''، لأن

ذلك يوجب عقد الأمر لغير الكامل، فلم يكن فيهم أحد يجوز أن يطلق

' في ب: في الحد وجهان   ' في ب: ناقل دفع   ' في ب: بالسدود   ' ساقطة في ب

' في ب: الوزارة   ' في أ: وأسدهم لقعده   ' ساقطة في ب   ' في ب: في

الامر الناس

ذلك فيه غيره، إذ كلهم قد زالت عنهم صفة الكمال التي أفسدنا خلق الإمام منها. فإذاً كان إطلاق ذلك في غير الكامل وفي الأمر الخاص فاسدا وكان إطلاقه في عليّ ثابتا بيّنا كماله واستحقاقُه[١] الأمرَ [١١٢ ب] واحتجوا أيضا بأن قالوا قد خولف في ولايته ونوزع وما ثبت له حق لقول الله، ولعمري ما تعدّى[٢] القائل بذلك حقاً. لقد اتوه طائعين، 〈وما كان في〉[٣] أمره الغلبة ما كان في أمره غيره فما حدّ فيه[٤] من ولايتهم عليه وأمر من يقتل من عاد إلى مثله ولم يوجب[٥] خلاف من خالفه فساد أمره إذ كان الحق ثابتا والبرهان عليه قائماً، وما أكثر من نوزع من أنبياء الله فلم يكن ذلك لدعوته مفسدا، ومن سلم له وترك منازعته من أئمة الجور قبل الإسلام وبعده فلم يكن ذلك [١١٣ أ] لدعوته مصححا له ولم[٦] ينكروا أنه قد كان فضل الأصحاب للنبي (صلع) وعلمائهم وأهل الحزم في حروبهم وآرائهم ، وأنه كان عالما بأخبار الجماعة التي نقلت إلينا. وقد أجمعوا 〈على تفضيل الصديق〉[٧] والفاروق عليه وأنهما كانا أولى بالإمامة منه، وأنه كان موضعا للشورى. وقالوا إن علياً كان عالماً فقيها ورعاً فاضلاً على ذلك أجمعوا من قبل أن يكون. ثم اختلفوا فيه عند ولايته فحاربوه جماعة كثيرة وأكثروا أن يكون أولاهم بها. فكنا[٨] معهم على ما أجمعوا عليه من أمره ثم وقفنا فيه وفيمن[٩] حاربه الاختلاف وتواتر

الشهادات منه ومن أهل حزبه[١]. [١١٣ ب] فنقول إنكم قد أقررتم بفضله وذكر محاسنه، فأما من زعمتم أن الأمة اجتمعت لهما بما ادعيتم، فلم نجد[٢] الأمة اجتمعت لهما على فضل ولا فقه ولا علم بل قد روى بعضهم أنهما[٣] كانا في أصحاب العقبة مع المشهور عند وليهما وعدوهما من خلوّهما من حمل الكتاب وبعدهما من نكاية أعداء الله وقرارهما[٤] في غير موقف من رسول الله (صلع) وما ظهر من سخفهما[٥] على أنفسهما من قول أحدهما: ولّيتكم ولست بخيركم، وإن[٦] لي شيطاناً[٧] يعتريني، ومن رجوع الآخر من غير حكم ربّه عنه[٨] على حكم قد كان حكم فيه بغير ما أنزل الله (تع) جهلاً وتخبطاً[٩] [١١٤ أ] في كل ذلك يقر بجهله ويقول كل أحد أفقه من عمر مع ما ظهر منه عما[١٠] كان قبل ذلك مستورا[١١] في يوم الحديبية من إنكار حكم رسول الله (صلع) والتحريض على دين الله وتشكيك الناس في أمر رسول الله (صلع). وقد كذبوا فيما ادّعوا من إجماع[١٢] الناس على تفضيلهما عليه وفي اختلاف الناس في ذلك واختلاف رواياتهم عن معنى[١٣] ما أبان كذبهم. وقد قدمنا أن إمامة علي (عليه السلام وكرم الله وجهه وصلى عليه) لم يثبت عندنا بإقرارهم فيزول خلاف بعضهم. بل إنما ثبت عندنا

---

[١] في كل من أ وب: خربه   [٢] في ب: مرددة مرتين   [٣] في أ: أنهم   [٤] في أ: وأقربها   [٥] في ب: إستخفهما   [٦] ساقطة في أ   [٧] في أ: شيطان   [٨] ساقطة في ب   [٩] في أ: وخيطا   [١٠] في أ: ما كان   [١١] في ب: سرّا   [١٢] في ب: جماع   [١٣] في أ: مضى

فضل من أجابه بأن أطاعه ونقص من فارقه بأن خالفه وقد قلنا في ذلك
ودللنا عليه بما فيه [١١٤ ب] كفاية. ولعمري لو كانت الامامة على ما
ذهبتم إليه من الشورى لكانت الحجة بإمامة علي أثبت منها بإمامة أبي
بكر، لأنه قد ثبت أن القوم أجمعوا[١] على بيعته 'خلا واحدا'[٢]، 'بل
إجماع[٣] الجماعة عند 'شذوذ الواحد'[٤] والأمر[٥] ثم نكث بيعته من يقيم[٦]
التسوية . قالوا: وجب على أصلكم أن العقد الذي أُبرم[٧] معهم لا
ينتقص[٨] إلا بإجماعهم على نقضه. وإذا كان عقد أصحاب الشورى
عندكم حجة على غيرهم حتى ولو خالفهم واحد أو[٩] اثنين من غيرهم
لم[١٠] يلتفت إليه[١١] كان عقد جمهور[١٢] محمد صلوات الله عليه وآله
أولى بقيام الحجة. [١١٥ أ] ولا أعلم أنكم تأتون على أصل قولكم أن ناكثا
لو نكث بيعة أبي بكر وأبى بيعة عثمان أنّه كان حلال الدم، ومن أبى
بيعة علي كذلك. 'فلو أن معتلّا[١٣] اعتلّ في معاوية على أصحاب هذه
المقالة، فكان معاوية خارجاً من أن يجب به على خلاف أن إمامة علي
لم تثبت عندنا من هذه الجهة وشبيهها[١٤] ما قدمنا ذكره، ولكن كنا
أردنا أن نخبر أن محاربته كانت ضلالا وأن إمرته[١٥] هدى بها من

---

[١] في أ: أجهدوا   [٢] في أ: خلا واحد، في ب: على واحد   [٣] في ب: بالإجماع[٤] في
أ: شدور الواحد، في ب: شرود الوعد   [٥] في أ: والأسر   [٦] في أ: هم   [٧] في
أ: أبرمهم [٨] ينقص   [٩] في ب: و   [١٠] في ب: ولم   [١١] في ب: إليه
[١٢] في ب: جمهور أصحاب   [١٣] ساقطة في أ   [١٤] في ب: وبينها   [١٥] في ب:
أمراته

الوجهين جميعاً. وقالوا ما لهدى الصدّيق والفاروق. وقد اجتمعت الأمة
عليهما. ثم وليّا فكانا على طريقة الهدى حتى توفّاهما الله معروفين
بالطهارة والفضل [١١٥ ب] ورضاء المسلمين لهما: لم يقتل(١) في ولايتهما
أحد. وقد اختلفوا في علي (ع م) حتى قُتل(٢) فيه ما بلغكم من الخلق
وأسس(٣) ممن حكم عليه بأنه كان مخطئا ولا يُحكم له للاختلاف. وقد
علمنا شجاعته وجرأته وإقدامه في زمن(٤) النبي (صلى الله عليه وآله)
ومبارزته، وأن مثل أبي بكر وعمر يصرفهما عن المبارزة، فنقول: إنكم
قد(٥) أبطلتم في دعواكم إجماع الأمة عليهما. ولعمري، لقد وليا ما حرم
الله عليهما ان يلياه(٦) فكان منهما خلاف الكتاب والسنة مع الذي ظهر
منهما في الأحكام وظلم آل(٧) بيت رسول الله(٨) ومنع الخمس وأشياء(٩)
كثيرة كراهة وحسبنا(١٠) ما قد تبين(١١) [١١٦ أ] من كذب(١٢) دعواكم في
غير موضع. (فأبو بكر في حكمه لكم خالف علياً(١٣) فإنا قد أخبرناكم أن
إمامة علي (ع م) لم تثبت عندنا بموافقتكم فيزول(١٤) بمخالفتهم وقد
قدمنا أن الأمور التي بها ثبت إمامته. وأما القتل(١٥) فإنه عندنا من بعض
فضائله التي تستكمل(١٦) عند الله رفيع منزلته. وإنما (عهد ديننا ودين

١ في ب: لم يقبل   ٢ في ب: قيل   ٣ في ب: واسا   ٤ في ب: حياة
٥ ساقطة في ب   ٦ في ب: يأتياه   ٧ في ب: أهل   ٨ في ب: رسول الله
صلى الله عليه وآله   ٩ في ب: وأشباه   ١٠ في ب: وحشيا   ١١ ساقطة في ب
١٢ في ب: قريب   ١٣ في أ: فأبو بكر حكم خلاف من خالف علياً؛ وفي ب: فأبا بكر
لكم خالف علياً   ١٤ في أ: فيزول   ١٥ في ب: القتال   ١٦ في ب: يستكمل

مخالفينا¹ النظر في الجهة التي فيها أثبتنا إمامته. فإذا لم يثبت له لم يكن لهذه الأمور معنى. فأما ما ذكرتم من جرأته ومبارزته فأمر لا يسع² جحده. ولعمري لقد ادعيتم من الظن مثل الذي ذكرتم³ من المبارزة أمر لا يختل ضعفه. ولقد أجمعت [١١٦ب] الأمة أن الله سبحانه ندب الناس كافة إلى جهاد عدوه وأن الرسول (صلعم) قد باشر في بعض حربه، وما فرّق⁴ الله بين المسلمين في الجهاد والندبة إليه، ولا تجهل الأمة فضله، ومن بذل مهجته⁵ على من ضنّ⁶ بها، ولا يعلم أحد عن المبارزة، فكيف يعقد لعمرو بن العاص على من يضنّ⁷ به عن المبارزة مرة ولا سامها⁸ مرة ولعمرها سره بل لعمري لقد كان يضن⁹ بها عند المبارزة لما خبر منهما من الهزيمة خوفا من توهين الدّين¹⁰ لا يعلم غير ذلك يصير¹¹ ما كان منهما في غير موطن وإلّا فلأي علة يضن¹² بهما وأي موقف أعظم من المبارزة قاما [١١٧أ] به قصّا على المبارزة. فعجباً لمن كان له أدنى مُسكة كيف يغلط هذا الغلط لولا غلبة الخذلان على قلبه. واحتجوا بأن النبي (صلعم) عقد لأبي بكر على الموسم وبعث بعلي (ع م) يقرأ كتابه، لأن من شأن الولاة يقرأ كتبهم من يكون تحت أيديهم. فنقول: قد أبطلتم فيما ادّعيتم ولاية الحج الذي صح¹³ من

---

¹ في أ: عهود ما بيننا وبين مخالفينا   ² في ب: يطاع   ³ في ب: ذكر   ⁴ في ب: مزق   ⁵ في ب: يهجته   ⁶ في كل من أ وب: ظن   ⁷ في كل من أ وب: يظن   ⁸ في أ: سلمتها   ⁹ في كل من أ وب: يظن   ¹⁰ في أ: الذين   ¹¹ في أ: ما يصر   ¹² في كل من أ وب: يظن   ¹³ في ب: احتج

الخبر أنه توجه، فهبط جبريل على رسول الله (صلع) فقال: يا محمد إن الله يأمرك ⟨أن لا⟩[١] يؤدي عنك إلا أنت أو رجل منك. فبعث علياً فلحقه وردّه ومضى إلى الموسم فبلّغ عن ابن عمّه. ولو كان علي على ما ذكرتم من أن ولاة الرسول (صلع)، قد دل [117 ب] ذلك على أنه أفضل لكانت الدلالة بفضل عمرو بن العاص قائمة. وكذلك أسامة. ولا يدافع بين الناس أن عمر قد وُلي عليهما، وأن الرسول[٢] مات وهما في عقد أسامة. وبعضهم قال: ⟨كان عمر⟩[٣] في جيش أسامة وحده[٤]. فأما علي وتوليته عليهما فما[٥] لا يحصى. وذكروا أنه كان يخبر بالغيوب ويؤدي الأمانات، وزعموا أن في أصحابه وشيعته من كان يزعم أنه نبي وأنه إله، ومنهم من روى أنه لا نبي بعدي. كما أنه لم يوصِ إلى أحد ممن ذكروا. فنقول: إنكم قد كذبتم على من ذكرتم أنه يخبر بالغيوب. والغيب أمر لا يعلمه [118 أ] إلا الله. ولكنا نقول: إن من فضله أن الرسول[٦] (صلعم) علّمه أشياء وأخبره بكونها. فكان يخبرها، فيكون كما يخبر. ومع كل خبر منها إخبارُه بأن الرسول (صلع) أخبره بذلك. وقوله[٧] (ع م): والله ما كَذَبتُ ولا كُذّبت. وأما ما ذكرتم من دعوى من ادّعى أنه نبي وأنه إله فإنّا نشهد على من قال ذلك بالكفر والشرك، وإن كنا لم نسمعه من أحد فيما قاله، فنحن منه براء. ولقد غلت طائفة

من الناس في عمر حتى قالوا فيه قريباً من ذلك. منه 'ما رووا وكذبوا على رسول الله (صلع) أنه قال'': لما نزل عذاب يوم بدر'ما نجا منه إلا عمر'' [١١٨ ب] 'ومنه أن عمر مصباح'' أهل الجنة وفيها النبيون، 'ومنه أنه'' كتب إلى نيل مصر ففتح'' عنه، ومنه أنه رأى سارية وهو في نهاوند''، ومنه أنه رأى شاعراً كان يُنشد النبي فدخل عمر فأمره بالإمساك'' ثم خرج فأمره بالإنشاد فسئل عن ذلك فقال: إنه لا يحب الباطل، ومنه: « ما أبطئ عني'' الوحي إلا خفت'' أن يخالفني إلى عمر ». ومثل''' هذا كثير. وأما تهمة من روى إنه لا نبي من بعدي كما اتهموه إنه لم يوصِ، فأين هذا من هذا؟ 'وهذا''' أمر نطق به الكتاب، وأجمعت عليه الأمة عن الرسول (صلع). قال الله (ع ج): ﴿وَخَاتَمَ النَّبِيِّينَ﴾''' وقال (صلع)''': « لا نبي من بعدي ». والوصية [١١٩ أ] أمر قد اختلفت فيه الأمة. ولم نعلم أحداً نقل أن رسول الله (صلع) لم يوصِ، ولم ينقل ذلك الناقلون. لما كان نقل إلا نفى كما لو شهد شاهد أن''' فلاناً لم يُعتق عبده لم يكن شاهداً. ثم ساءلونا: أخبرونا''' عن النبي (صلعم): أمن تلقائه ولّى أم بوحي 'يوحى إليه'''؟ فالذي''' يقول''' إنه جائز 'أن يكون''' الله

____

' في ب: ما روي أنه   ' في ب: ما نجا منه إلا عمر ومنهم رسول الله صلى الله عليه وآله   ' في ب: ومنهم عبر مصباح   ' في ب: وأنه   ' في ب: مفتح   ' في ب: منها وند   ' في ب: بأمساك   ' في ب: على   ' في ب: ما خفت   ''' في ب: مثل   ''' ساقطة في ب   ''' سورة الأحزاب (٣٣):٤٠   ''' في ب: تعالى   ''' في ب: مرددة مرتين   ''' في ب: خبرنا   ''' ساقطة في ب

(تع) قد علّمه كيف يختاره ووفقه وأمّنه من الخطأ في اختياره وعصمه من الزلل في أمره، ثم أمره أن يختار ويولي من اختار. فهو مأمون الخطأ فيمن ولى سمى له أو لم يسمِّ له. ثم قالوا في الثاني الذي ولاه الإمام[1] (أمن تلقائه)[2] [119 ب] أو[3] يوحى من الله إليه[4] فهو إذاً نبي وسمّاه له النبي (صلع). قالوا فإن زُعم أن النبي سمّاه[5]؟ قيل له ذلك[6] وكذلك الثاني والثالث كل ذلك بالتسمية[7] إلى يوم الدين. أو برأي الإمام، قالوا فإن أخبروا وقال كل واحد منهم فسمى[8] له جميع من يكون إلى يوم القيامة؟ قيل: وكذلك قولنا في ذلك ‹قيل: وكذلك كل›[9] من ولّى أحكامه على البلدان. إذاً[10] كان النبي لم يسمِّ له. قيل له: وأيضاً[11] في الإمامة مثل ذلك. وقولنا في ذلك: إن الإمام لا يوحى إليه. فإن[12] هذه مرتبة لا يبلغها إلا النبيّون عليهم السلام. ‹وجائز›[13] أن النبي عرّف الإمام جميع من [120 أ] يكون إلى يوم القيامة، وعدّهم بأسمائهم، وجائز ألاّ[14] يكون فعل ذلك ويكون أمرُ الإمام بعده أن ينص على الأفضل من أقاربهم، وقد علّمه كيف الخيار. وقد[15] قدّمنا أن الإمام لا يكون إلا موثّقاً ‹مأموناً من الخطأ›[16] فاجتباه أنه يحتمل لعلمه، فعلّمه ونصّ عليه

---

١٧ في ب: والذي   ١٨ في أ: نقول   ١٩ في أ: يكن   ١ ساقطة في ب

٢ ساقطة في ب   ٣ ساقطة في ب   ٤ ساقطة في أ   ٥ ساقطة في ب

٦ ساقطة في ب   ٧ في ب: بالقسمة   ٨ في كل من أ وب: فسما   ٩ ساقطة في ب

١٠ في أ: إذ   ١١ في ب: أيضاً   ١٢ في أ: وأن   ١٣ في ب: وهو

١٤ في ب: أن له   ١٥ في ب مرددة مرتين   ١٦ في ب: مأمون الخطأ

بعده، فإن كان الرسول نصّ على الأئمة بعده، وليس ذلك يوجب أنه قد نص على ﴿مَن يولّى البلدان كما قد ينص[1]﴾ على والي البلد، ولا يجب كذلك أن ينص على عمّال والي البلد، وكما ينص على أمير الجيش، ولا يجب أن ينص على صاحب الميمنة والميسرة ولا صاحب العلم. قالو: وسألونا [120 ب] عن النبي (صلع) قبل ذلك أم غيره. قالوا: فإن قلنا لم يقبله عن النبي (صلع) فقد جوّزوا له ألّا يكون متّبعاً للنبي (ع م). وإن قال قَبِلَه عن النبي (صلع) بالنظر فقد دخل فيما غاب علينا من تجويز النظر، وأن ذلك يكون قبولاً عن النبي (صلع). وإن زعم أنه سمى له من تولى له على البلدان إلى يوم القيامة، قيل وكذلك ما يخبر شهادة الشهود في جميع ما يحكم به من ولاة الأمر إلى يوم القيامة. قالوا: وقد يستقيم بدون هذا من اختلاط الخصوم وادّعاء[2] الباطل. فنقول إنه لا يفعل إلا ما قَبِله عن النبي (صلى الله عليه وآله) وقد قلنا: جائز أن يكون سمّى له وجائز أن يكون [121 أ] أمر باختيار مَن تولّى. فإن[3] كان سمى[4] ﴿فعن أمره ولى وإن كلف أمر بالاختيار فعن أمره اختار[5]﴾ ولن يخلوا من أن ﴿يخبر محتملاً[6]﴾ لعلمه. فإذا يخبر فوجده مولاه[7] كان قد أطاع الله وكان ﴿مأموناً من الخطأ[8]﴾ في ذلك وكان على رعيّته الانقياد لِمَن نصّ له عليه. وكيف كانت الحال في ذلك فقد خرج من أن يكون قبل ذلك نظراً[9]

---

[1] ساقطة في ب [2] في ب: وادعاء الله [3] في ب: بأن [4] في ب:
سمى له [5] في ب: وجائز وإن أمر بالاختيار فعن أمره اختار [6] في ب: الخبر يحتمل
[7] في ب: مولاه [8] في ب: مأمون الخطأ [9] في ب: لأنه

لأنه يكون مأموراً(١) إما بتولية(٢) مسمّى(٣) وإما مأموراً بالاختيار لمحتمِل
بعد أن يعلم كيف المحتمل(٤) ويؤمّن بالله من الخطأ(٥) في ذلك. وقد
سأله، وبعد التفسير(٦) لهم وبعد قولهم(٧) النبي(٨) « أولى بكم من
أنفسكم » احتجاجاً [121 ب] عليهم، لأن الرسول لا يجوز أن يقول قولاً
يحتج به إلّا عرف مخاطبه(٩) ما معناه(١٠) إما بأخبار تقدمت أو(١١) أمور
منه عُلِمت يعلم بها خروج معنى قوله أو دلالة لضرب من الضروب كما
علم معنى قول الرسول من قوله « المؤمنون بعضهم أولياء بعض »، وأن
ذلك قد جمع للنبي وغيره ومعرفة العرب(١٢) أن قوله مولى الرجل مولى
ابن عمه، قلنا كان هذا معلوماً(١٣) عندهم، وكان لا يجوز أن يخبرهم
النبي (صلى الله عليه وآله) بخبر لا يعلمون ما عنى به وإذا قاله فقد علم
أصحابه بما ظهر فيهم من ذكره، إنما أراد بذلك معنى كذا دون كذا
فقد علم القوم جميعاً(١٤) أن الله قد أوجب لرسوله(١٥) ما لم يوجبه
بعضهم على بعض(١٦) وأن الرسول قد قرّرهم(١٧) بذلك وعقد لعلي (ع م)
عليهم ما كان يجب له من الولاية والطاعة والحكم الجائز ما
خصّه الله وما نطق به الكتاب مما تخلّفوا(١٨) في من طاعة الله [122 أ]

---

¹ في ب: مأمور ² في ب: توله ³ في ب: مسمى ⁴ في ب: المتحمل ⁵ في
أ: الخطاب؛ في ب: الخطا به ⁶ في أ: النقرير ⁷ في أ: قوله ⁸ ساقطة في ب
⁹ في ب: مخاطبة ¹⁰ في ب: معناه ¹¹ في كل من أ وب: و ¹² في ب:
القرب ¹³ في ب: معلوم ¹⁴ ساقطة في أ ¹⁵ في ب: رسوله ¹⁶ ساقطة في أ
¹⁷ في أ: أقررهم ¹⁸ في ب: يخلون

وطاعة رسوله(١) (صلع)، واحتجوا بأن زعموا بأن اختيار الإمام إلى
الفقهاء، وقد ذكرنا في غير موضع من كتابنا أن الفقهاء مختلفون.
ولعمري إن الأمر إذا كان على ما ذكرتم مع الاختلاف بين أهل الفرق
ليكون المستحقون لاختيار الإمام غير معلومين ولا معروفين ولا
مستحقين لاسم الفقه، إذاً ليس كل فرقة عند مخالفتها بمقبولٍ قولُها ولا
صواب مذهبها، إذ كانوا لم يجمعوا لأهل فرقة بالصواب في مذهبها [لم
يستحق من لم ينصح صواب أن يكون فقيهاً ولكل فريق](٢) يرميه بالبدعة
والضلالة وليس المختار على أصلكم للإمام إلا مَن أُجمع على عدله
وفضله(٣) ولم يجتمع الأمة [١٢٢ب] لأحد على ذلك. لأنه ليس في
إجماع أهل فرقة على رجل منهم أو على جماعة منهم ما أوجب لهم
الحجة. لأن كل فرقة تساويهم في الإجماع على من ادّعوا فقههم منهم.
وأمّا ادعاؤهم ليخالفوهم، وذلك إذا كان كذلك راجع إلى ما ذكرت
وصح(٤) أنه ليس أحد يعلم بإجماع أنه فقيه. ورجع الأمر الآن عليهم ترك
إقامة إمام لهم(٥) لم(٦) ينص له الكتاب أنه إمام. ولم يخبر(٧) لرسوله
(صلى الله عليه وآله) بذلك وترك تعاطي ما لم يفترض عليهم لأن ما لم
ينصه الكتاب والرسول فغير خارج من الظن والرأي. وقد قدّمنا من
التفرقة بين الإمام والشهود وغيره(٨) [١٢٣أ] ما يغني عن [إعادة ذكره](٩) إن

شاء الله تعالو ﴿حَسْبُنَا اللَّهُ وَنِعْمَ الْوَكِيلُ﴾[1] و﴿نِعْمَ الْمَوْلَى وَنِعْمَ النَّصِيرُ﴾[2] ولا حول ولا قوة إلا بالله العلي العظيم.

«اللهم صل على محمد وآل محمد كما صليت على إبراهيم وآل إبراهيم إنك ﴿حَمِيدٌ مَجِيدٌ﴾[3]»[4]

«قد وقع الفراغ من هذه النسخة الميمونة نهار الثامن والعشرين من ذي الحجة سنة ١٣٢٩ بخط الأقل أحمد علي ابن ملا يوسف علي، غفر الله له ولوالديه بحق الأئمة الأطهار عليهم صلاة الملك الغفار آمين»[5].

---

[1] سورة آل عمران (٣):١٧٣   [2] سورة الأنفال (٨):٤٠.   [3] سورة هود (١١):٧٣
[4] في ب: وصلى الله على محمد نبيه وأبرار عترته وسلم تسليماً   [5] في ب: وقع الفراغ من تنسيخ هذا الكتاب المسمى بتثبيت الإمامة...في شهر الله المعظم - ١٣١٠ من سنة ألف وثلثمائة وعشر من الهجرة النبوية صلعم غفر الله لكاتبه وبعثه مع وليه وإمام عصره ودهره ونقله بعد نقلته إلى دار كرامته بحق سيدنا محمد وآله الطاهرين صلع

فهرس الآيات

al-Manṣūr bi'llāh Ismāʿīl

Tathbīt al-imāma

Arabic Text